Finance and the Good Society

Finance and the Good Society

Robert J. Shiller

With a new preface by the author

Princeton University Press
Princeton and Oxford

Robert J. Shiller is the Arthur M. Okun Professor of Economics at the Cowles Foundation for Research in Economics and professor of finance at the International Center for Finance, Yale University. He is a research associate at the National Bureau of Economic Research in Cambridge, Massachusetts. He is also the co-creator of the Standard & Poor's / Case-Shiller Home Price Indices, and he serves on the index committee for these indices at Standard & Poor's, New York. At the CME Group in Chicago he is a member of the Competitive Markets Advisory Council. He is currently engaged in the joint analysis and development of exchange-traded notes with Barclays Capital in London. He writes regular columns for Project Syndicate and the *New York Times.* The views expressed in this book are solely those of the author and do not necessarily reflect the views of these institutions.

Copyright © 2012 by Princeton University Press

Published by Princeton University Press, 41 William Street, Princeton, New Jersey 08540
In the United Kingdom: Princeton University Press, 6 Oxford Street, Woodstock, Oxfordshire OX20 1TW
press.princeton.edu

Third printing, and first paperback printing, with a new preface by the author, 2013
Paperback ISBN 978-0-691-15809-9

The Library of Congress has cataloged the cloth edition of this book as follows

Shiller, Robert J.
    Finance and the good society / Robert J. Shiller.
        p.   cm.
    Includes bibliographical references and index.
    ISBN 978-0-691-15488-6 (hardcover : alk. paper)
    1. Finance—History.   2. Capitalism—History.   3. Social justice—
History.   I. Title.
HG171.S52   2012
332—dc23   2011053481

British Library Cataloging-in-Publication Data is available

This book has been composed in Adobe Palatino and Berkeley Old Style Book and Black by Princeton Editorial Associates Inc., Scottsdale, Arizona

Printed on acid-free paper. ∞

Printed in the United States of America

10 9 8 7 6 5 4 3

Contents

Part Two
Finance and Its Discontents

Preface to the Paperback Edition

As I prepare the paperback edition of this book, *Finance and the Good Society*, tens of thousands of students around the world are about to enroll in university courses on economics and finance, just as even more young people are about to embark on careers that get them involved, one way or another, in financial activities. These young people comprise the most significant audience for the paperback edition as they ponder their role in an expanding world of financial capitalism.

While there is nothing especially novel about a new generation of students and young professionals assuming their places in classrooms and corporations and nonprofits and regulatory agencies, in recent years there is something very new about the culture in which they will learn. That is, the part played by the new financial technologies in precipitating the ongoing financial crisis has become a matter of public as well as intellectual concern. Although the "Occupy Wall Street" and "Occupy London" movements and their variants have passed, their legacy of anger and criticism lives on.

Anger is still today being nurtured by a major segment of the general public around the world. There is anger at bankers, brokers, money managers, mortgage brokers, derivatives producers, and the whole army of people in professions related to finance who, as the popular story would have it, created the financial bubble that enriched them and impoverished the rest of us.

The "Occupy" protesters have left the financial centers around the world where they set up their encampments. But the smoldering public resentment and skepticism at advanced financial solutions to the world's problems remains, and will likely produce new outbreaks of visible discontent.

Did the financial community create the financial crisis after 2007 that has done so much to diminish the economic prosperity of so many people around the world? More to the point, do the practices of modern finance as seen in the work of highly visible enterprises from Goldman Sachs through Société Générale, through Sberbank, through HSBC, support or subvert the goals of a healthy society, a market democracy built on broad-based prosperity and fairness? Put differently, what is the proper role of a robust financial sector in promoting the good society?

These are the questions that motivated the work that went into this book, beginning with the Walter E. Edge Lecture I delivered at Princeton University in 2010; and with my plenary address in 2010 before the United Nations General Assembly, as keynote speaker for the opening of the 65th session of the Second Committee; and finally with the twenty lectures on financial markets I gave to my own students at Yale, and to the world through Open Yale free on the Internet. Beginning with these lectures, and continuing through the 2012 publication of the hardcover edition of this book and its reviews, a series of subsequent articles and op-eds, adoption and discussion of the book in finance courses, and a number of lectures to academic as well as professional groups, this book has served as a focal point for an ongoing conversation. This conversation is at various points and turns full of heat or full of light, but it is a conversation nonetheless.

There is an old saying, attributed to various authors, that "books [as works of art or science] are never finished. They are merely abandoned." An author needs to step aside at some point, but the thinking a book initiates never really ends. It is carried on by a multitude of others and intertwined with thinking in other books and other new public dialogues.

This book is about progress and change, and even more than with most books it is intended as a conversation starter. It is in this spirit—the spirit of discussion, collaboration, and dialogue, leading to invention and change—that I invite finance students and young professionals to take part in the effort to try to define a clear and compelling connection between finance and the good society.

This book consists of two parts, following an introductory chapter. The introductory chapter establishes the context of financial capitalism in modern history and global society, emphasizing the centrality of financial innovations, from stock markets through mortgages, in contributing to the achievement of all of the varied long-term goals people have, and the role of the finance professions as "stewards" of society's wealth. Part 1, "Roles and Responsibilities," then goes on to build accounts of the roles played by finance professionals—including bankers, accountants, lawyers, investment bankers, regulators, and others—in performing their respective parts in the good society. Part 2, "Finance and Its Discontents," written in a different key, raises a series of questions about the morality and substance of finance in an evolving society.

In reading this book young finance students and professionals are likely to find Part 1 of the most inherent interest, because it provides a smorgasbord-like presentation of the various professional positions that collectively comprise the field of finance, jobs young readers may profitably occupy through their working lives. And it is about the often doubted and often obscured *moral purposes* of these occupations.

To underscore the relevance of this new preface, I have asked my publisher to include an article of mine, published by newspapers and magazines around the world via Project Syndicate in May 2012, "My Speech to the Finance Graduates."[1] This piece was motivated by the "Roles and Responsibilities" part of this book, and served to augment it by specifying the central missions for each part of the finance profession today's students are about to enter. It appears at the end of this preface.

Beyond the didactic role played by *Finance and the Good Society* in specifying the relevance of modern finance and raising questions as to its ongoing economic and social role, the discussion that has followed the hardcover edition of this book has only served to strengthen my conviction that there is a widespread and profound misunderstanding of the role that financial markets and institutions play in the good society.

It is not the reviewers of the book in newspapers and magazines who have shown this misunderstanding. It has been more in evidence among many of the people who came to my book talks or who emailed me about the book.

Among the general public, there is clearly a tendency to think of the financial professions as focused on *conspiring* against them instead of *contributing* as constructive organs of civil society. Of course, conspiracies here and there are part of history, and part of finance too, but we should not assume the universality of those instances of calculated manipulation and deception.

There is a plea in this book, and it is a plea for well-meaning people—idealists, even—to consider learning finance and working with its powerful tools to help all individuals in our society achieve their varied goals. Given the imperfections of human nature, there will be chaos and crashes over the course of a lifetime, part of the inevitable consequences of a society that encourages people to pursue their goals instead of just keeping their heads down to play it safe. Financiers will be blamed for these dislocations. But idealists should not shrink from getting involved in the financial system, even if it is tainted in the public eye. For they should know in their hearts that engaging with the financial community provides for them the tools and the opportunities to make a real mark on society.

---

1. "My Speech to the Finance Graduates" copyright © 2012 by Project Syndicate, reproduced by permission.

As noted above, this book, more than any other book I have written, serves as the basis for an ongoing conversation. It is my great hope that my colleagues teaching the principles of economic and financial theory, corporate finance, investments, and financial markets and institutions will see fit to join this conversation by continuing it with their students. Discussion of the ethics and sociology of finance does not fit naturally into courses dedicated to technical training in economic and financial modeling and strategy, but the reality of life, especially in the wake of the financial crisis, makes this discussion necessary. And so I offer this book in the spirit of constructive conversation and ongoing experimentation with financial ideas that will, in the best intellectual spirit, make the world not only a richer, but a genuinely better, place.

My Speech to the Finance Graduates

NEW HAVEN—At this time of year, at graduation ceremonies in America and elsewhere, those about to leave university often hear some final words of advice before receiving their diplomas. To those interested in pursuing careers in finance—or related careers in insurance, accounting, auditing, law, or corporate management—I submit the following address:

Best of luck to you as you leave the academy for your chosen professions in finance. Over the course of your careers, Wall Street and its kindred institutions will need you. Your training in financial theory, economics, mathematics, and statistics will serve you well. But your lessons in history, philosophy, and literature will be just as important, because it is vital not only that you have the right tools, but also that you never lose sight of the purposes and overriding social goals of finance.

Unless you have been studying at the bottom of the ocean, you know that the financial sector has come under severe criticism—much of it justified—for thrusting the world economy into its worst crisis since the Great Depression. And you need only check in with some of your classmates who have populated the Occupy movements around the world to sense the widespread resentment of financiers and the top 1 percent of income earners to whom they largely cater (and often belong).

While some of this criticism may be overstated or misplaced, it nonetheless underscores the need to reform financial institutions and practices. Finance has long been central to thriving market democracies, which is why its current problems need to be addressed. With your improved sense of our interconnectedness and diverse needs, you can do that. Indeed, it is the real professional challenge ahead of you, and you should embrace it as an opportunity.

Young finance professionals need to familiarize themselves with the history of banking, and recognize that it is at its best when it serves ever-broadening spheres of society. Here, the savings-bank movement in the United Kingdom and Europe in the nineteenth century, and the microfinance movement pioneered by the Grameen Bank in Bangladesh in the twentieth century, come to mind. Today, the best way forward is to update financial and communications technology to offer a full array of enlightened banking services to the lower middle class and the poor.

Graduates going into mortgage banking are faced with a different, but equally vital, challenge: to design new, more flexible loans that will better help homeowners to weather the kind of economic turbulence that has buried millions of people today in debt.

Young investment bankers, for their part, have a great opportunity to devise more participatory forms of venture capital—embodied in the new crowd-funding Web sites—to spur the growth of innovative new small businesses. Meanwhile, opportunities will abound for rookie insurance professionals to devise new ways to hedge risks that real people worry about, and that really matter—those involving their jobs, livelihoods, and home values.

Beyond investment banks and brokerage houses, modern finance has a public and governmental dimension, which clearly needs reinventing in the wake of the recent financial crisis. Setting the rules of the game for a robust, socially useful financial sector has never been more important. Recent graduates are needed in legislative and administrative agencies to analyze the legal infrastructure of finance, and regulate it so that it produces the greatest results for society.

A new generation of political leaders needs to understand the importance of financial literacy and find ways to supply citizens with the legal and financial advice that they need. Meanwhile, economic policymakers face the great challenge of designing new financial institutions, such as pension systems and public entitlements based on the solid grounding of intergenerational risk-sharing.

Those of you deciding to pursue careers as economists and finance scholars need to develop a better understanding of asset bubbles—and better ways to communicate this understanding to the finance profession and to the public. As much as Wall Street had a hand in the current crisis, it began as a broadly held belief that housing prices could not fall—a belief that fueled a full-blown social contagion. Learning how to spot such bubbles and deal with them before they infect entire economies will be a major challenge for the next generation of finance scholars.

Equipped with sophisticated financial ideas ranging from the capital asset pricing model to intricate options-pricing formulas, you are certainly and justifiably interested in building materially rewarding careers. There is no shame in this, and your financial success will reflect to a large degree your effectiveness in producing strong results for the firms that employ you. But, however imperceptibly, the rewards for success on Wall Street, and in finance more generally, are changing, just as the definition of finance must change if is to reclaim its stature in society and the trust of citizens and leaders.

Finance, at its best, does not merely manage risk, but also acts as the steward of society's assets and an advocate of its deepest goals. Beyond compensation, the next generation of finance professionals will be paid its truest rewards in the satisfaction that comes with the gains made in democratizing finance—extending its benefits into corners of society where they are most needed. This is a new challenge for a new generation, and will require all of the imagination and skill that you can bring to bear.

Good luck in reinventing finance. The world needs you to succeed.

Preface

I started writing this book initially for my students in the finance class I have been teaching for twenty-five years at Yale University. Many of these young people, I believe, still have not figured out their places in the world and are wondering how their goals and dreams will meet hard reality. In writing this book, I wanted to help them understand the modern system of financial capitalism in which they must live, now and in decades hence, whatever their career choices.

Since 2008 this class has been available online via the videos of all my lectures produced for the public by Open Yale Courses, and a new video version of my lectures is appearing in 2012.[1] The needs of my distant students who watch the lectures online from all over the world have also contributed to my motivation to write this book.

But since I started working on it this book has taken on a larger and more urgent purpose, and not just for students. We all live our lives in a world of financial capitalism—an economic system that is increasingly guided by financial institutions and that, in the wake of the severe financial crisis that began in 2007, appears to many to be broken. We all need to consider whether this society is even going in the right direction, in both our lifetimes and the lifetimes of our children.

Financial capitalism is an invention, and the process of inventing it is hardly over. The system has to be thoughtfully guided into the future. Most importantly, it has to be further expanded and democratized and humanized, so that we may reach a time when financial institutions will be even more pervasive and positive in their impact. That means giving people the ability to participate in the financial system as equals, with full access to information and with the resources, both human and electronic, to make active and intelligent use of their opportunities. It will mean that they truly consider themselves part of modern financial capitalism, and not the victims of the aggressive and selfish acts of a cynical financial establishment. It will mean designing new financial inventions that take account of the most up-to-date financial theory, as well as the research revolution in behavioral economics and behavioral finance that has explored the real human limitations that inhibit rational and humane decision making. Creating and implementing such inventions will be the best tactic to deal with economic inequality. This future is in the hands of the people, old as well as young, who might read this book.

This matter is especially apparent at the time of this writing, as many countries around the world still struggle with the effects of the financial crisis that began in 2007. It is hard to be precise in dating this crisis, since as I write in 2012 we certainly do not believe that it is over yet, and the worst may be yet to come. Efforts by governments to solve the underlying problems responsible for the crisis have still not gotten very far, and the "stress tests" that governments have used to encourage optimism about our financial institutions were of questionable thoroughness.

Public street protests against both government and the financial establishment were front-page news in 2011, long after the writing of this book had gotten under way. The protests apparently took their inspiration from those of the Arab Spring against dictatorial governments in the Middle East. They began to be directed against the financial establishment with the Movimiento 15-M in Madrid, then with Occupy Wall Street in New York, along with Occupy Boston, Occupy Los Angeles, Occupy London, Occupy Melbourne, Occupy Rome, and other variants. The December 2011 election protests in Russia reflected dissatisfaction with the cozy situation of rich "business oligarchs." The most consistent theme in all these movements has been a plea for better democracy, lamenting a perceived conspiracy between governments and their associated financial establishments. While their arguments and rhetoric are not always coherent, the protests represent, in substantial measure, a welcome assertion of democratic values and citizen responsibility.

The movements are not necessarily left-wing. Even those who consider themselves the ideological opposite of Occupy Wall Street in the United States, the right-wing Tea Party activists, also seem upset by the apparent concentration of wealth and power in New York and other financial centers, while "middle America" does all the work. There seems to be almost universal agreement, by those of all political persuasions, that wealthy financial interests should not use their influence over government to grab more wealth, as seems to have been the case in events leading up to and following the crisis. But as to what should be done next, there is much less agreement.

Many people seem fixed on the idea that those responsible for the financial crisis should go to jail. In late 2011 I gave an evening talk, sponsored by the Chicago Council on Global Affairs, to a large audience, apparently mostly businesspeople. Some in the audience angrily criticized me afterward for failing to stress the many charges of fraud leveled against financial firms in the wake of the crisis. I was surprised to hear such anger from those in the business community—hardly street protesters and probably both Republicans and Democrats. I was equally surprised to see that my basic theme—the need to democratize finance by making the financial markets work better for all people—was not seen as more sympathetic to their concerns. In fact, this theme would appear to promote the deepest objectives of Occupy Wall Street.

While it is impossible to overlook illegality as one cause of the current financial breakdown, I believe that in situating the problem there we fail to appreciate the big picture. We have a financial system that malfunctioned because of a host of factors. If we do not address the deeper sources of these problems by improving the system, we will have missed the point of the problem—and the opportunity to correct it.

Certainly anyone who committed fraud should suffer penalties. But it is hard to blame the crisis on a sudden outbreak of malevolence. The situation during the boom that created the crisis was rather more like that on a highway where most cars are going a just a little too much over the speed limit. In that situation, well-meaning drivers will just flow with the traffic. The U.S. Financial Crisis Inquiry Commission, in its final 2011 report, described the boom as "madness,"[2] but, whatever it was, it was not for the most part criminal.

And, pursuing this highway metaphor a bit further, we may suggest that automotive designers would best stay focused on how new technology can help us better manage vehicular traffic, with improved cruise control, external electronic feedback to cars, and ultimately even self-driving cars—complex new systems that will enable people to reach their travel destinations more easily and more safely. If that's the future for our highways, something like it should be the future for our financial institutions as well.

All of these protest movements are only the most manifest signs of discontent that have been discernible in conversations and blogs ever since the financial crisis began. The words of street protesters and angry businesspeople alike are without focus and offer us no clarity about what is wrong or what should be done. And yet the underlying dissatisfaction with our financial system, in the wake of the financial crisis, reflects real problems with the system that need to be fixed—problems that have not yet been solved by the new legislation and regulations put forward in the wake of the crisis.

The financial crisis became visible in the United States when home prices started to fall after 2006. According to our Standard & Poor's / Case-Shiller national home price index, real U.S. home prices fell 40% over the five years from 2006 to 2011. By 2007 this decline had brought prices of home mortgage securities down far enough to create a crisis for investors in these securities. It was called the *subprime crisis* because the price falls were especially striking among mortgages issued to subprime borrowers, that is, home buyers who are judged more likely to default because of factors including their past payment and employment histories. Financial innovations related to these subprime loans were blamed for the crisis. But the crisis did not remain confined to subprime mortgages; that was only the initial shock in a vast catastrophe. The consequence was a drop in real estate prices and the collapse of financial institutions, not only in the United States but also in Europe and elsewhere. By the spring of 2009 the crisis was so severe that it was described as the biggest financial calamity since the Great Depression of the 1930s—bigger than the Asian financial crisis of the 1990s and bigger than the oil-price-induced crises of 1974–75 and 1981–82. Beginning in 2010 it was complicated by a European sovereign debt and banking crisis, which by 2012 resulted in many downgrades of governments' debt, and even of the Eurozone's bailout fund, the European Financial Stability Facility. This crisis continues to have repercussions around the world.

Despite the problems in the mortgage business and many large financial institutions—some based simply on overenthusiasm and naïveté, others on outright efforts to manipulate and to defraud—I never felt, as did so many, that these problems were a damning indictment of our entire financial system. Imperfect as our financial system is, I still find myself admiring it for what it does, and imagining how much more impressive it can be in the future.

I realize that critics might think that preparing students for careers in finance merely exacerbates a trend toward greater economic travail for the many. Certainly some who work in finance or related fields often reap great material rewards for their efforts, while others earn far less. Modern society is indeed currently on a trend toward higher levels of economic inequality,[3] and contributing to that trend has been the tendency to reward especially well some of those who go into activities that relate to finance, while those who make their livings primarily in other sectors of the economy, including most of the middle class and the poor, lose ground. The government bailouts of well-to-do bankers have redoubled public concerns about inequality.

But finance should not be viewed as inherently or exclusively elitist or as an engine of economic injustice. Finance, despite its flaws and excesses, is a force that potentially can help us create a better, more prosperous, and more equitable society. In fact, finance has been central to the rise of prosperous market economies in the modern age—indeed this rise would be unimaginable without it. Beyond headlines incriminating bankers and financiers as self-aggrandizing perpetrators of economic dislocation and suffering, finance remains an essential social institution, necessary for managing the risks that enable society to transform creative impulses into vital products and services, from improved surgical protocols to advanced manufacturing technologies to sophisticated scientific research enterprises to entire public welfare systems.

The connections between financial institutions and individual people are fundamental for society. Clarifying the terms of these connections and establishing a proper context for implementing and enhancing them is the subject of this book.

It seems a paradox that the very financial system that is the facilitator of some of our greatest achievements can also implode and create such a disaster. Yet the best way for society to proceed is not to restrain financial innovation but instead to release it. Such an approach can reduce the impact of such disasters and at the same time democratize finance. At various points in this book I describe financial innovations currently being developed, and I also propose newer innovations, as examples of how creative and well-meaning people can still further improve our society and democratize its finance.

But the financial crisis reminds us that innovation has to be accomplished in a way that supports the stewardship of society's assets. And the best way to do this is to build good moral behavior into the culture of Wall Street through the creation and observance of best practices in its various professions—CEOs, traders, accountants, investment bankers, lawyers, philanthropists.

When Adam Smith wrote his classic *Wealth of Nations* in 1776, a book long acclaimed as marking the beginning of modern economics, the pressing issue for thinkers and critics of the day was tariffs.[4] Private interests lobbied governments to put their interests ahead of public interests and push tariffs up so high as to make it impossible for lower-cost foreign producers to compete. But Adam Smith and other economists who followed him were successful in clarifying the importance of trade for the widespread wealth of nations. Since Adam Smith, lobbyists for special interests have found it much harder to push up tariffs, and trade is substantially free today—a vital institution in creating the remarkable growth and widespread prosperity we have seen since the revolutions of the eighteenth century.

At this time of severe financial crisis the point of contention among thinkers and critics is not trade but finance itself. Hostility runs high toward societal institutions that are even tangentially associated in people's minds with finance. This hostility is reminiscent of the public state of mind during the last major world financial crisis—the Great Depression after 1929—which led ultimately to a degree of unrest that shut down much of the world economy and contributed to the tensions that led to World War II.

Hostility among the general public generated by the crisis may have the unfortunate effect of inhibiting financial progress. Ironically, better financial instruments, not less activity in finance, is what we need to reduce the probability of financial crises in the future. There is a high level of public anger about the perceived unfairness of the amounts of money people in finance have been earning, and this anger inhibits innovation: anything new is viewed with suspicion. The political climate may well stifle innovation and prevent financial capitalism from progressing in ways that could benefit all citizens.

To be sure, financial innovation is still percolating, at a slow and conservative level, but major new financial inventions cannot be launched now because of fear. In this book I contend that the financial crisis was not due simply to the greed or dishonesty of players in the world of finance; it was ultimately due to fundamental structural shortcomings in our financial institutions. Yet such shortcomings as a failure to manage real estate risk or a failure to regulate leverage are still not really being addressed; the response to the crisis has not been to innovate confidently to address areas where our institutions failed. Instead, the main focus has been on avoiding bailouts and reducing national debt by curtailing government spending. Initiatives developed by politicians in response to public anger have been shaped by what the public perceives as the problem, not by the contributions of visionaries.

Socially productive financial innovations could be moving forward rapidly, given the information revolution and with so many more countries experimenting with different economic structures and competing in the world marketplace. In coming decades we could see rapid development in the breadth of financial contracts, with extensions in the scope of markets, for the purpose of safeguarding our fundamental economic assets. Innovations could include the implementation of new and better safeguards against economic depression, including the proliferation of new kinds of insurance contracts to allow people to be more adventuresome in their lives without fear of economic catastrophe. We could also see innovative measures developed to curtail the rising plague of economic inequality that threatens to create serious social problems in our society.

What I want most for my students—near and far, young and old—to know is that finance truly has the potential to offer hope for a more fair and just world, and that their energy and intelligence are needed to help serve this goal.

Acknowledgments

My student research assistants here at Yale—Oliver Bunn, George Cook, Duck Ju Kang, Bin Li, Michael Love, Lindsey Raymond, Kate Stratton, Argyris Tsiaras, and Rachel Wang—were my eyes and ears as I wrote this book. I also got important feedback from the students in my finance class at Yale, where an early draft of this book was assigned as a supplement to the textbook. I wanted a youthful perspective. I wanted to see the financial world from the vantage point of those whose lives are still taking shape, who are launching their careers, whether in finance or in other fields—and they came through wonderfully for me.

My colleagues Karl Case, John Cochrane, Darrell Duffie, Seth Fischof, John Geanakoplos, Gary Gorton, Henry Hansmann, Daeyeol Lee, Bill Leigh, Shlomo Maital, Wayne Moore, and Pasko Rakic, as well as anonymous reviewers, gave me helpful comments and suggestions. They are not responsible for any errors I may have made.

My administrative assistants Carol Copeland and Melissa Studer were a source of constant support.

My wife Virginia, who is a psychologist in private practice and a clinical instructor at the Yale Child Study Center, was, as always, a deep collaborator in all my thinking. She has made possible all the things I do.

I thank the Public Lectures Committee at Princeton University, who invited me to give the 2010 Walter Edge Lecture, "Finance and the Good Society," in which I presented, and received feedback on, an earlier version of the ideas set forth in this book.

I am indebted to Peter Dougherty, director of Princeton University Press, for his great help in conceptualizing and developing the book. Thanks are also due to everyone at the press and indeed to the book publishing industry as a whole, for promoting the broader discourse that ultimately made this book possible.

I am a believer in achieving understanding through *books*, not just scholarly articles in professional journals, since I believe that the more comprehensive discussion of a topic that books permit ultimately leads to a broader understanding of any subject. This book began as a work for my students, and I included many references to books for them, as any good teacher would. Yet even after I had decided that this was really a book for the general public and not just for students, I persisted in including numerous references. I believe it is important for all readers, including my professional colleagues, to spend time with whole, readable books on broad topics rather than just the specialized scholarly literature. I do not think of these books as popularizers, but as synthesizers, originators, provokers, and inducers. That is how I view this book—and hope others will as well.

Finance and the Good Society

Introduction:
Finance, Stewardship, and Our Goals

What are we to make of a book called *Finance and the Good Society?* To some readers, this may seem an incongruous coupling of concepts. The word *finance* is commonly thought of as the science and practice of wealth management—of enlarging portfolios, managing their risks and tax liabilities, ensuring that the rich grow richer. We will revisit—and challenge—this definition of finance later in this chapter. The phrase *good society* is a term used by generations of philosophers, historians, and economists to describe the kind of society in which we should aspire to live; it is usually understood as an egalitarian society, one in which all people respect and appreciate each other. So at first glance *finance*, at least as commonly understood, seems to be working *against* the achievement of the *good society*.

But it is not so simple. Finance has become ever more associated with *capitalism*. Since the Industrial Revolution, intellectuals have focused their often heated debates about the good society on issues related to capitalism, including the system of markets, private property, legal rules, and class relations. These institutions and issues have increasingly come to define modern society throughout the world. Along with democracy, few ideas have been as pervasive and contentious in defining the good society as capitalism.

Debates about capitalism and the good society, from Karl Marx's incendiary criticisms in the nineteenth century through Milton Friedman's spirited defenses of free markets in the twentieth, have tended to center on *industrial capitalism*: the system of production, banking, and trade that shaped modern society up through the end of World War II. But the past several decades have

1

witnessed the rise of *financial capitalism:* a system in which finance, once the handmaiden of industry, has taken the lead as the engine driving capitalism. Much ink has been spilled over the purely economic aspects of financial capitalism. I too have contributed to this discussion, in my scholarly writings on market volatility and in books such as *Irrational Exuberance.* The current severe financial crisis has called forth questions not only about the system's parts but also about financial capitalism as a whole. This crisis—dubbed by Carmen Reinhart and Kenneth Rogoff as the "Second Great Contraction," a period of weakened economies around the world starting in 2007 but continuing for years after, mirroring the Great Contraction that followed the financial crisis of 1929—has led to angry rejections of the value of financial capitalism.

Given this experience, many wonder, what is the role of finance in the good society? How can finance, as a science, a practice, and a source of economic innovation, be used to advance the goals of the good society? How can finance promote freedom, prosperity, equality, and economic security? How can we democratize finance, so as to make it work better for all of us?

What's in a Phrase? Financial Capitalism Evolving

The term *financial capitalism* developed negative connotations as soon as it first became popular in the 1930s with the publication of George W. Edwards's *The Evolution of Finance Capitalism.*[1] Edwards saw a conspiracy of large financial institutions, with J. P. Morgan at the lead. He called it the *Pax Morgana.* During the Great Depression critics and much of the public at large blamed the financial system for their plight; they viewed the system as almost feudal, with financiers replacing the lords.

The term has recently been revived, and again it is used with hostility. President Nicolas Sarkozy of France has said,

> Purely financial capitalism has perverted the logic of capitalism. Financial capitalism is a system of irresponsibility and is . . . amoral. It is a system where the logic of the market excuses everything.[2]

Tony Blair, former British prime minister, speaking of the severe financial crisis that began in 2007, remarked,

> What is plain is that the financial system has altered its fundamentals, and can never be the same again. What is needed is radical action to deal with the fallout of the crisis.[3]

Grigory Yavlinsky wrote the 500 Days Program of 1990, which outlined the Russian transition to a free-market economy, and was promoted to deputy prime minister to implement it. He began to express similar doubts after the crisis. In his 2011 book *Realpolitik,* in a section entitled "Structural Shift: From Industrial Capitalism to Financial Capitalism," he noted that the fundamental structural shifts [are] directly related to a gradual slackening of moral constraints in developed countries. Structural shifts like these follow very fast growth of the financial sector and services directly related to it.[4]

I argue in this book that while critics are correct in some of their indictments, the changes that must be made, rather than having the effect of constraining the innovative power of financial capitalism, should instead broaden its scope. We will make little progress if we simply condemn financial capitalism as a "system of irresponsibility." But we have the potential to support the greater goals of good societies—prosperous and free societies in the industrialized as well as the developing world—if we expand, correct, and realign finance.

The Inexorable Spread of Financial Capitalism

At the time of this writing we are still stuck in the severe financial crisis that began in 2007. As such we tend to associate finance with recent problems, such as the mortgage and debt hangovers in the United States and Europe, and with the legal and regulatory errors that preceded these events. But we should not lose sight of the bigger picture. The more important story is the proliferation and transformation of successful financial ideas. Financial innovations emanating from Amsterdam, London, and New York are developing further in Buenos Aires, Dubai, and Tokyo.

The socialist market economy, with its increasingly advanced financial structures, was introduced to China by Deng Xiaoping starting in 1978, adapting to the Chinese environment the examples of other highly successful Chinese-speaking cities: Hong Kong, Singapore, and Taipei. The economic liberalization of India, which allowed freer application of modern finance, was inaugurated in 1991 under Prime Minister P. V. Narasimha Rao by his finance minister (later prime minister) Manmohan Singh, who was educated in economics at Nuffield College, Oxford University. The voucher privatization system introduced to Russia in 1992–94 under Prime Minister Boris Yeltsin by his minister Anatoly Chubais, following a modification of the Yavlinsky plan, was a deliberate and aggressive strategy to transform Russia's economy. The intent was not simply to match the rest of the world in the degree to which finance permeated the daily lives of the Russian people, but to have Russia rank first in the world in public ownership of capital.

Such sudden integrations of sophisticated financial structures, originally designed in more financially advanced countries, were not achieved entirely smoothly in these countries, and there was a degree of anger about the inequality of benefits that accrued to some, as opportunists amassed great wealth quickly during the transitions. But China, India, and Russia have seen a flourishing of financial sophistication and amazingly high economic growth rates. And it is not just these countries. According to International Monetary Fund data, the entire emerging world—including the Commonwealth of Independent States, the entire Middle East, Sub-Saharan Africa, and Latin America—has proved able to generate annual gross domestic product (GDP) growth of over 6% during the past decade, when not compromised by world financial crises.[5]

In addition, a host of international agreements have created institutions that work for the betterment of humankind using sophisticated financial tools. The World Bank, founded in 1944 and today expanded into the massive World Bank Group, has engraved on its headquarters in Washington, D.C., the motto "Working for a World Free of Poverty." The World Bank was only the first of the multilateral development banks: the African Development Bank, the Asian Development Bank, the European Bank for Reconstruction and Development, the Inter-American Development Bank Group, and many others.

Modern financial institutions are pervasive throughout the world today. Moreover, it is not just stocks or bonds that represent financial markets. One might not at first consider the price of agricultural commodities as relevant to a discussion of financial instruments, but the prices that they fetch on futures exchanges are entirely analogous to prices in the stock and bond markets. Wheat and rice markets are financial markets too, in the sense that they engage in similar activities and rely on comparable technical apparatus, and they are similar in their fluctuations and their impact on the economy. The fact that the very lives of low-income people around the world depend on food prices in some of these markets only underscores the significance of our financial institutions—and the importance of getting these institutions right.

Financial Capitalism and Marxian Communism

The triumph of financial capitalism or its analogues since the 1970s, even in formerly Marxian communist countries, is one of the most significant revolutions in history, and a radical departure from the past.

Communism, in its modern form, had its defining moment in 1848, the year that saw a number of popular uprisings in cities around Europe. Those revolts of the working class did not have an effective leader and were not by themselves communist in nature. They sprang forth from general dissatisfaction at the roots of society. But they created an opportunity for the communist movement to take hold.

Karl Marx and Friedrich Engels recognized the significance of these events and in the same year, with the support of the Communist League (originally a Christian organization), published their brief *Communist Manifesto*—which came across as quite radical and un-Christian. It advocated violent revolution, and Marx and Engels were eventually perceived by many as filling the leadership void in the revolutions of 1848. Even though those revolutions were short lived, their manifesto came to be seen as speaking for the many who had previously remained silent.

The word *communism* comes from the old French *commun*, meaning common, and refers to the original central tenet of this belief system: the common ownership of capital, the means of production. In this book I refer to the traditional form of communism, not the socialist market economy promoted by the Communist Party in China today, which allows—and even actively encourages—private ownership among members of the public.

The central argument for public ownership of capital was, according to Marx in his *Capital*, to break a vicious cycle of poverty:

> It is not because he is a leader of industry that a man is a capitalist; on the contrary, he is a leader of industry because he is a capitalist. The leadership of industry is an attribute of capital, just as in feudal times the functions of general and judge were attributes of landed property. . . . The capitalist system presupposes the complete separation of the laborers from all property in the means by which they can realize their labor. . . . The process, therefore, that clears the way for the capitalist system, can be none other than the process which takes away from the laborer the means of his production; a process that transforms on one hand, the social means of subsistence and of production into capital, on the other, the immediate producers into wage laborers.[6]

Marx never explains clearly why it is that laborers do not have access to capital. He implies that under capitalism the goals of society are set by those at the top—those with access to capital—and not by all the people. It remains an unstated assumption that a poor laborer could never start a business by getting credit from a bank or capital from wealthy investors.

But in an ideal capitalist system, people with good business ideas can, in principle at least, do just that. Our capitalist institutions do not yet fully live up to this ideal, but throughout history there has been a long trend toward the democratization of finance, the opening of financial opportunities to everyone. It is a trend we must hope will continue into the future.

It is true that social barriers prevent some from realizing, and profiting from, their talents. An illiterate farm boy from a remote area finds it difficult to walk into the offices of a bank in a big city to ask for capital to start a business. There is a very real barrier to such people's accessing capital, and there is substantial evidence of such a barrier in the extreme variation in interest rates paid by borrowers in different regions and different categories. Development economist Esther Duflo summarizes: "This body of evidence makes it very hard to believe that credit markets, at least in the developing world, are anywhere near the ideal market that would make the distribution of wealth irrelevant for investment."[7]

But this is not a fundamental problem of financial capitalism. It is rather a problem of *democratizing and humanizing and expanding the scope of financial capitalism*. The same basic issue would remain in Marx's new society. It is a social dilemma that can be addressed by changes in our educational system. Indeed we have already started to change the system around the world with improved public education and communications.[8]

Financial Capitalism Comes of Age

We do indeed live in the age of financial capitalism. We should not regret that. Regulations and restrictions can and should be placed on financial institutions to help them function in the best interests of society, but the underlying logic and power of these institutions remains central to their role. Financial institutions and financial variables are as much a source of direction and an ordering principle in our lives as the rising and setting sun, the seasons, and the tides.

Indeed there appears to be no viable alternative. We never hear talk of *nonfinancial* capitalism as a model—although one could use such a term to refer to a market economy with poorly developed financial institutions, as we still see today in some poorer regions of the world. As much as we might like to criticize finance, no one seems to view these alternatives as suitable models for anyone's future.

Our task, both in the financial sector and in civil society, is to help people find meaning and a larger social purpose in the economic system. This is no small feat, with all the seemingly absurd concentrations of wealth the system brings about, the often bewildering complexity of its structures, and the games—often unsatisfying and unpleasant—it forces people to play.

Definitions matter, and so how we define financial capitalism—getting that definition right—will help us develop a working theory of this most important force. It should set a norm for how finance works and what leaders within business, the public sector, and civil society must do to harness emerging developments within the field of finance to support the goals of a robust and prosperous economy, to curb its excesses, to smooth its volatility, and to consider how finance can be brought to bear to address the needs of advanced and developing economies alike.

Toward a Working Theory of Financial Capitalism

At its broadest level, finance is the science of goal architecture—of the structuring of the economic arrangements necessary to achieve a set of goals and of the stewardship of the assets needed for that achievement. The goals may be those of households, small businesses, corporations, civic institutions, governments, and of society itself. Once an objective has been specified—such as payment for a college education, a couple's comfortable retirement, the opening of a restaurant, the addition of a new wing on a hospital, the creation of a social security system, or a trip to the moon—the parties involved need the right financial tools, and often expert guidance, to help achieve the goal. In this sense, finance is analogous to engineering.

It is a curious and generally overlooked fact that the very word *finance* actually derives from a classical Latin term for "goal." The dictionary tells us that the word derives from the classical Latin word *finis*, which is usually translated as *end* or *completion*. One dictionary notes that *finis* developed into the word *finance* since one aspect of finance is the completion, or repayment, of debts. But it is convenient for our purposes to recall that *finis*, even in ancient times, was also used to mean "goal," as with the modern English word *end*.

Most people define finance more narrowly. Yet financing an activity really is creating the architecture for reaching a goal—and providing stewardship to protect and preserve the assets needed for the achievement and maintenance of that goal.

The goals served by finance originate within us. They reflect our interests in careers, hopes for our families, ambitions for our businesses, aspirations for our culture, and ideals for our society; finance in and of itself does not tell us what the goals should be. Finance does not embody a goal. Finance is not about "making money" per se. It is a "functional" science in that it exists to support other goals—those of the society. The better aligned a society's financial institutions are with its goals and ideals, the stronger and more successful the society will be. If its mechanisms fail, finance has the power to subvert such goals, as it did in the subprime mortgage market of the past decade. But if it is functioning properly it has a unique potential to promote great levels of prosperity.

The attainment of significant goals and the stewardship of the assets needed for their achievement almost always require the cooperation of many people. Those people have to pool their information appropriately. They must ensure that everyone's incentives are aligned. Imagine the development of a new laboratory, the funding of a medical research project, the building of a new university, or the construction of a new city subway system. Finance provides structure to these and other enterprises and institutions throughout society. If finance succeeds for all of us, it helps to build a good society. The better we understand this point, the better we will grasp the need for ongoing financial innovation.

What Finance Does

Economists and finance professionals tend to define and discuss finance in narrower terms than those we've been employing here. Much research in academic finance is focused on short-term trading strategies and results, and on the related topic of risk management. In its canonical form, academic finance is the science of designing optimal portfolios of investments. Day-to-day activities on Wall Street likewise tend to be concentrated on highly specified activities. But this is only part of what finance really involves.

An essential part of what finance professionals actually do is dealmaking—the structuring of projects, enterprises, and systems, large and small—an activity that brings convergence to individuals' often divergent goals. Financial arrangements—including the structuring of payments, loans, collateral, shares, incentive options, and exit strategies—are just the surface elements of these deals. Dealmaking means facilitating arrangements that will motivate real actions by real people—and often by very large groups of people. Most of us can achieve little of lasting value without the cooperation of others. Even the archetypal solitary poet requires financing to practice her or his art. An income to live on, publishers, printers, arrangers of public readings, the construction of suitable halls for public readings—there is a hidden financial architecture behind all of this.

All parties to an agreement have to want to embrace the goal, do the work, and accept the risks; they also have to believe that others involved in the deal will actually work productively toward the common goal and do all the things that the best information suggests should be done. Finance provides the incentive structure necessary to tailor these activities and secure these goals.

In addition, finance involves discovery of the world and its opportunities, which ties it in to information technology. Whenever there is trading, there is price discovery—that is, the opportunity to learn the market value of whatever is being traded. This in turn involves the revelation of people's feelings and motivations, and of the opportunities that exist among groups of people, which may in turn make even more ambitious goals possible.

Along with being the science that structures the achievement of goals, finance embodies a vital technology. As such, it has demonstrated continuous progress over the centuries, from the beginnings of money lending in the ancient world through the development of modern mortgage markets as well as the legal and regulatory structures necessary to sustain these innovations. And it will continue to progress. Finance, suitably configured for the future, can be the strongest force for promoting the well-being and fulfillment of an expanding global population—for achieving the greater goals of the good society.

Finance Meets the Good Society

The real cure for the problem that Marx addressed lies not in destroying the capitalist system but in improving and democratizing it—and improving it means serving the greater goals of the good society. That has always been the best response, to the dismay of radicals.

The essential challenge for leaders to contemplate in coming to terms with the future of finance is to understand that it can be used to help broaden prosperity across an increasingly wide range of social classes, and that its products can be made easier for people to use and can be better integrated into the economy as a whole.

On the first point, there is nothing in financial theory that specifies that control of capital should be confined to a few "fat cats." Think of the broadly democratic proliferation of insurance, mortgages, and pensions—all basic financial innovations—in underwriting the prosperity of millions of people in the past century. Further perfecting financial institutions and instruments through innovations large and small will enable society to enlarge the scope of this prosperity and reverse the growing trend toward social inequality.

Regarding the second point, designing financial institutions around real human quirks will make it easier for people to adapt financial innovations to their lives and for the financial system as a whole to function more smoothly. This means that psychologists have to be on the financial team, and we must also take account of the revolution in behavioral economics and behavioral finance that has occurred in the past few decades.[9] It means that we must smooth the rough edges off our financial system—those aspects that can cause trouble when people make mistakes. It means that people have to be told the truth about the financial contracts into which they enter, and about the ways in which those contracts could be hurtful in the future, so that they can take full account of their emotions and wants before they sign a contract.

If we extrapolate historical trends, it will be possible to further extend the scope and range of financial capitalism and render Marx's criticism—the fundamental basis for his vision of the communist extreme—forever obsolete. Accomplishing this goal will require a degree of government intervention, but not intervention that would frustrate market solutions. Government's task in this endeavor is to provide a clear set of rules for the game, one that protects consumers and promotes the public interest while enabling the players to compete in doing what they do best: delivering better products and services. A real challenge in this regard is that these rules must have an international dimension, as today's financial markets are both global in reach and instantaneous in effect.

Tomorrow's Opportunity:
Financial Capitalism in the Information Age

In his 1995 book *The Road Ahead*, Bill Gates made a number of predictions about our future in the information age, most of them fanciful. The majority of the more amusing predictions have not yet come to pass. For example, he predicted that some of us will record our entire lives, running video recorders all the time and storing our entire video biographies for future viewing. That idea made for thought-provoking reading, but it hasn't yet become a reality. What Gates did not predict were numerous other fundamental developments, including the web sites eBay (founded in 1995, the very year his book appeared), Wikipedia, Facebook.com, LinkedIn.com, Zipcar.com, CouchSurfing .org, and a million others that have changed the way we live our lives. He shouldn't be faulted for failing to predict these—no one could have. Instead we should consider the process through which such innovations happen, and why they happen more in certain environments than in others. That is the real subject of finance.

Bill Gates was not presenting a vision of the future of capitalism or of the good society; he was captivated by the engineering details. His predictions seemed to center on little things, on gimmicks. He also did not choose to look very far ahead. The real issue is: What can capitalism do for the good society, with all of the complexity and information linkages a society involves? What little things, in concert with other little things, have the potential to strengthen our sense of fulfillment in our lives? Consider a "little" thing like Facebook, not predicted by Bill Gates in 1995, which can reunite old friends across the years. Is this an important innovation for achieving the good society? It could be, in the sense that it gives people a sense of completion in their lives.

The rapid advance of information technology in this century portends numerous—and often frightening—changes, for machines are rapidly replacing human intelligence. A computer program named Soar has the ability not only to play games against humans but also to learn how to play new kinds of games as well.[10] The DeepQA program invented at IBM by a group led by David Ferruci can recognize speech and answer general-knowledge questions. The program has been tested in simulated appearances on the television quiz show *Jeopardy*, and it appears to be able to beat human contestants.[11]

Hearing about such innovations can be demoralizing. We all want to develop our skills to compete as effectively as possible and be successful in the working world. There is no sense in acquiring talents that will be replaced by machines. Unfortunately, it is hard to predict which talents will ultimately matter.

In their 2005 book *The New Division of Labor: How Computers Are Creating the Next Job Market*, labor economists Frank Levy and Richard J. Murnane argue that computers are replacing routine tasks yet cannot perform what they call "expert thinking" or "complex communication." In fact, computers are more likely to *create* jobs requiring these human talents than displace humans from them.[12]

Expert thinking means thinking broadly, interpolating different sources of information and information from different perspectives—information about what is new and current as well as what is perennial and has been forgotten. An example of an expert thinker given by Levy and Murnane is the auto mechanic who is familiar with the computerized diagnostic routines required by modern automobile makers, knows where parts can be found cheaply, is aware of the needs of a variety of customers, and can sense by test driving a car what really should be done.

Complex communication refers to the combination of interpersonal skills and understanding complex situations. An example offered by the authors is that of a lawyer, who not only knows the intricacies of the law but also understands what is really in the best interest of the client, given the client's situation, and can communicate this knowledge to the client persuasively.

It is not possible to predict which broad job categories will survive in the face of increasingly sophisticated information technology, for every major occupational group will continue to include some jobs that provide opportunities for both expert thinking and complex communication. But finance, broadly construed, is a field in which such jobs may be especially likely to survive and perhaps even proliferate. Jobs that involve finance are a little like those of the auto mechanic and the lawyer. One must understand the technicalities of financial engineering just as the auto mechanic understands mechanical engineering, and be able to apply that knowledge and sensibility to human problems. One must understand the intricacies of financial institutions (and the legal framework that defines them) and be able to communicate that knowledge to a client.

This process has been defining the history of financial innovation for generations. On the streets of New York in the 1840s one would see boys running back and forth, delivering checks, drafts, and other negotiable instruments to the various windows inside banks, and receiving gold and banknotes in exchange. All that disappeared after 1853, with the founding of the New York Clearing House, which soon had fifty-four bank members. This was an important innovation in information technology, even though it might not meet our current idea of such technology since it did not involve any electronics. At ten o'clock every morning representatives of all the major banks would sit down in a large room, each at a designated desk, with all the desks arranged in a circle. A clerk for each of the representatives would then get up from his desk and, simultaneously with all the other clerks, make a round of all the other fifty-three desks, dropping off fifty-three bundles of documents, one for each of the other banks. The whole process took no more than six minutes. Any imbalances would then be summed and paid in gold or banknotes, not by the banks to one another, but to the Clearing House. The jobs of delivering documents and cash on the street faded. But finance itself had not faded.[13]

The technology of clearing improved even more markedly with the advent of the computer. Indeed artificial intelligence systems like DeepQA will soon be available that will be able to answer *Jeopardy*-like questions about finance. With all these continuing advances in technology, one may wonder what will be left of many jobs in the future. But, for the foreseeable future, computers will not be able to counsel people effectively on what they really need to do with their portfolios, nor to make deals among companies, nor to advise a university department about a new research project, nor to do any of a large number of other jobs. For finance is still about achieving human goals—a task that machines cannot handle in any but the most basic of ways.

We shall see in this book that democratizing finance entails the development of both human arrangements—such as those for financial advice, legal advice, and financial education—and technology that works together with these human arrangements to make it possible for everyone to participate intelligently in the financial system.

Financial Activities in the Economy

Financial activities consume an enormous amount of time and resources, increasingly so over the years. The gross value added by financial corporate business was 9.1% of U.S. GDP in 2010, continuing a long upward trend. By comparison it was only 2.3% of GDP in 1948.[14] These figures exclude many more finance-related jobs, such as insurance.[15] Information technology certainly hasn't diminished the number or scope of jobs in finance.

To some critics, the current percentage of financial activity in the economy as a whole seems too high, and the upward trend is cause for concern. But how are we to know whether it really is too high or whether the trend is in fact warranted by our advancing economy? What standard do we have? People in the United States spend 40% as much (3.7% of GDP) eating out at restaurants as the corporate financial sector consumes.[16] Is eating out a wasteful activity when people could just as well stay home and eat?

Surely at least a part of what all these finance professionals are doing is productive: a good number of them are evaluating businesses and directing resources to the more promising of these. But other types of financial activity—trying to outguess the psychology of the market, carrying out high-frequency trading, or advertising dubious financial products—seem not to be very productive.

Arjun Jayadev and Samuel Bowles have estimated that 19.7% of the U.S. labor force in 2002—supervisors, security personnel, members of the military—was involved in guarding in some form.[17] The high percentage of our citizens paid to guard us and our installations and possessions is at its essence surely more troubling than the percentage engaged in the substantially productive activities of finance. Yet relatively few of us seem bothered by this statistic.

Financial Capitalism and the
Challenge of Financial Innovation

While financial capitalism inevitably must be made to serve the good society, it cannot be summarized in simple terms. This is so because it represents a bewilderingly broad and cross-cutting array of institutions, instruments, and markets, each element of which evolved through a process of invention not unlike the processes that produced our automobiles and airplanes, and through which they continue to evolve.

Financial innovation is an underappreciated phenomenon. According to Google Ngrams, the term *financial innovation* was hardly ever used until the late 1970s and 1980s. The term seems to have been applied first to the controversial financial futures markets that developed around that time. It was shortly thereafter that patent offices began to accept claims for financial innovations. For example, the U.S. Patent and Trademark Office granted patent number 4,346,442 to what is now Merrill Lynch in 1982 for its Cash Management Account (CMA).

That was a landmark change. Why had the patent authorities not previously thought of financial methods as patentable? A clue can be found in a 1908 U.S. Second Circuit Court decision in the case of *Hotel Security Checking Co. v. Lorraine*, which set a "business method exemption doctrine" that held sway until around the time of the Merrill CMA decision. The 1908 court held that business methods, whether original or not, are uniformly unpatentable.[18] In its decision, the court emphasized that the patent granted, a method for detecting fraud in accounting, used only paper and ink and business common sense. The wording suggested that the court was looking for some proof of concrete innovation as manifested in the "physical means employed."[19] Financial patents thus awaited the application of computers to financial innovation, as in Merrill Lynch's 1982 patent; a computer programmed to perform a financial service could, at least by the 1908 standard, be considered a physical means.

A problem with patenting financial innovations is that they interact with the whole economy; they may produce consequences—including winners and losers—that are evident only years later. The applicant for a financial patent cannot prove the efficacy of the invention as can the inventor of a device submitted for an engineering patent. Since financial innovations interact with people's foibles—their hopes, their promises, their life savings—patents on them seem to be inherently more controversial than engineering patents. Most financial patents that do not require complex computerized implementation would seem likely to have a long history of prior art that was implemented in some rudimentary form, if never well documented. Indeed a common reaction to many financial patents (including the original 1982 Merrill Lynch CMA patent) has been that they lack the kind of originality underlying inventions of physical devices.

But the process of financial innovation is still important, even if it is more at the level of corporate and societal innovation than lone-inventor-in-the-lab creativity. When we describe finance, and how it succeeds, we are aiming at a moving target. Leaders must understand that financial innovation is a messy and sometimes disruptive process. In this book, descriptions of financial products and institutions will have interspersed among them possible directions for future innovation and change.

What Follows in This Book

This book develops a working theory of financial capitalism to help guide the greater discussion of finance and the good society. It begins, in Part One, with the realities of financial capitalism, as it is constituted today and will be constituted in the future. This part looks at the roles and responsibilities that people take on in the field of finance, from investment bankers through lawyers through regulators and educators. It examines the various organs of the body of financial capitalism—organs that function together to produce a living economic entity, organs that take the form of groups of people bound together in organizations and with particular traditions and ways of operating.

There is an unfortunate tendency to talk about the financial system in the abstract, as if it is all about stocks and bonds, or about mathematical equations. But the drivers of financial capitalism are real men and women, who adopt certain personae in our society and make the goals inherent in these roles their own personal goals and the responsibilities associated with these roles their own personal responsibilities. Each such role has its own code of ethics and professional conduct, and it depends on the people filling that role to uphold that code. Here we consider a wide array of such roles, to give a broad picture of the real workings of financial capitalism. As these various roles are discussed, we will consider how they might be improved, and how financial innovation will alter these roles and make the people who assume them more effective.

The public hostility that we see today toward financial capitalism often takes the form of anger directed toward the people who fill certain of these roles. An important mission of Part One is to take account of this public hostility, to try to understand, on a role-by-role basis, why particular roles in the financial system are so controversial.

Part Two of the book takes a more critical look at the financial system that all the people described in the first part have created, and it offers some ideas about how it can and will be improved in the future. It looks at some of the system's strengths and inspirations, but also at its anxieties and breakdowns—all of which are relevant to any discussion of the role of finance in the good society. The financial system conforms to a large degree to financial theory, which has a sort of beauty that can inspire minds, but also a sort of ugliness, at least in its present form. The financial crises that we experience from time to time are only part of the story. That ugliness can provoke some to dismiss the whole concept of financial capitalism. But it would be foolish to do so, for that would cost us the ability to accomplish some of our most cherished goals.

The history of the economic development that has brought the world to its current state of prosperity and enlightenment is a history of many technical adjustments to our financial system, of innovations inspired by financial theory but also based on realistic assessments of human nature. This part of the book indulges in extrapolations of past trends that have resulted in better and better financial systems; it also puts forth a number of concrete ideas for how the system can be improved in coming decades.

The epilogue offers some final thoughts on how power is actually wielded in finance, on our negative feelings about the concentration of power we see in the financial world, and on how in a financial democracy such power might be managed and reconciled with basic human values.

Part One

———

Roles and Responsibilities

A n old saying holds that while the problem with socialism is socialism, the
problem with capitalism is capitalists. Some of the headlines of the past
decade—from the exploits of the executives of Enron and Satyam to those of
the likes of Bernard Madoff—would seem to confirm that the problem with
financial capitalism is indeed financial capitalists. But achievement of the
good society is dependent on a healthy and robust financial sector—including
the people who occupy the roles that enable the financial system to run, and
thus help the economy to run. If finance is the science of goal architecture,
those who work in the field are the architects who structure these goals and
manage the risks of small businesses, families, school systems, cities, corporations, and all the other vital institutions throughout society. If finance, properly understood in the good society, is the stewardship of society's assets, it
is these same people who are entrusted with the management and cultivation
of those assets.

In this part of the book we review a full array of roles played by financial
professionals, from CEOs through accountants and philanthropists. The idea
is not to biopsy these roles for their flaws. Rather it is to get to the heart of
their value; to understand their functions; to better appreciate how factors
such as rewards, reputation effects, and codes of conduct promote best professional practices; and also to predict how these roles are likely to change in the
future. And it is also to try to understand why so much of the public does not
seem to appreciate the value of these roles, and why there is so often hostility

toward those who fill them. For all the talk of critics and apologists alike about Wall Street, a clear, succinct account of the various roles and relationships that actually make it work has not existed until now. But any discussion of the future of finance and its connection to the goals of the good society presumes an understanding of these roles, so we begin here.

Chapter 1

Chief Executive Officers

The CEO of a company is in a very special position, because he or she stands for an idea—the core idea behind the company's activities, a way of thinking that defines the work of all the company's employees, and a culture that includes its corporate values, connecting the company to the larger society.

The CEO is responsible for the formulation of short-run goals that promote that very idea. The CEO embodies the purpose of the company. This responsibility has to be put, to a significant extent, into the hands of an individual and not a committee of equals, just as the writing of a novel usually has to be put into the hands of one individual. Human society has natural tendencies that can coordinate the activities of teams of people in performing routine tasks; teams seem to form naturally, but they are also vulnerable to conflict and to being sidetracked by the individual goals of their members. We still need the prefrontal cortex of one individual—however it may work—coordinating the activities of large groups of people. Large groups of people cannot be strategic or purposeful if they are leaderless.

A Succession of CEOs

That said, the corporation has a fundamental problem: it has to deal with a succession of CEOs. Companies, with luck, may live for centuries. CEOs, subject to human mortality, cannot.

The essence of a corporation is its longevity. Successful corporations have no termination date, no shelf life, no inherent limits on how long they can operate. The succession of CEOs of a corporation is like a succession of kings of an empire, each one of whom takes up the flag from a fallen predecessor and reinterprets and further develops the cause. Except CEOs cannot relax to enjoy the lives of kings: they have to work especially hard.

A CEO typically serves for only a few years, during which time she or he has to set goals for a company that is much longer lived than the CEO's own tenure. Thus there has to be an effective reward system that focuses the CEO on the long term. And this is a problem that lends itself to financial solutions.

CEOs have egos and personal interests that do not necessarily coincide with the long-term interests of the firm. Companies must find ways to keep their leaders focused on their jobs, attending to the boring and often un-appreciated tasks that take up much of their time. A corporation needs a leader who will do an inspired job of keeping everything running over the long term, anticipating trends and shifts and providing a vision for the company, while putting his own needs and wants second.

The ego of a CEO is most naturally satisfied if he or she is the *founding* CEO of a company, for being first in any succession carries with it the greatest ego gratification. The founding CEO of a company is of special importance. If the company endures, the founding CEO may well become a legendary figure to later generations. Years or even centuries later, the founding CEO may be remembered by employees as an almost mythic figure.

Anthropologists have noted a human universal called a creation myth—a story that everyone in a given society knows, one that describes their origins.[1] Such a myth is typically humanized by the identity of a major leader. A found-ing CEO is part of the creation myth for a company. The founding CEO knows this and instinctively pursues such legendary status, living out a new version of that same ancient story. But that is only the *first* CEO.

Behind the succession of CEOs lies a financial structure, which indeed makes each CEO's employment possible. The CEO of a modern corporation is technically just an employee, serving at the discretion of the board of direc-tors. He or she is defined by a financial contract, with terms relating compen-sation to the performance of the company and its stock. The CEO depends on a certain financial structure, a financial invention, for motivation.

Even though the CEO is usually not the founding CEO, he or she is still expected to be a visionary. The modern corporation must be reinvented again and again, in response to new information and new market demands.

Success in reinventing the company is reflected in financial prices. When the CEO is successful, the price of shares in the company goes up. When the CEO fails, the price falls. A CEO avidly watches the company's share price—it is like a continual report card on his or her activities, issued minute by minute. It is the reward signal for the cognitive center of the company, and there is an analogy to the reward system for the decision-making apparatus in the human brain, a point to which we shall return later in this book. In the corporation, as in the brain, the reward system is imperfect but essential.

The financial arrangement for the typical CEO is carefully human engineered, designed to incentivize that person to stay in the position long enough and prominently enough that his or her relationship to others as their leader becomes firmly established in everyone's minds.

The dispensation to CEOs of stock or options on the company's own shares is a method of aligning the CEO's incentives with those of the company. An option to buy a share in the company at a specified price is valuable only if the actual market price is higher, and so granting options to the CEO creates an incentive to take actions that will boost the firm's share price.

A share of stock does not have a termination date, as does the CEO's tenure. Assuming that the stock market price of a share in the company is a good indication of its true *long-term* value, then the change in the stock price is a measure of the CEO's contribution to the long-term value of the company. The stock price signals a reward only if there is good news. It responds to actual news, and it does not encourage gloating over past successes. The CEO is thereby incentivized to be the bearer, to attentive investors, of good news about the company's long-run potential—news about the long run, but news that is delivered today, *right now*—and thus to plan for the indefinite future, not just his or her own tenure.

Incentivizing by stock options can be a lot better than awarding bonuses to the CEO for achieving high profits: profits-based bonuses might encourage the CEO to merely milk the company in the short run, neglecting longer-term problems and leaving a disastrous situation for his or her successor. With stock-price-related incentives, on the other hand, the CEO is encouraged to steer the company toward opportunities that could improve its *long-term* value.

Setting the Level of the Reward

The salaries and bonuses of CEOs are the subject of many news accounts, owing to their extraordinarily high levels, especially in recent decades and especially in the United States. The anger and resentment over executive compensation account for much of the public hostility toward financial capitalism in general.

But sometimes a high level of compensation for a CEO is readily understandable. Consider the example of a man who was the very successful CEO of Corporation A, who has turned the company around, taking it from the brink of failure to success. Along the way he handled numerous unpleasant tasks like firing key people, waging policy battles against entrenched forces within the company, and shutting down operations—and he did so in such a politically deft way that those who remained in place were not resentful, and indeed were motivated to take the company to new levels. He was paid handsomely for his work, and he now presides over a well-managed, successful company. He may be thinking about retiring early and enjoying some of his fortune.

Now suppose the board of directors of Corporation B feels it needs to take those same drastic actions. It is entirely plausible that they would ask our CEO to quit his present job and become their new CEO. They *could* ask someone with no such experience to do what he did, but that other person would not have the same personality, the same judgment. They want *him*.

It is entirely possible that our CEO will respond that he has had enough of this unpleasant business and in fact has more money than he could ever spend. No, he doesn't want to go through all that again.

So it is plausible in turn that the board of Corporation B would offer a really attractive package to lure the CEO—a package that might, say, offer options on the company's stock potentially worth $30–50 million if he is successful. That amount is not enormous relative to the earnings of a large company. A diligent board exercising its fiduciary responsibility in presiding over a company with billions in revenue might consider a highly qualified, proven CEO worth all of this.

Running, or turning around, a business all over again, after one has already done it, may not seem all that glorious in and of itself the second or even third time around—yet it is precisely those who have done such an important job before who have the best credentials to do it again. CEOs, even those of Fortune 500 companies, are not usually particularly beloved or famous, with only a few exceptions. Thus high compensation is the best way to attract qualified candidates to such jobs.

It is often observed that in decades past, when CEO salaries were much lower, companies still found people who were willing to do the job. As president of American Motors from 1954 to 1962, George Romney, Mitt Romney's father, turned down huge bonuses.[2] In 1978 Lee Iacocca offered to serve as the CEO of Chrysler, to save it from bankruptcy, for a salary of only one dollar.[3] These are fine examples, but they do not mean that companies can always cheaply hire the CEOs they want. Romney and Iacocca were rare exceptions: each had a strong public moral persona, and for them such symbolic gestures may have been especially important. Romney later became governor of Michigan, and Iacocca later wrote three best-selling books about his business philosophy. At one time or another both showed signs of running for president.[4]

Moreover, the growth in high salaries that we have seen in recent decades might in part be explained as the result of improvements in our capitalist system, as the system comes to recognize the importance of qualified leaders and refuses to be bound by arbitrary pay conventions.

This is why the Squam Lake Group (a nonpartisan, nonaffiliated group of fifteen academics who offer counsel on financial regulation, of which I am a member) advised in its 2009 report that the government should not regulate the *level* of CEO compensation. Some CEOs are, and always will be, worth a great deal to their firms. On the other hand, the group *did* believe that regulation of the *structure* of CEO compensation is called for.[5]

Moral Hazard and Deferred Compensation

There *is* a reason for the government to intervene in the process of determining executive salaries: to mitigate a specific moral hazard that seems to have played a substantial role in causing the financial crisis that began in 2007—at least for big and so-called systemically important firms. This moral hazard arises because the CEOs and other top officers of such key firms have incentives to take extraordinary risks. They believe that their companies are too big to be allowed to fail. Because the failure of their companies would be simply too disruptive to the economy as a whole, they reason that the government will not allow that to happen.

Given such a mindset, the CEO may not very much care about the risk of precipitating an international financial crisis. He may on the other hand be very interested in taking a gamble that gives him a 50% chance of achieving a huge increase in the stock price and so reaping a windfall on his stock options—even if that same gamble has a 50% chance of wiping out the company and taking much of the global economy with it. In the one case, he ends up rich. In the other, well, his options are worth nothing—but they might have been worth nothing *for sure* if he had not taken the gamble.

Moreover, a CEO with a stock-option-based compensation scheme has an incentive to manipulate the flow of information out of the company and to doctor financial reports—to delay the release of unfavorable information until after he has received his compensation. And such practices do not conflict with the efficient markets theory—the theory, to be discussed in various places later in this book, that market prices efficiently and quickly incorporate all public information about a company. The CEO is a company insider and knows things that are being deliberately kept secret from the market.

Therefore, the Squam Lake Group recommended that government require that systemically important firms defer a substantial part of their CEOs' compensation for an extended period, say, five years.

The 2010 Dodd-Frank Wall Street Reform and Consumer Protection Act in the United States contains terms that resemble the Squam Lake Group's recommendation. Notably, the act includes provisions that require a CEO to give back "erroneously awarded compensation" that was the result of "material noncompliance of the issuer with any financial reporting requirement under the securities laws."[6] Yet the Squam Lake proposal is more far-reaching, in that it would deprive the CEO of the rest of the compensation if ever there were a bailout or failure of the company.

Cronyism in the Boardroom

Of course there are different circumstances under which a CEO might receive an especially high salary. It could be fraud. It could be that the board of directors votes in favor of a high salary out of a sense of professional courtesy or class sympathy. There may even be individual expectations of being repaid in kind later on.

Lucian Bebchuk and Jesse Fried, both professors at Harvard Law School, have argued in their 2006 book *Pay without Performance* that the growth of top executive salaries has largely been the result of a breakdown in the arms-length bargaining process between boards of directors and the top executives they hire. When the "bargaining" is among close friends, it may have only the appearance of being fair: "Directors have had various economic incentives to support, or at least go along with, arrangements favorable to the company's top executives. Various social and psychological factors—collegiality, team spirit, a natural desire to avoid conflict within the board team, and sometimes friendship and loyalty—have also pulled board members in that direction."[7]

Thus it is ultimately psychological tendencies that underlie the problem of cronyism in the boardroom. There has been public awareness of this problem, and reforms strengthening director independence have already been introduced by lawmakers. But the problem persists.

The issue, Bebchuk and Fried argue, is not with financial capitalism, but with certain details of its implementation. To reduce the problem of board favoritism, they propose reform of the election of board members, measures to make it easier to replace a board, and procedures to give shareholders the power to initiate changes in corporate charters.

The rise over the second half of the twentieth century of venture capital firms—which specialize in providing funding to unproven startup companies that have a high probability of failure, hoping to profit from the few that succeed—has helped deal with such problems, at least for startup or early-stage firms. They have replaced many of the angel investors—independently wealthy individuals who have supported startup firms in the past, investors who are not investment professionals and who, through inexperience, are vulnerable to error.

Venture capital firms have learned some things about CEO talent and compensation over the years. They have learned that the talent and dedication of the CEO and top executives make an enormous difference to the success of the firm, but that these talented people—at the stage in their lives when they are most hungry and most energetic—are not necessarily expensive to hire. Venture capital firms do make sure that the top executives in the firms they fund will participate substantially in the possible success of their companies; the firms have learned how to structure contracts, typically including stock options, that motivate executives well and protect them against the high risk of failure. A venture capital firm almost always demands a seat on the board of directors—a vantage point from which it will stop in its tracks any non-arms-length deals excessively rewarding CEOs. Venture capital firms also are more likely than angel investors to replace the founder with an outside CEO when things go badly.[8] Unfortunately, venture capital firms typically sell their shares and exit the business as firms in which they have invested succeed and grow larger.

Institutional investors—portfolio managers, to be discussed later—can sometimes enforce similar limits on executive overcompensation. Yet there is still a need to improve their methods and organization to help them do a better job of this.

Another ultimate cause of excessive CEO compensation is a public failure to understand the problem that Bebchuk and Fried have described. The general public, at least in the United States, cannot really appreciate all the issues surrounding the extremely high salaries paid to some executives, and the public has therefore been excessively willing to acquiesce in those salaries.

Failure to recognize the problem of non-arms-length negotiations between their boards and their top executives was a sign of the times in the late twentieth century, when there was excessive complacency about the ability of an unregulated free-market system to work perfectly. The late twentieth century was the era of the "charismatic CEO," overvalued by the public and incentivized to take excessive risks to perform miracles to justify his or her salary.[9] Indeed there was a bubble in executive salaries that mirrored the bubbles in home prices and stock prices.

The Universality of the CEO Incentivization Problem

The fundamental nature of the problem of CEO compensation can be seen from the fact that the same issues arose even in communist countries.

Yugoslav economist Milovan Djilas, in his 1957 book *The New Class: An Analysis of the Communist System,* showed frank parallels between executive behavior in communist countries and that in western countries.[10] His criticism of the communist system derailed Djilas' hopes of succeeding Josip Broz Tito as leader of Yugoslavia. It candidly exposed problems, including the reward system for government executives—a system that resembled the bonus system of western corporations. Government officials would receive an expensive house and other perks if they performed well. Communist managers form a crony system to milk the enterprise to their own advantage, just as certain managers do in capitalist countries.

David Granick, in his 1960 book *The Red Executive,* pointed out many more parallels between the Soviet *nomenklatura* and the western financial class. Business management in the Soviet Union relied on party committees, city committees, and regional committees who had an interest in the success of an enterprise and who played much the same role that stockholders and their appointed boards of directors do in western countries: choosing, motivating, and sometimes disciplining managers.[11] The Soviets had rediscovered the advantages of a system that awarded incentives to executives who would work hard to make an enterprise successful.[12]

The problem of motivating CEOs is a basic one, and difficult to solve. But as our understanding of the workings of the economy evolves, we find ourselves somewhat freed from the mistakes of the past. The roles of top managers (as well as their titles) are bound to change over time as we discover better ways to find and incentivize people to take on leadership roles and to take to heart the deepest goals of the organizations they lead.

In the future, we will still hear about some CEOs with extraordinarily high(-sounding) salaries and benefits. That will be part of the story of financial capitalism, but we can hope that there will be more sense to the process of awarding these benefits and so better public acceptance of them. This—and a better public appreciation of the principles underlying the corporation— would better align the interests of the corporation with those of the larger society.

Chapter 2

Investment Managers

Investment managers—those who manage portfolios of shares in companies, bonds, and other investments—are among the most important stewards of our wealth and thus vitally important players in the service of healthy and prosperous market democracies—in the service of the good society. They are employed by all kinds of organizations, from multinational corporations and union pension funds through city governments, universities, libraries, and churches. The funds they manage are of many different types and legal forms, with names like "mutual funds," "unit investment trusts," "exchange-traded funds," "hedge funds," or "private equity funds." In this chapter we lump the managers of all these different kinds of funds together according to their common purpose: they determine the composition of portfolios of investments on behalf of their clients and buy and hold those portfolios for those clients, the ultimate investors.

These managers provide many services to the investors who entrust their money to them, including such routine services as safekeeping of securities; spreading out investments into broadly diversified portfolios; recordkeeping; and minimizing the tax impact of investments in consideration of the client's particular tax status. They also deal with clients' special concerns, related to their long- or short-term goals; their needs for liquidity; risks they face, such as regional or political risks; and their priorities in terms of "green" or ethical investing. But they do much more than that, for they are a guiding force in the economy. When they actively select investments, they are directing capital toward particular uses at the expense of others, and they have an incentive to try to direct capital to its best uses. Investment managers serve millions of people worldwide, including those with special needs: the retired, the sick, teachers, police, the dependent, young students. They are of fundamental importance.

And yet investment managers are, like the CEOs discussed in the previous chapter, subject to public hostility. This hostility comes in part from the same public sense that they are overpaid, that they are making "obscene" incomes. But public hostility toward investment managers also arises from another source: a sense that they cannot in fact do what they claim to do, to achieve better-than-average returns on the investments they manage. Hence the lack of trust between investment managers and the public they serve.

Beating the Market

Despite the wide variety of services investment managers provide, most advertise themselves as achieving superior returns, through active management of their portfolios and picking stocks that they predict will do well in the future. For much of history, most investment managers have *really* been in the business of "beating the market."

The popular efficient markets theory that has taken hold in academia is seen by many as implying that such investment managers are in fact, to put it bluntly, frauds. If statistical evidence proves that no one can outperform a strategy of choosing investments randomly, then their attempts to claim that they do so must be fundamentally dishonest. There is an element of truth to this academic view: many investment managers have succeeded in creating false impressions as to their superiority as investors.

Evidence in the academic finance literature shows that actively managed stock market mutual funds have generally been worse investments in recent decades than funds that follow a passive investment strategy and merely invest in all shares in the stock market. For example, Martin Gruber found in 1996 that mutual funds underperformed a diversified investment in the stock market by about 1.5% a year.[1] This underperformance reflected the regularly scheduled management fees imposed by the mutual funds on their investors, but not the load fees (large one-time-only fees that are collected when money is invested or taken out), so the actual performance of mutual funds was even worse.

Professional investment managers do not seem to do particularly well in selecting their own personal portfolios either. A 2011 study by Andriy Bodnaruk and Andrei Simonov obtained data on the personal portfolios of mutual fund managers in Sweden.[2] (It is possible to get these data in Sweden because the country levied a wealth tax until 2007, and so wealthy people had to report their entire personal portfolios to the government.) They found that the investment managers did no better on their investments than the average investor, nor were they more diversified.

And yet, in the past half century, investments in actively managed funds have grown dramatically. It would seem that investors, by entrusting their assets to these managers, must have been irrational. In his study Gruber concluded that not *all* mutual fund investors were irrational, since there is *some* persistence through time in mutual fund investment performance, and some investors, who are quick to follow the best mutual funds with their money, exploit this situation. But most people who invest in mutual funds are not so sophisticated, and they stay in poorly performing mutual funds. In many cases they do so because their mutual funds are held in retirement plans that do not give them a free choice of funds.

The basic diversification and portfolio services provided by mutual funds still make sense for many, and it is not that investors are terribly served by the current system. Certainly there may be many investors who do not choose their investment managers well—an issue to be addressed and remedied in the future. But we should not reach the unwarranted conclusion that investment managers, like mutual funds, are not providing a service to the public.

Modern academic finance sometimes seems to take the evidence on underperformance of investment managers as proof that no one should be leaving their assets in the hands of a professional investment manager since, given extremely efficient markets, there is nothing for these managers to do. Carried to its logical conclusion, this same efficient markets theory also appears to imply that *anyone* who trades in financial markets is making a mistake. By this logic, one should just buy a diversified portfolio and be done with it, except perhaps for periodic rebalancing to keep the portfolio diversified. It would mean there is nothing investment managers can do to beat the market.

The modern theory, which has held great influence in recent decades, asserts that there is no way to be smart about investment returns. In the words of Andrew Redleaf and Richard Vigilante, who are themselves hedge fund managers, "If the ideology of modern finance had a motto, it might be 'thinking doesn't work.'"[3]

But this cannot be the right conclusion to draw about investment managers. Surely professional attention to the investment of individuals' wealth cannot in the long run be detrimental to society. These professionals are paid to think about what should be done for investors.

There are problems with the efficient markets theory, and in particular with the notion that the market is so perfectly efficient because smart traders have made it so. If everyone is so rational, then why is there so much trading in these markets? If you can't make a profit trading, how can it be rational that there is so much trading going on?

Maybe the trades are made because some traders have inside information that others do not. But in a much-talked-about 1982 paper financial theorists Paul Milgrom and Nancy Stokey argued—assuming perfectly rational markets that incorporate all public information into prices—that even people with private information, information not known to the public, would not trade. Reducing their argument to its simplest form, they said they would not trade because they could not find trading partners among people who do not share their information, and they could not find trading partners because any potential trading partner would refuse to trade with someone who was motivated to trade only because of superior information.[4]

We *do* observe trading in financial markets—massive amounts of trading— and so, leveraging from Milgrom and Stokey, one might conclude that all this trade is ill advised from the standpoint of at least one of the two trading parties. One is led to wonder if psychological principles, such as overconfidence, are the dominant reason for trade in financial markets—or if those who profit from such trades, including stockbrokers and others, are not making suckers out of at least half of their customers.

But perhaps the Milgrom and Stokey theory is not really evidence that such overconfidence dominates. We might instead regard the theory as a reductio ad absurdum for the efficient markets theory. How can markets become efficient if that very result would imply that nobody trades?

If markets are going to display prices that efficiently incorporate all information, there has to be some activity. Part of this activity would involve trading, and other parts of it would involve information gathering. All this takes time and effort, and costs money. Who would undertake such activities if all markets were perfectly efficient? This viewpoint is reflected in another classic paper in financial theory, "The Impossibility of Informationally Efficient Markets," written by financial theorists Sanford Grossman and Joseph Stiglitz.[5] They frame their conclusion in terms of the "nonexistence" of an efficient markets "equilibrium." In other words, it just doesn't make sense to suppose that markets are really generally completely efficient.

Persistence of Investment Manager Performance

It is of course a truism that the average investor can never beat the market since the market is itself the definition of the average investor. And, as professional investors increasingly dominate trading, the average professional investor is fast becoming that average investor. But still there remains something useful for society in a competition among these professionals—a competition that eventually rewards the smartest institutional investors—for this competition leads to the best people rising to the top of the investment management world and taking control of the allocation of capital in our economy.

This theory relies, however, on the assumption that the smarter investors do tend to win. There is nothing in financial theory to deny that smarter investors should tend to win. There are only doubts that the financial system really rewards the smarter investors—doubts based on empirical research that some interpret as saying that financial outcomes are really just random, like the tossing of dice.

Casual observation indeed suggests that smarter investors do tend to win. The investment endowments at top U.S. universities have performed exceptionally well. My own university, Yale, leads the pack, with a 14.2% average annual return on its endowment portfolio under David Swensen in the twenty-six years since he began managing Yale's endowment in 1985, even including the years of the financial crisis since 2007.[6] Other universities have done nearly as well in recent years, notably Harvard and Princeton. Yet these universities haven't always done so well with their endowments: it was not until they established modern finance departments and cultivated a real sense of intellectual discipline about investing that their trustees would allow such thinking, rather than permitting traditional investing by conventional wisdom to dictate the composition of their portfolios.

But these isolated examples do not constitute proof that smarter investors tend to do better. It is hard to find out if smarter people generally can beat the market since it is hard to measure who is smarter. But we can find the names of the colleges investment managers attended, and there are data on average Scholastic Aptitude Test scores for students entering those colleges. Judith Chevalier and Glenn Ellison found evidence that smartness does generate performance for mutual fund managers.[7] Haitao Li, Xiaoyan Zhang, and Rui Zhao found similar results for hedge fund managers.[8] Mark Grinblatt, Matti Keloharju, and Juhani Linnainmaa found that individuals in Finland with higher IQ scores (measured when they first reported for that country's mandatory military service) showed evidence of better performance on their choices of investments, after correcting for risk.[9]

Another tack is to look at the *persistence* of performance of professional investors. We can measure their intelligence indirectly by looking at their investment performance up to a point in time, and see whether their subsequent investment performance is similarly high or low. That will allow us to determine whether investment success is just random from year to year or instead related to some characteristic, presumably intelligence, of the manager.

A number of studies have found modest persistence of mutual fund managers' performance, though the persistence seems to last no more than a year.

Harry Kat and Faye Menexe studied hedge funds. They found a small degree of persistence in hedge fund average return, though their ability to measure it was swamped by the enormous variability of their returns.[10]

Steven Kaplan and Antoinette Schoar studied private equity firms, firms that invest in stocks that are not publicly traded on stock exchanges. They concluded that "General partners . . . whose funds outperform the industry in one fund are likely to outperform the industry in the next and vice versa."[11] In judging the amount of persistence, which often seems small, one must consider that for an investment professional managing a large portfolio of a billion dollars, the extra return that this manager must earn to justify compensation of a million dollars a year is only 0.1% a year. Standard economic theory implies that competition among investment managers should drive them to the point where they just earn their keep, and so the excess return that they generate might be driven down to such a small number that it would be hard to detect among all the noise—yet they are earning their compensation. Competition should drive their returns down to the level at which they are on the point of looking for a job in another line of business. Part of the competition takes the form of new investment managers arriving in the business, hoping to compete with the existing ones, and thereby depriving the existing ones of investment opportunities. Another part of the competition takes the form of investors asking a successful existing portfolio manager to invest more money for them; faced with an ever larger portfolio to manage, the manager runs out of good investment opportunities and sees fund performance decline.[12]

Bubbles in Investment Manager Remuneration

Are top investment managers smart enough that they could routinely expect to earn a million dollars a year in another line of work? If so, and if the alternative incomes are predictable, they will have an incentive to leave investment management after their investment returns sink to this level or below, and the million-dollar-a-year income for investment managers will tend, by basic principles of economics, to be conserved. Workers' arbitrage across occupations will tend to keep the returns to skilled investing down to this level, and not let it fall below this level either. If investment managers' ability to earn excess returns through investing fell below this level, some of them would exit to their alternative jobs.

However, there is a complication: one cannot know exactly what the prospective excess return one can earn as an investment manager will be in the future, and one cannot easily move into another million-dollar-a-year occupation. Both learning about prospective excess returns and preparing for an occupation take so many years that the process of equilibrating alternative career earnings may take a generation or more.

In the meantime, there may be speculative bubbles—both positive and negative—in investment managers' salaries. If at any point there has been a shortage of skilled investment managers, then those who are in the business will earn high returns. It will be hard for others, in other lines of business, to train themselves quickly to perform at the pinnacle in investment management, and it will take years for new young people to come into the business to compete with them. It will likewise take years before the potential competitors appreciate that the existing managers really have achieved high returns by investing intelligently.

Eventually many more people will attempt to move into the investment management business. The field will become overcrowded, and investment returns will become disappointing. Then, after more years have passed, investors will become less willing to pay high compensation to investment managers and the bubble will burst; the compensation trend may even overshoot in the downward direction.

Bubbles in investment manager compensation may tend to occur in synchrony with bubbles in the markets themselves, to the extent that investors who allocate funds to investment managers are confused and assume that returns due only to the market are attributable to manager skill. We apparently have seen such a bubble in investment manager compensation in the bubble years of the late 1990s and early 2000s, when the stock markets of the world did very well. The bubble has generated such significant anger among the general public that there have been many calls to restrict the earnings of investment managers, along with those of top executives.

But it is perhaps not necessary for governments to put any caps on the salaries that investment managers earn, for the market forces needed to bring them down may already be in place. If we are seeing the bursting of a bubble in investment manager compensation, we may see relatively lean times in coming years for people in this line of business. Anyone contemplating going into this line of work must take such considerations into mind.

In his book *Enough! True Measures of Money, Business, and Life*, the founder of the Vanguard Funds, John C. Bogle, laments that many in the financial community are milking society based on their false hopes of extraordinary profits. There must be some element of truth here, but the true magnitude of this "milking" is hard to pin down, as Bogle himself recognizes: "I know of not one academic study that has systematically attempted to calculate the value extracted by our financial system from the returns earned by investors."[13]

It will be just as hard to measure the benefit that the financial community provides in improving the allocation of resources and incentives to achieve business success. Taking a simple approach, one might note that the United States and Switzerland are the two countries with the highest per capita income, and are also among the countries with the most advanced financial sectors. Ross Levine has taken such comparisons to a higher and more systematic level, comparing many countries.[14] But it is hard to sort out real causality. Are the more advanced countries successful because of their advanced financial markets, or is their success the cause of the financial development?

The real problem is that it is difficult to prove to what extent things would be different if the financial community did not exist. It is possible to compute how much those in the financial community are paid, and the combined impact of that compensation on investor returns has been documented.[15] Yet the aggregate benefit of all these people, offsetting this cost, is hard to measure. Much of this benefit is in a form that is external to the individual investor's decision: the process of investment management makes markets more efficient and thus directs resources in a better way.

Deceptive Games Investment Managers Play

Financial theorists have developed a substantial literature on how to evaluate the success of portfolio managers. An important fundamental problem is that investment managers can appear to do very well for a long time by investing in assets that other investors shun because of perceived risks, so long as there is no current news about such risks. The manager can take home high management fees for all the years that the risks do not show up, and then walk away when the catastrophe finally comes.

For years, finance students have been taught to use the Sharpe ratio to evaluate whether a portfolio manager is really beating the market. The Sharpe ratio, named after Stanford University finance professor William Sharpe, is the average excess return over the historical life of the manager's portfolio above the return of the market of all possible investments as a whole divided by the standard deviation of the return over the historical life of the manager's portfolio. A high Sharpe ratio is taken as a sign of a good investment manager. If the manager is outperforming the market consistently, then the numerator of the ratio should be large. But if the manager is taking significant risks to achieve a high return relative to the market, that will show up in the denominator as high variability in the manager's portfolio return, and thus bring down the Sharpe ratio.

But the Sharpe ratio is not necessarily a reliable indicator of a manager's performance, as the risks do not necessarily show up in a high standard deviation of returns for the portfolio over most of its life. If there is no news about the risks, then prices will not change, until the catastrophe comes.

Consider for example the risk of investing in politically unstable economies. Those investments are inherently very risky. But suppose the country was Egypt under Hosni Mubarak. The end of his regime came with shocking suddenness in 2011. It can be traced to an outbreak of riots in neighboring Tunisia. Within a month the quick fall of the Tunisian government had encouraged similar rioting in Egypt by those who sensed that Tunisia marked an important turning point and that the time was ripe for a popular revolt against Mubarak.

Investment managers can seek out investments like those in Egypt under Mubarak, ones that will blow up only in the future. If their sole objective is to pocket management fees right now, and they have no sense of integrity or commitment to their clients, they have a strong incentive to do just that. They know they cannot be prosecuted for negligence: who could really be blamed for not predicting something like Mubarak's overthrow? So if they are cynical they won't give such risks a moment's thought.

William Goetzmann and some of his colleagues in the Yale finance group have calculated the optimal strategy for a manager of an investment fund who wishes to deceive investors by producing good returns for a number of years, and then to take the investment fees and run in that rare year when the fund does very badly for its investors.[16] Such a nefarious strategy generates "tail risk," risk in the tails of the probability distribution of investment returns, or, in other words, "black swan events" that are so rare that investors may not see them coming, even though they are huge when they do occur. In the meantime, the investment fund can profit from the appearance of good and safe returns. The optimal strategy involves adding options to the portfolio, in such a way as to sell off the benefit of any (rare) unusually high portfolio returns (sell out-of-the-money call options on the portfolio) and also to profit in the short run by redoubling any (rare) unusually bad portfolio returns (sell out-of-the-money put options on the portfolio).

Investment companies can legally engage in such shenanigans if they disclose them. The private investment company Integral Investment Management, managed by former biologist Conrad Seghers, advertised, according to a *Wall Street Journal* story, an extremely high Sharpe ratio but disclosed that it was pursuing some unusual derivatives activities.[17] According to Goetzmann and his co-authors, Integral was coming close to the optimal Sharpe ratio manipulation because of massive sales of out-of-the-money puts on U.S. equity indices and a short call position implicit in the hedge fund fees. The manipulation worked, and Integral managed to persuade the Art Institute of Chicago to invest $43 million of its endowment in Integral and related funds. After the stock market collapse in 2001, and at least a $20 million loss on its investment, the Art Institute sued Integral. Integral was caught on a number of securities law violations, but it was not penalized for its unusual Sharpe ratio strategy.[18]

This example illustrates why investing cannot be done by the numbers alone. Integral Investment Management looked great in terms of the numbers. But the advantages were illusory. Other firms that pursue similar strategies that are not based on options trades may be even more successful at the same game Integral played. That is why one cannot merely allocate funds to the investment company that has had the highest historic returns or Sharpe ratios or any other statistic. These high numbers may be evidence of something very different than the competence of the managers. One must judge the integrity of the people who run the fund by the broad picture of their actions over time, and by other clues to their behavior. Character matters, and it is reflected in the reputation of certain firms, for better and worse.

Regulations can make it more difficult for retail investment companies to pursue such tricks. Securities laws in the United States and other countries prohibit investment companies from failing to state a material fact if such an omission would make their report of past returns misleading. These regula-tions are, however, necessarily imperfect. What "material fact" before 2011 could a fund have been accused of omitting that would have predicted the overthrow of Mubarak? The regulations were unsuccessful in preventing the deceptions that contributed substantially to the severity of the financial crisis that began in 2007.[19]

Integrity in Investment Management

The efficient markets theory works as well as it appears to because the theory is most routinely tested with assets that are heavily traded—assets that profes-sional managers have done their best to price accurately, and hence have effectively endorsed as honest investments at the current price. In this way, the investment profession—including its self-regulatory organizations, which work with government regulators—is collectively responsible for the integrity that exists in our financial markets. We trust the market prices of investment-grade assets not just because they have had a market test but because we trust the integrity of the many analysts who evaluate them.

As Henry Kaufman, a managing director of Salomon Brothers, concluded in his 2001 book *On Money and Markets:* "Trust is the cornerstone of most relationships in life. Financial institutions and markets must rest on a founda-tion of trust as well."[20]

It is also a conclusion reached by Anna Bernasek in her 2010 book *The Economics of Integrity.* She refers to the "constant temptation to cut corners to save money or exploit the trust of others." But businesspeople with moral standards resist that temptation: "Integrity works to create wealth by making the economy more efficient."[21]

Ultimately, the idea that investment managers as a group are "frauds" because they cannot as a group outperform the market is mistaken. They are providing a multitude of services, including honestly watching over portfolios with sympathy for the needs of their clients—and the better among them apparently *are* outperforming the market. The intellectual community that they provide also constitutes an externality that benefits society, in directing resources and incorporating information into market prices. In the future, better regulation and better financial advice for general investors can help improve the overall state of the investment management industry.

Chapter 3

Bankers

Banks—and bankers—have survived centuries of financial evolution, and thus have found an important ecological niche in the economy. The form taken by banks evolves steadily; their function remains much the same. Their activities are fundamental to the economic environment; notably they provide transaction services and contribute to the money supply, which in turn facilitates commerce. They are so involved in our daily lives that they are known by everyone, and banking is a concept integral to modern world culture.

And yet there is immense hostility today toward bankers. The word *bankster* (rhymes with *gangster*) has come back into vogue to describe them. The word was first coined amidst the anger of the Great Depression of the 1930s, and it has returned with the public anger directed toward the financial community today. Much of this venom is directed at bankers because they were bailed out by the government, their compensation continuing at high levels while the economy remained in the doldrums.

Governments have put in place elaborate sets of laws and regulations to make it possible for such institutions to minimize the faults that have generated such ill will. In particular governments want to prevent instabilities in the banking system from creating economic recessions and depressions, as they have many times in history. And yet banks themselves are constantly and fundamentally changing, becoming much more sophisticated and universal in their activities—a trend that makes the problem of their regulation tougher and tougher, to the consternation and despair of bank regulators.

It is a curious fact that while there is much criticism of bankers, people do not carry over to them the criticism they aim at investment managers for their claims that they can beat the market. Of course, bankers are in much the same business as investment managers: when bankers make loans they are in effect making risky investments, just as investment managers do. But somehow it is thought that bankers must know what they are doing. This distinction must in part have to do with the fact that bankers typically stay out of the most volatile, headline-grabbing markets. But perhaps too it is because bankers, in contrast to hedge fund managers and the like, are following a long and time-honored tradition, extending back hundreds of years, which has evolved to solve certain problems—including liquidity, moral hazard and selection bias, and transaction service problems—to the satisfaction of most people most of the time.

The anger toward bankers takes a very different form. It seems to be anger at their power and presumption, at their single-minded pursuit of money. And the anger flares up whenever there is a banking crisis and the governments of the world come to the rescue of these wealthy interests.

But the public also has a sense of the centrality, sobriety, and safety of banks, and they must know that those who manage banks are highly influential in determining the economic outcomes in our society. The people who run banks indeed find themselves in a guidance or management role for the whole community.

Banking has historically been a pillar-of-the-community line of business, one that provides a degree of extra-monetary reward for those who go into it, at least in normal times when things are going well. But these days—at least as of the time of this writing—that feeling of reward is not so apparent.

The Origins of Banks

The current metaphor for a bank is a safe or vault for storing gold or money. The metaphor has become so ingrained in our thinking that the bank is thought of, viscerally, as providing a safe and practical investment option. In reality, the modern word *bank* was derived not from the word *safe* but, by the fifteenth century, from the Old Italian *banca*, related to the English word *bench*, referring to the tables on which bankers counted money in front of their customers. Still, metaphor counts for more than etymology in popular culture, and part of the ecological niche that banks occupy is still as a perfectly safe place to put one's money.

There will always be anxieties about money and a demand for the safest place to put it. Protecting wealth from theft or loss is a fundamental problem that has animated people from the very beginnings of the exchange economy. Even in today's anti-finance climate, people remain grateful for the services banks provide, and they still trust them.

For thousands of years, the best way to safeguard precious metals, jewels, or money was actually not to put them in a bank but just to bury them in an unmarked spot in a yard. Unfortunately burying valuables in a yard has drawbacks, too, as illustrated in Moliere's play *The Miser*, in which the rich man Harpagon has buried his fortune in his garden. His continual worries about whether it is still there eventually cause him unwittingly to reveal its location, and it is stolen. Moreover, burying gold is no longer as safe as it once was, as modern metal detectors can find it. We can't go back to ancient ways. We all need a modern provider of safety in saving.

The metaphor of the bank that developed after the Renaissance was the ancient citadel, or fortress, in the center of a city, like the Acropolis in ancient Greece. The wealthiest and most influential people could put their money there for safekeeping. That is part of the reason why bank buildings for centuries were built to resemble the Acropolis and other such classical buildings of a type found in citadels.

Bankers as Providers of Safe Return with Liquidity

A problem with burying gold or storing it in the citadel is that it earns no interest. People thus learned to trade off some safety for return, and even in ancient times they would leave some of their gold with money lenders. In ancient Rome, these establishments were called *tabernae argentariae* (literally, shops of money). They would pay interest on deposits left with them and make a profit by charging a higher interest rate on loans they made. About seven first-century examples of these *tabernae argentariae*, little more than small storefronts along a street, were found (with some of the coins still there) near the Pantheon in the ruins of ancient Pompeii. These were simple shops that housed a money lender with a few assistants; they were not large organizations like banks today. Pedestals for the oblong tables on which the money lenders counted the money are still visible. With so many to choose from, a depositor of the time could easily diversify the risk and deposit with several of them.

So banks are managers of investments on behalf of clients, just like other kinds of investment managers, but with greater claims to safety. The defining characteristic of banks has generally been that their investments take the form of deposits which pay a fixed interest rate, rather than an uncertain return, and that the deposits are usually liquid; that is, the money can be withdrawn with no more than short notice. Bank deposits are thus as freely available as money buried in the garden, but they improve on that approach in terms of safety and expected return.

The safety and return that banks offer bear further examination. How is it that they can offer a respectable return with great liquidity and little risk? Is it just because they are backed by the government, which won't let them fail out of concern for the economy? Banks flourished long before governments were generally involved in insuring their deposits or bailing them out when they were in trouble.

Banks solve a fundamental problem potentially encountered by anyone who seeks a return on an investment. If you as an individual loan money to another individual, who in turn uses the money to start or expand a business, or to buy a house, you can't demand it back with interest at a moment's notice. You have to wait until the business matures and starts yielding profits, or until the house can be sold at a profit. You probably can't easily sell your loan to another investor either. So in terms of ready cash flow you are in a bind— you are illiquid.

Banks also can't get their money back quickly from most of their investments. But banks achieve liquidity for their depositors by another means: pooling the investments of many depositors. They do not invest all the money that is deposited with them in illiquid investments. They keep in liquid form an amount of capital sufficient to cover the normal volume of withdrawals. So everyone can make deposits that are backed by illiquid investments yet have their individual deposits remain highly liquid. It seems almost a miracle.

This system usually works as intended, though it is vulnerable to sudden panic or bank runs: if people begin to distrust the bank, too many of them may ask to withdraw their money at one time and they will exhaust the bank's supply of liquid funds.[1] Even then, and even if there is no deposit insurance, if the government allows the bank to suspend liquidity temporarily, then depositors will still in all likelihood eventually get paid most of what they were owed, as the bank converts some of its illiquid holdings into cash.

Bank regulators in modern times attempt to further reduce the problem of bank runs by demanding that banks maintain an adequate amount of reserves (cash in the vault or deposits at other banks, to make good immediately on any sudden withdrawals by depositors) and of capital (the total cushion of assets, after subtracting liabilities, available to make good on promises to depositors), so that they will not put the government in the position of having to bail out the banks. In the United States, explicit reserve requirements date back to the early days of the Federal Reserve, in 1917.[2] Capital requirements for banks began to be enforced by the United States in 1982.[3] International capital agreements began with the Basel Accord in 1988, and they were reformed by the Basel Committee in response to the financial crisis that began in 2007, to avoid more government bailouts in future crises. Bank regulation becomes more and more complex as the years go by, as does the banking business itself.

In addition to providing liquidity, banks address another problem that individuals seeking a return on their investments face if they try to invest directly—a moral hazard problem. If individuals invest directly in companies, by lending money to them or buying their securities, they may in effect be robbed by the people with whom they invest. There are numerous ways for the managers of a business to funnel money out of the company and into the hands of friends, thereby in effect stealing money from their investors. They may pay inflated invoices from supplier companies run by cronies, enriching them and expecting a kickback later. They may deliberately destroy the business (in which they may never have really believed in the first place), liquidating its assets in the interest of redirecting the money to associates. Or the business could simply launch especially risky activities, with but a small probability of gain and a much larger probability of loss. The company may not care about the losses since they will be visited on the "sucker" investors.[4]

On the other hand, many banks have been in business for a long time—sometimes centuries—and thus have a reputation to uphold. (Reputation is still important even with deposit insurance, for many of the deposits in a successful bank will be above the statutorily insured limit.) The public perception is that banks are adept at sniffing out and avoiding such bad investments. And even if they do make the occasional bad call, they have numerous other investments in their portfolios, a strategy that generally helps them maintain their integrity and reputations—except for the occasional severe financial crisis, during which, admittedly, some may fail or be bailed out.

Banks solve yet another problem that less-skilled investors face: a selection bias problem. Those who are paying less attention to researching their investments will tend to be the more easily victimized; they will wind up with the "lemons" among investments because more skilled investors will snap up the better ones.

Most individuals have no way of evaluating the trustworthiness of businesses in which they might invest. They can try to read published reports on the businesses in newspapers or magazines, or reports issued by rating agencies. But these reports tend to be reliable only for the biggest of companies: there is little incentive for reporters or investment analysts to get into the nitty-gritty of really evaluating every business that is looking for money to expand. Such reports are not profitable for their providers because they are not really of interest to a broad audience, only to those actively looking for investing tips. Moreover, any time one of those reports is issued, there is a free-rider problem: people will spread investing tips gleaned from the report to others (the free riders) who did not even pay for the report.

Companies, at least large companies, do issue debt directly to the public, and some people try to avoid the need for bankers as intermediaries and invest directly in such company debt. They may find such investments safe enough because they know that many other investors, supposedly in the know, are investing in the same companies. But here again *they* are free-riding on the vigilance of other investors in the debt, and so there is the risk that the other investors may be free-riding too. It can turn out that *none* of the investors is really paying attention to the machinations of a company in which they are all investing, and this fact will become apparent only later—and alarmingly quickly—during a crisis.

A bank, on the other hand, stays connected, and it usually has branches in the communities in which it does business. The officers in those branches deal on a personal basis with the businesses to which they lend money, and they collect detailed information about what is really going on with these businesses, right down to evaluating those who run the companies—their trustworthiness, their real motivations and likely future behavior. There is no free-rider problem associated with the collection of this information since the bank does not publish it. Bankers traditionally make short-term renewable loans and demand regular reporting from the companies to which they lend, and the managers of these companies know they had better maintain a good relationship with their bankers or risk having their loans called.

These bank procedures have endured for centuries because, in normal times at least, they work. And they work especially well, relative to direct borrowing from the public, in less-developed countries, where there are fewer analysts, rating agencies, and newspapers and magazines to provide evaluation of investments. Hence banking plays an even bigger role in the economies of less-developed countries.[5]

In contrast, the role of traditional banks in the economies of more advanced countries has been in decline for decades: the fraction of these countries' debt that is accounted for by traditional bank loans has been falling.[6] This is so because the quality of publicly available information about securities is improving, and so the moral hazard and selection bias problems are reduced.

Banks will increasingly be transformed into more complex institutions, but their traditional banking business will not go away entirely. Such banking meets too many of society's needs, and banks' public persona—current events notwithstanding—is too strong.

The Evolution and Future of Banking

Indeed the severe financial crisis that began in 2007 was not due to any failures in the traditional banking business model, but instead to certain new kinds of business models, in which loans made to homeowners were not retained on the books of banks and other mortgage originators but bundled together into securities and sold off to other investors, including other banks—reintroducing the very problem of moral hazard that banks were supposed to solve.

Regulators, notably in the United States, have been increasingly permissive of alternative forms of banking. Over the past generation they have allowed an unregulated "shadow banking" system to develop, which is not subject to the same regulatory oversight as the commercial banking system. Shadow banks are merely financial institutions that manage to escape banking regulation by designing themselves so that they do not fit the definition of commercial banks. They do not literally accept deposits, but instead get the money they lend in slightly different ways.

Examples of shadow banks include the now-failed Bear Stearns and Lehman Brothers, which were called investment banks but were not regulated as commercial banks, since they did not accept deposits. They became shadow banks when they began to *act* like commercial banks. Another example is the structured investment vehicle (SIV), which was created by commercial banks before the financial crisis of 2007; they hoped to escape regulation by putting some of their business into the SIVs, which were considered separate (and unregulated) entities.

Shadow banks may obtain commercial securitized loans or mortgages and enter into repurchase agreements with institutional investors, using the securities as collateral. That business creates liquid investments for institutional investors, which resemble deposits, and so the shadow bankers are in effect creating money as well. Thus their activities may involve a risk of collapse of the entire economic system, just as with commercial banks.[7]

A bank's business—which may have had significant "charter value" because of barriers to entry into banking that serve to inhibit new competitors—is adversely affected by these new competitors. Thus traditional banks may feel an imperative to branch out, and they may start behaving like the shadow banks if they can, entering unconventional new lines of activity like originating subprime mortgage securities and thus creating risks to the economic system that may not be noticed by regulators of traditional banks.[8] That is what led to the current financial crisis.

New regulations, notably the Dodd-Frank Act in the United States, are designed to put many of these shadow banking activities under stronger regulation, to help prevent a repeat of the crisis. But that process has been slow and cumbersome. And it will be difficult to develop regulation to keep pace with, and prevent problems with, new kinds of shadow banks as they are invented. Critics of the financial system are right to be wary of this situation.

The Democratization of Banking

The business model that bankers have evolved over the centuries is a great idea, and people who know this well have sought to encourage a broader and broader application of this model. That is, they have been trying to democratize banking, moving it beyond its original role in serving primarily the wealthy and the financially sophisticated. This initiative stands as an excellent example of finance performing its role in the stewardship of society's assets.

There have been a number of historical movements to democratize banking. In the early nineteenth century there was the savings bank movement in Great Britain, followed by a similar one in the United States. These banks were initially set up as mutuals by philanthropists to give those with low incomes the means and incentive to save; hence they were nonprofit. That same century saw the beginnings of the building society movement in the United Kingdom, followed by the savings and loan association movement in the United States, both of which were aimed at providing people the wherewithal to buy a home.

Postal savings banks arose in that century and in the early twentieth century to provide savings vehicles to every town that had a post office. The twentieth century saw the microfinance movement, exemplified by Muhammad Yunus's Grameen Bank, which specializes in making very small loans to people who traditionally have been ignored by banks.[9] Evidence from randomly assigned individual liability loans shows that lending programs like those of Grameen Bank "increase ability to cope with risk, strengthen community ties, and increase access to informal credit."[10] Today microfinance loans are further promoted by a web site, kiva.org, that allows individual lenders all over the world to lend small sums via microfinance institutions to individual entrepreneurs in poorer regions and, through the power of the Internet, to deal one-on-one with the very people who benefit from their loans.

The democratization of banking is a slow process, occurring over centuries, benefiting from technological progress of various sorts, and still far from complete, even in advanced countries. A Federal Reserve study based on 2007 data showed that 25.1% of U.S. families in the bottom fifth of income have no transactions accounts at all.[11] Because of the absence of elementary banking services, these families find it difficult to save, thus undermining their ability to acquire important skills, send their children to college, and plan for their future.[12]

A number of government policies to encourage the democratization of banking have been proposed, including explicit incentives to banks to provide services to low-income people and the automatic opening of bank accounts for tax refunds and welfare payments.[13] We should also consider another drive to encourage more people to avail themselves of financial services: a repeat of the nineteenth-century savings bank movement for the twenty-first century.

For the better part of two centuries there has been an effort to deliver the full range of banking services to the broadest cross section of society, but the job is not yet complete. The democratization of finance is a route to the good society, and the democratization of banking is a trend—admittedly slow and long-term—that should play an important role in that process. Further democratization of banking is also the best means of dealing with the hostility currently felt toward bankers.

Chapter 4

Investment Bankers

Investment bankers are the people who help organizations sell new securities. In particular, they arrange for companies to issue shares to investors. If it is the first time the company has sold shares to the public, investment bankers help with what is called the initial public offering (IPO). If the company wants to raise yet more money by selling even more shares to the public, investment bankers help organize what is called a seasoned offering. Either way, the investment banker is facilitating the acquisition of capital by the company, dividing up the company into shares that appeal to investors, and helping manage risk.

Investment bankers, in their pure form, differ from conventional bankers in that they do not accept deposits and do not make loans. They specialize in *underwriting* securities, such as new shares, which means they perform due diligence on the issuing company, design the terms of the issue, place the shares with long-term investors, put their own reputation behind the new issue, and perform a variety of other tasks necessary to meet administrative and regulatory requirements.

Because the general public does not usually deal directly with investment bankers, the bankers are largely invisible to them and therefore do not usually elicit as much public hostility as other financial professionals—until there is a crisis that spotlights their activities. In the current financial crisis, major investment banking firms—such as Bear Stearns, Goldman Sachs, and Lehman Brothers—became objects of loathing for some. But in fact investment bankers are really responsible for the origins of our securities markets, including stock markets. Without them, we would not have these markets.

The stock market is a wonderful invention. It is important that companies be able to sell shares to the public, for that process engages a large number of people in their economic undertakings. It allows people to indulge their naturally adventurous spirit but also allows them to choose how much exposure they can tolerate. It decentralizes the allocation of capital, potentially to involve any member of society. And, in the case of corporate acquisitions, it allows individuals or entities to take control of an enterprise and run it as they see fit.

The idea of issuing shares in an enterprise is probably so old that it cannot be dated. It is known that shares (Latin *partes*) in corporations (Latin *publicani*) were traded near the Temple of Castor in the ancient Roman Forum. Records of the share prices do not survive, but evidence that these prices were talked about does.[1]

We know even less about what sort of investment bankers may have existed back then. Perhaps an important reason why there were so few shares in companies in ancient times is that the profession of investment banker had not yet developed very far. Modern methods of investment banking were as yet unheard of.

Shareholding gained momentum in Renaissance Italy, but even then it was not well developed. A notable advance occurred in 1602 with the founding of the Dutch East India Company in Amsterdam, for this corporation soon had a market designed to facilitate daily trading of its shares. The company opened its books to record new shareholders only once a year, but the law allowed for trading of these shares every day. Effectively people could buy shares and hold ownership in what is now called "street name," meaning that the shares are really in the physical possession of and recorded in the name of the broker, on behalf of the beneficial owner. The ownership was guaranteed by a broker, even though the company at first knew nothing about it. The daily trading of shares in a corporation had a profound psychological impact. The price fluctuations from day to day were widely noted, and this in turn generated increased interest in the investment. The freedom to get in or out of the investment day by day built a sense of excitement. This advance both democratized and humanized finance: it brought many more people into the market even as it respected their demand for liquidity and need for pride of ownership while they held shares.

The Amsterdam stock market became regulated when short selling (the sale of borrowed shares, not even owned by the seller) in 1609 led to market turmoil and the temporary abolition of that practice. The invention of the newspaper came soon after, and it was not long before the prices of the East India Company's shares were reported regularly, spurring immense public interest in the investment.

The issuance of shares in joint stock companies (companies owned jointly by a number of people through shares) was limited at first. To mount an IPO, each corporation needed its own special charter, which was hard to get. The Bank of England was chartered as a joint-stock company in 1694, but at the same time it was given a monopoly on joint stock banking. No other bank could have more than six partners, making it virtually impossible to compete with the Bank of England.

A quarter century later, in 1720, Parliament further restricted joint stock companies by mandating—in what later became known as the Bubble Act—that no joint stock company could ever be started without a royal charter. Perhaps this was an effort to support the rise in the price of shares in the South Sea Company, which was at the time soaring in an obvious bubble.

But as time went on pressures to democratize finance prevailed, enabling more corporations to be formed. Parliament restricted the Bank of England's monopoly to an area within sixty-five miles of London in 1826, and in 1844 the monopoly was eliminated altogether. This led to an expansion of banking activities, and within two decades England had seen bank offices proliferate to even small towns.[2]

The Democratization of Investment Banking

Investment banking received further impetus on the other side of the Atlantic in 1811 with the passage of a corporate law in New York State that made it clear that anyone who satisfied minimal requirements could set up a corporation, without special action by the government, and that clearly established limited liability for corporations. The law further democratized finance. By clarifying that shareholders would never be held liable for the debts of the corporation, the law made it possible for the first time for an investor to hold a diversified portfolio, consisting of stocks in many companies. Prior to the advent of limited liability, one could not have done such a thing, for fear of a lawsuit from any of the companies held. This development created a ready pool of investors with whom investment bankers could place newly issued shares. After seeing how steady a supply of capital for new businesses this innovation produced, countries all over the world copied it.

The framers of the New York law probably did not see themselves as the inventors of a brand new kind of market. Instead they apparently thought of themselves as merely responding in an imaginative manner to an economic crisis. The U.S. Congress had imposed an embargo on trade with Britain starting in 1807, citing grievances related to British behavior toward the United States as Britain fought a war with France. By 1811 the extended trade embargo was causing massive economic pain at home, for America had been an exporter of cotton and other fibers to British textile mills. There was a need to finance U.S. textile mills, but few wanted to start a local mill, thinking it would be hard to compete with Britain when the embargo was eventually lifted. The provisions of the bill were thought of merely as expedients to deal with this crisis. The bill followed a 1784 measure granting automatic incorporation to religious congregations, and similar measures for colleges and academies in 1781, municipalities in 1788, libraries in 1792, medical societies in 1806, and turnpikes in 1807.[3] Yet only by 1811 did general business have the status within New York society to win the same right. Equally important, the bill clarified that stockholders in these new corporations had limited liability: they could not lose more than the money they had put in in purchasing their shares.

The full name of the act was "A Bill to Encourage the Manufacture of Woolen Cloth, also Cotton, Hemp and Flax, and for other Purposes." As it turned out, it was the "other purposes" that would have lasting importance. Once again, dealing with a short-term crisis led to a financial innovation that would change the world, for the 1811 New York law became the model for new corporate law all over the world.[4]

Underlying the concept of free incorporation and the unrestrained trading of shares is a hoped-for result: an imaginative application of capital to new ideas and new business directions. We continue to improve the ability of our investment banking institutions to achieve this; the recent development of "crowd funding" Web sites, enabled by the U.S. JOBS Act of 2012, is an example. Even if most of these ideas fail, some will succeed.

It has been argued by many that share trading is little more than gambling. Contributing to this idea is the "fact" that most entities traded on stock exchanges are big companies that do not regularly issue new shares. Stewart Myers offered a theory of corporate finance according to which there is a pecking order of new capital sources, and new issues of shares are last in the order. Seasoned issues of shares are, Myers asserted, relatively unimportant sources of capital for corporations.[5]

But it turns out that Myers's evidence was not as impressive as one might think. Eugene Fama and Kenneth French argued that, at the time Myers wrote, issues of seasoned shares *were* rare. But that merely reflected the situation in the economy at that time. At other times, including more recently, share issuance is a more important source for new capital.[6] Since Myers wrote, share issuance has also tended to come about as part of incentive packages given to employees of firms. Even though those shares are issued in special circumstances, they are still shares issued. The firm continues to depend on market valuations to maintain its ability to raise capital.

How Investment Banking Keeps Incentives Up to Date

As anyone who has ever lived in a family knows, there are profound difficulties in motivating everyone to do their work. Usually one person in the household shoulders most of the work and is responsible for keeping things running. The same would tend be true in any business organization. Fortunately, ever since fractional interests in corporations were developed, there has been a better way: allocate shares in the corporation, or bonuses or options paid in shares, to key people to reward them directly for bearing responsibility.

Facebook was founded by Eduardo Saverin and Mark Zuckerberg. According to recent news accounts Saverin currently owns only about 5% of the company, down from about 34%, while Zuckerberg's share has fallen from 66% to 24%. Why did their ownership stakes both decrease? They did so because Saverin and Zuckerberg needed to bring in other investors to grow the company. Why did Saverin's share fall more? Certainly no one took Saverin's stock away from him. He lost much of his percentage share of the company by dilution: new shares were issued to incentivize newly hired employees, and still more shares were awarded to Zuckerberg. Why? This is a sensitive subject, and one of the determinants of his share was a legal settlement. In part it—quite logically—has to do with the board of directors' opinion that Saverin needed less incentivization than Zuckerberg in order to move the company forward.

The process of issuing new shares in a company that unevenly dilute the ownership stakes of existing shareholders can become one of the fiercest battlegrounds in modern finance, as fortunes are wiped out, rivalries are created, and political machinations are indulged. There is no way to make this process appear fair to all involved. Lawyers may smooth some of the rough edges and ruffled feathers, but it is still a killing field where the absurd and the tragic often go hand in hand.

But the overall process of share issuance and incentivization is far kinder and gentler than armed conflict, and it provides a civilized outlet for human aggression that can ultimately lead to more productive corporations and thus beneficial outcomes for society as a whole. Investment bankers in a sense serve as diplomats negotiating an understanding between contentious powers—an understanding that ultimately allows them to cooperate and get on with their business. In the corporate world, investment bankers are, in the final analysis, keepers of the peace and promoters of progress.

Chapter 5

Mortgage Lenders and Securitizers

Housing is one of the most fundamental of economic needs. The need for housing tends to come at an early point in the life of a family, when it first has children or sees the immediate prospect of them, yet when resources may be low. There is a strong motive for the financial industry to help with this fundamental problem. Society, as we have already noted, regards the subsidizing of homeownership as beneficial, and so sees a public good in promoting mortgage lending.

And yet, particularly in the United States, public disgust has been directed toward mortgage lenders and securitizers today. They are seen as the instigators of the financial crisis that has spread from America around the world. The crisis began with the collapse of the subprime mortgage securities market in the United States, and so anger about the crisis has generalized to anger directed at those who made those loans initially.

Mortgage lending is a process of dealmaking among three major parties: the home buyer, the ultimate lender, and the government, which typically wishes to promote homeownership. Each of these three parties has different needs, concerns, and time horizons. Efficiently selecting and matching among all these parties is a problem that can benefit from financial innovation. It is also a process prone to error and even catastrophe.

A method for mortgage lending developed in the United States was being increasingly copied in other parts of the world until the advent of the severe financial crisis that began in 2007. The first stage of the process is mortgage origination, in which a local office works directly with the home buyer to arrange the terms of the loan and get the contract signed. The mortgage originator then sells the mortgage to a mortgage securitizer, who in turn bundles a large group of mortgages into a residential mortgage–backed security (RMBS), which may then be sold to investors.

Mortgage Origination

The process of originating mortgages is perhaps the most delicate link in the chain, for it involves crafting a deal between the least financially informed party, the future homeowner(s), and sophisticated professional financial representatives. The potential for neglect of the real needs of the borrowers, or even outright abuse, is high.

Most mortgage originators operate with integrity, and indeed they find that maintaining their reputations is part of what keeps them in business. The mortgage origination process works well when they feel part of their communities and are motivated to do well for their clients by that personal sense of integrity. But the process does not always work well.

The financial crisis of 2007 can in part be traced back to abuses of the mortgage origination process. Borrowers were given mortgages they couldn't afford or the wrong kind of mortgages.

The problem was not a new one, and the U.S. Congress had already tried to remedy the situation over the years. The Riegle Community Development and Regulatory Improvement Act of 1994 created a new legal entity, the community development financial institution, to ensure that people seeking home mortgages would be protected, and there are now over a thousand such community organizations. Congress also tried to help with its Home Ownership and Equity Protection Act of 1994, which established standards for mortgage lending—but its provisions were too easily evaded. Mortgage brokers at that time were not subject to licensing, and the industry had no professional code of ethics. Brokers would often talk clients into buying large homes with adjustable-rate mortgages, without clearly informing them that the rates would likely go up and the homes become unaffordable. State governments in the United States have now instituted licensing for mortgage brokers. The Dodd-Frank Act of 2010 forbids mortgage companies from incentivizing their loan officers to steer borrowers toward profitable mortgages that are not right for them, and it also requires mortgage originators to verify their borrowers' ability to repay.

Nevertheless all these government efforts have been only partly successful. There remains so much in the process of issuing a mortgage that simply cannot be seen and policed by the government. The weaknesses in the mortgage origination market—and in the behavior of certain market participants— reflects a genuine deficiency in the modern financial system and a prime site for innovative solutions.

Nonprofit organizations like the Center for Responsible Lending and the Center for Community Self-Help offer advice to homeowners, but they are just not big enough to reach most borrowers. Properly reforming finance means that at the very least we have to think about how such grass-roots assistance organizations can be expanded in the future.

Mortgage Securitization

The next step in the mortgage lending process, as we have seen, is that the mortgage originators sell their individual mortgages to a mortgage securitizer so that they can be bundled into a form that will allow them to be placed in investor portfolios. At this point there has often been another step in the process. The RMBSs will in turn be placed into a trust to allow a set of collateralized debt obligations (CDOs) to be issued based on the mortgage pool. The CDOs are divided up into pieces known as tranches, according to the perceived repayment ability of the holders of the underlying mortgages; in case of default on some of those mortgages, the senior tranche is paid first, followed by the second tranche, the third tranche, and so on. The various tranches, with their different levels of risk and accordingly varying pricing, are designed to appeal to different kinds of investors. The last tranche—the residual tranche, known colloquially in the industry as "toxic waste"—is paid last, and holders of it receive no income at all unless very few of the underlying mortgages default. All of these tranches, except for the last, the toxic waste, which is retained by the securitizer, are sold separately by the securitizer to investors.

According to the logic, the first tranche, the senior tranche, is very unlikely to default, and so securities rating agencies routinely gave these tranches AAA ratings before the financial crisis. They were easy to sell to the ultimate investors.

Yet the whole process became suspect after the collapse of the securities that were backed by subprime (low-quality) mortgages, resulting in a domino effect around the world. Something was indeed wrong with the process as it had developed by the early 2000s.

Many of the AAA-rated CDOs ultimately lost substantial value. The rating agencies—like so many lenient teachers who give out too many As—had grown complacent and distributed too many high ratings. The ratings were faulty, and so was the whole system based upon them.

And yet the tranching system and the rating system have nevertheless functioned fairly well so far in this crisis—a little-known fact. Research by Sun Young Park, recently a graduate student at Yale and now at the Korea Advanced Institute of Science and Technology, found that, contrary to popular belief, only a very small fraction (0.17%) of the principal of U.S. AAA-rated subprime mortgage–backed security tranches issued between 2004 and 2007 had experienced losses owing to underlying mortgage default as of 2011.[1]

News accounts of a few AAA subprime securities that suffered major default losses, of the significant default losses in the lower-rated tranches, and of major market price declines have all left people with a faulty impression of the failures of the tranching system.[2]

Mortgage securitization was all part of a design by—indeed was an invention of—the U.S. government. Mortgage securities were first issued by government-sponsored enterprises (GSEs): the Federal Home Loan Mortgage Corporation (Freddie Mac) in 1971 and the Federal National Mortgage Association (Fannie Mae) in 1981.[3] The process appeared to go well at first. Yet the mortgage credit risk of Freddie and Fannie together rose 16% a year from 1980 to 2007.[4]

But both enterprises later went bankrupt and came under U.S. government conservatorship in 2008, after the collapse in home prices left many mortgages in foreclosure and brought on the financial crisis. These GSEs had never thought a home price decline of such magnitude was possible, and so they did not plan for it. In common with the so-called systemically important private firms considered earlier, they enjoyed "too big to fail" status. The government could never let them fail as that might bring down the whole economy; it was therefore clear that the government would inevitably bail them out with taxpayer money. There was faulty oversight of their aggressive pursuit of advantages from their implicit government guarantee.[5]

Why did this system crash so terribly? The crash appears to have been the result of a combination of factors. The first and foremost was the near-universal assumption that home prices could never fall. If you believe this, then you will conclude that mortgage securities are a pretty safe investment: if anyone fails to repay a mortgage, the lender can simply foreclose and sell the home to recover the loan balance. Actually, in most cases there would not even be a foreclosure, since the homeowner who can no longer pay on the mortgage can, with a little prompting from the lender, just sell the house and avoid foreclosure.

I myself wondered, in the years just before the financial crisis, why so many people thought home prices could never fall. To me, the extraordinarily rapid ascent of home prices from around 1997 to 2006 suggested there was a housing bubble, which might burst, producing rapid price declines. But practically no one in the mortgage industry seemed to think that was even a remote possibility. I asked some of these people why they thought prices could never fall. They would sometimes reply that home prices had never fallen since the Great Depression. And the Depression was so long ago that it just didn't seem relevant anymore. Needless to say, they were wrong about that.

Another puzzle also presented itself in those days: why did the RMBS market become so important, when people had seen no need for it before the 1970s? We know that securitizers were creating new investment vehicles based on mortgages. But what is the difference, really, whether one invests in RMBSs or in shares in banks that own mortgages, as was the practice before Freddie and Fannie started issuing these?

Securitization was indeed never really popular in most parts of the world. The movement toward securitization of home mortgage debt became particularly strong in the United States thanks to powerful impetus from government support. But, lacking the subsidy effectively given by the U.S. government via Fannie Mae and Freddie Mac, mortgage securitization has not been common anywhere else.[6]

Before the crisis of 2007 finance theorists saw clear innovation in mortgage securitization. Securitized mortgages are, in the abstract, a way of solving an information asymmetry problem—more particularly the problem of "lemons." This problem, first given a theoretical explanation by George Akerlof, refers to the aversion many people have to buying anything on the used market, like a used car. They worry that they can't judge whether the item has defects, and that they will get stuck with a lemon. The seller knows whether a particular item is of good quality or not, but the buyer does not—at least not without expending a good deal of costly effort to find out.[7] In a nutshell, Akerlof's theory holds that if you think that the seller is going to pass off the bad stuff on you, you won't pay more for it than the lowest price. So the seller won't even try to offer the good stuff to the market, and the market becomes a repository for only the bad stuff. That is why people tend to keep (what they perceive as) good used cars in the family, but to dump the lemons onto the used market.[8] This all makes for a poorly functioning market.

Claire Hill, in her article "Securitization: A Low-Cost Sweetener for Lemons," written before the crisis, argued persuasively that an important reason the securitization and CDO market can function well is that it helps solve the lemons problem.[9] Bundling mortgages into securities that are evaluated by independent rating agencies, and dividing up a company's securities into tranches that allow specialized evaluators to do their job, efficiently lowers the risk to investors of getting stuck with lemons. They should be able to trust the higher-tranche CDOs more than any pool of mortgages or any share in a complex and difficult-to-understand mortgage-lending institution.

So there was a valid theory as to why the splitting of securitized mortgage debt into tranches was a good idea. Of course it turns out not to have worked superbly well in practice, but this is largely because of the erroneous assumption noted earlier—that everyone, including the rating agencies, thought home prices just couldn't fall. That mistake, and not any flaw in the logic of Claire Hill's theory, was the real problem.

And that is the problem that so often plagues finance. We can build beautiful models and theories about what kinds of financial products to provide, but thanks to human foibles we are always vulnerable to bubbles and their bursting.

The enormous growth of mortgage securitization in the United States also arose in part from regulatory arbitrage, that is, from businesses trying to please the regulators as efficiently as possible, and from bureaucrats who were not thinking deeply about the rules they were enforcing.

Ever since the Basel I agreement in 1988, which set the first important international bank regulatory standards, banks around the world have been subject to capital requirements that are tied by a formula to their so-called risk-weighted assets. Banks have to hold more capital, to hold back on their lending, if their investments include relatively risky assets as measured using this formula. But a neat trick on the regulators is possible: a bank that originates mortgages (which have a high risk weight and so significantly increase their risk-weighted assets) can bundle them into a security and sell them off in exchange for any other asset—even for more mortgages. Selling off the mortgages frees up the bank from its capital requirements and enables it to issue more mortgages. Under U.S. law, the bank can even go out and buy highly rated RMBSs with the money, on the assumption that these are nearly riskless. It may end up holding essentially the same mortgages as it started out with, but the regulators' formula quantifies the change as meaningful, and so banks that pursue this strategy are freer to lend.[10]

Part of the motivation for the creation of RMBSs was essentially to allow banks to escape capital controls. In 2001 the Federal Deposit Insurance Corporation, the Federal Reserve, the Comptroller of the Currency, and the Office of Thrift Supervision promulgated a new regulation, called the Recourse Rule, that offered special incentives for banks to hold securitized mortgages rather than mortgages themselves. For computing risk-weighted capital, an input in determining the capital requirements for banks, any securitized mortgages rated AAA or AA would qualify for 20% risk weighting, rather than the 50% risk weighting typically applied to mortgages. Consider what this means, for example, for two banks, both making most of their loans in the form of mortgages. Imagine that the banks are virtually identical, and that both have lent out about as much money as the regulators allow them to, given their current capital. Suppose they each package part of their mortgages into AAA securities and swap the securities with one another: each thus holds mortgages that the other originated—in the new, securitized form. You might think that nothing essential has changed. But think again. Because capital requirements are based on risk-weighted assets, and because the securities fall into a different asset class than the underlying mortgages, the effect is to loosen regulation and allow the banks to lend more.

You might ask, how could regulators be so stupid as not to see the potential for disaster here? They were not stupid. But they were operating on the assumption that the rating agencies were infallible—an assumption that they did not feel it was within their purview to examine, as they did not regulate the rating agencies. They were also politically constrained, following rules that had to be agreed upon nationally, and rules ultimately based on international agreements. Ultimately the problem was not stupidity; it was rather a problem of assigning responsibility to and coordinating the efforts of a diverse group of people.

And yet not everything was flawed: many features of the mortgage lending process will be corrected and developed into better institutions for the future. In principle, if the ratings of the RMBSs had been accurate, if they had taken accurate account of a possible collapse in housing prices, and if regulators had not given any special advantages to holders of those securities, then the system would have worked.

The defects of the mortgage securitization process were very visible in this crisis, and they will now be corrected. The benefits to society of mortgage securitization were hard to see because they take the form of lower borrowing rates for homeowners. People have no clear knowledge of what the rates might have been without the benefit of securitization. Certainly they have not thought about the possibility that they might not be living in a house at all, and that certain things that they value in life (e.g., having a home of one's own from the time the children are young) might have been made possible by it.

It is important to encourage financial innovation to proceed, to develop new and better mortgage institutions, despite the debacle with the innovative mortgage products associated with the financial crisis. Creative people in mortgage finance have a good deal of work ahead of them to make for still better deals between the parties to mortgage contracts. The mortgage contract could be made more flexible for the homeowner, with a preplanned workout.[11] Other kinds of mortgage financing innovations are possible, such as shared equity arrangements like the home equity fractional interests promoted by John O'Brien, which allow homeowners to sell shares in their homes, or the housing market partnerships promoted by Andrew Caplin and his colleagues, which allow homeowners to become partners with an institution in purchasing their homes.[12]

The rocky road that mortgage lenders have trod during the financial crisis is ample warning that we may yet experience further dislocations. But the jobs of mortgage originator and mortgage securitizer will still be with us, if perhaps in modified form, because they do help solve a basic economic problem. Next time, we won't believe that home prices can never fall, and we will do better. That is the painful process of learning that we see in financial markets—but it is a process that ultimately leads us to better financial institutions.

Chapter 6

Traders and Market Makers

The classic example of a trader is the specialist on a traditional stock exchange, who stands at a post where certain stocks are traded on the floor of the exchange, and who buys and sells from his personal inventory of these stocks in order to maintain an orderly market. But the specialist is only one of many people whose job involves trading minute by minute. In addition to market makers, there are also execution traders, who help others make transactions efficiently at good prices without disturbing the market to their own disadvantage, and proprietary traders, who trade on their own account to profit from short-run price movements, including doing risk arbitrage, that is, profiting from price discrepancies across markets. As the stock markets of the world become increasingly electronic, the majority of traders never even see the floor of an exchange, and mostly they feel no commitment to maintaining an orderly market. But together they do in general have the effect of making markets more orderly and prices more reflective of true value.

In the current environment the greatest hostility is often reserved for the traders, since they usually do not present themselves as helping society in any direct way. They are just buying and selling to try to make money for themselves. Their activities remind people of gambling—and the successes of some who excel in trading can be galling.

Traders are very different from investment managers who manage large portfolios of investments, who set portfolios on their course for years on behalf of clients and their long-term goals. Traders put themselves at risk every minute of every day, and for no one's benefit but their own.

Each of us gets involved in short-run trading to some extent at some point in life. One discovers a certain unpleasantness in confronting other people and having to bargain with them. It leaves one wondering: Are we on good terms or not? Am I concealing information, taking advantage of this other person? Yet traders have to specialize in doing just that all day long.

Of course, society needs traders. A market economy needs people who stand ready to buy and sell necessary items. We need traders in the same way we need used furniture dealers and scrap metal dealers.

People who trade for much of their lives learn a sort of bland professionalism that guides them, a sort of practical ethics that allows them to consistently stop just short of actions that would anger others. As Charles de Montesquieu observed in his 1748 book *The Spirit of the Laws*, "The spirit of trade produces in the mind of man a certain sense of exact justice, opposite on the one hand to robbery, and on the other to those moral virtues which forbid our always adhering rigidly to our own private interest, and suffer us to neglect it for the advantage of others."[1] Having long since thought through their own practices, traders find boring the anger that some of their counterparties show at what they perceive to be mistreatment; to experienced traders, it is business, pure and simple.

Those who spend a lifetime trading develop an expertise that involves an intuitive appreciation of market forces. Other financial professionals respect traders; they consider them a breed apart and often consult them for their insights in important decisions. That traders should have such expertise in no way contradicts the notion that markets are basically efficient. There is no respectable theory according to which there is not a normal return to be had in trading. Trading is a necessary activity for a market economy, and so there should be a normal return to expertise in trading.

Part of traders' expertise will be in the form of knowledge about how to "take advantage" of others. Only if they understand such things can they survive. Traders' professionalism may dictate that they not talk too freely about such things. Any profession develops certain dark secrets about behavior that, while not really unethical, is difficult to justify to outsiders.

Traders as Managers of a Financial Reward System

The existence of traders allows financial markets to respond almost instantly to new developments. When the price of a share of stock goes up, those who had bet on that stock are rewarded. Because of traders' activities, the reward is virtually instantaneous, and it serves to encourage similar activities again and again.

The markets that traders make are a "valuation machine" that assesses the value of various actions in a constantly changing environment and that gives nearly instant feedback and corrections in the form of meaningful price movements.

According to neuroscientist Read Montague, "Once life started to move, valuation mechanisms were an inevitable consequence."[2] Even the simplest motile microorganisms have a valuation mechanism and an impulse to pursue value. Montague points out that single-celled *Escherichia coli* bacteria have a mechanism to estimate the concentration in their fluid environment of the amino acid L-aspartate, which they consume, and a mechanism to propel them toward higher concentrations of it. The human brain is vastly more sophisticated, but its basic units are essentially similar to single-celled animalcules like *E. coli*. How does it achieve such masterful coordination of all these agents?

One theory about how it does this, called the dopamine gating hypothesis, has been proposed by quantitative psychologists Randy O'Reilly, D. C. Noelle, Jon Cohen, and Todd Braver.[3] The theory involves the dopamine system, which is in the brainstem but sends signals over long axons to many parts of the brain, notably the prefrontal cortex, which in turn sends signals back to the dopamine system.

The dopamine system responds to rewards and makes estimates of how advantageous the environment is. It is well known that this system sends signals to many areas of the brain, including the prefrontal cortex, which is an information integration center and helps in the maintenance of goals and associated actions.[4] It has recently been learned that the dopamine reward system also permeates "the gray matter in nearly every subdivision of the brain."[5]

The neuroscientist Wolfram Schultz has monitored the signals sent by the dopamine system and shown that it responds only to surprises—only to *unanticipated* rewards.[6] Furthermore the system responds not when a treat (say some food) is actually experienced, but when information about it is received. Thus if the brain gets an unanticipated signal that a treat is expected, the dopamine system broadcasts a stronger set of signals. It does not send out a stronger signal when the treat actually comes; it continues to fire at its normal background level. If on the other hand the brain is expecting a treat and is disappointed, the dopamine system's signals drop to an unusually low level at the moment the deficit is discovered.[7]

The reward stimulus from the dopamine system, according to the dopamine gating hypothesis, has the effect of turning off an information shield, and in response the prefrontal cortex selects a certain pattern of neural activity. The prefrontal cortex stabilizes the selected pattern into a goal and then uses the goal as the basis for a signal to other brain regions.

Since the dopamine system records rewards in much the same way the stock market does, it functions analogously to the stock market. When a company announces that a new special dividend will be paid to shareholders, traders bid up the stock in the market immediately after the announcement. They thereby send out a signal to the whole world that the stock is more valuable, just as the dopamine system sends out a signal to the whole brain. When the company actually pays the dividend on the stock at a later date, there is no higher return on the stock on that day. Just as with the dopamine system, the market reacts when the information about a future reward comes, not when the reward is actually received.

There is an uncanny resemblance between the plots Schultz has made of the signals fired by the dopamine system from a few seconds before to a few seconds after the time information appeared that a reward was coming and the "event study" plots produced by financial researchers of the daily returns on stock prices from just before to just after the time a special dividend is announced.[8] Just as with the dopamine reward system, the stock returns jump when an extra dividend is announced, not when it is paid. And that kind of instantaneous response to new information is exactly what is needed to make a reward system function well—whether in the brain or in the economy.

So-called parallel evolution may lead to the development of similar mechanisms or structures in different species. For example, there were sabertooth tigers and sabertooth marsupials, who developed similar tooth structure entirely independently. Another such example is that of ants and termites, insects that evolved separately but that share a complex colony structure and that build their own habitats. The reinvention in the course of economic evolution of a reward system similar to that in the brain may be regarded as a type of parallel evolution.

High-Frequency Trading

Rapid-fire electronic trading has been a source of concern for much longer than one might think. In 1847 a newspaper article lamented the fact that "Orders . . . were received by magnetic telegraph from New York to sell, and the consequence was a fall, the market closing unusually heavy—many sellers and few buyers."[9] As far back as the middle of the nineteenth century, information could be communicated at the speed of electricity.

And that was only the beginning of the apparent anomalies due to what we now call high-frequency or millisecond trading. There are certainly some more recent examples as well. On May 6, 2010, the Dow Jones Industrial Average suddenly dropped 9%, only to rebound within minutes. According to a postmortem of this "flash crash" by the Commodity Futures Trading Commission and the Securities and Exchange Commission (SEC), the crash followed a single $4.1 billion sell order, executed using an automated sell algorithm, and the sudden cessation of buying by high-frequency traders.[10] But events like this are merely among the growing pains to be expected whenever new technology is being adopted; they should become less frequent as market participants gain more experience and as regulators learn how to reduce their probability.

The real change that electronics has brought to trading has been more in the organization of information than in the speed at which trading is carried out. Once computers are involved, it is much easier for people to collect, collate, and store information about investments. A related but much less significant benefit is the enhanced speed at which trading can take place. In a competitive world, speedy trading becomes a necessity to maintain competitiveness, but it does not change the basic activities of the participants. They are still serving clients who do not think in milliseconds. The advent of this form of trading may be compared to engineers' move from slide rules to calculators: high-frequency trading helps traders do their job faster, but it is still the same job.

High-Scope Trading

Far more important than high-*frequency* trading is trading of a broader *scope*—trading of more different kinds of things. The scope of trading has been gradually increasing over the past century. But progress has been slow, and still there are some extremely important assets for which there are no liquid markets. With the advent of high-scope trading, many more things are traded.

An example would be the "prediction markets" that set prices based on the probabilities that a specified event will transpire. The earliest prediction markets, dating back to 1988 at the Iowa Electronic Markets, traded contracts that paid out according to the outcome of a specified event, such as a candidate receiving a certain share of the popular vote. The price of such a contract turns out to be a useful estimate of the probability of that outcome.[11] Since prediction markets focus on a well-defined event in the near future and give quick feedback to participants, they are probably less likely to be influenced by speculative excesses than other markets, such as stock markets. Today there are many such prediction markets, including Intrade.com, Lumenogic at newsfutures.com, and the Foresight Exchange at ideasphere.com.

There have been attempts to start markets for macroeconomic aggregates.[12] In 1985 the U.S. Coffee, Sugar and Cocoa Exchange launched a market for the U.S. consumer price index, and in 2002 Goldman Sachs launched a market for nonfarm labor force statistics. Analogous markets have since been trading at the CME Group in Chicago.[13] The European Investment Bank in 2004 attempted to start a market for longevity risk—the risk that, because of developments in medical research and changing environmental conditions, people will on average live longer than expected (a problem for defined-benefit pension funds, which have to make payments for as long as retirees live) or less long than expected (a problem for life insurance companies, which will have to pay benefits early).[14]

Many of these markets have not yet achieved liquidity, and there is little volume of trade. Often, as in prediction markets, the volume is so low that the market seems more a game among enthusiasts than a significant economic institution. This problem poses a challenge for market makers, and it is instructive to understand the role they play in launching such markets.

For example, there was, until recently, no derivatives market for residential real estate prices, for single-family home prices. There are markets for commercial real estate prices, but not for the much bigger category of real estate represented by our homes. The subprime crisis, which triggered the severe financial crisis that began in 2007, was caused by a bursting bubble in U.S. home prices. Perhaps this crisis could have been averted if there had been a market that revealed public opinions about future home prices.

My colleagues and I worked with the Chicago Mercantile Exchange (CME) to launch a futures market in single-family home prices.[15] Futures market prices of single-family homes for ten U.S. cities—Boston, Chicago, Denver, Las Vegas, Los Angeles, Miami, New York, San Diego, San Francisco, and Washington, D.C.—as well as a market for an aggregate index of all ten of them together were launched at the CME on May 22, 2006. Options on futures were also offered at that time.[16] We had every reason to think that these markets would be fundamentally important, for real estate was a significant risk for which there were at the time no risk management vehicles.

I talked with some of the market makers for these contracts, and I was impressed by their spirit. They seemed genuinely committed to creating an important new market, excited by the prospect. These encounters confirmed for me once again that the vast majority of financial professionals are not in the business just to make money.

On the other hand, they had to be careful, for as market makers they were committing their own capital. If they were to make a market too aggressively— that is, fill large orders in such a way as to leave them exposed to market risk—they would put themselves in danger of sudden and catastrophic loss.

The problem at the time was that our contracts didn't become liquid enough to attract attention. I spoke to portfolio managers who might have taken a position in these markets, and they told me that the number of shares they could trade without causing large moves in market price was just too small to be worth considering.

It was a classic "chicken-or-egg" problem. To start an important new market, you need liquidity. To have liquidity, you need an important market. Market makers can sometimes create new markets, despite the chicken-or-egg problem, if they have enough capital and courage and commitment to make the market work. But it is a slow process, and we still have relatively few markets for individual fundamentals.

In this connection I would advocate tax incentives for market makers—at least market makers in fundamental and important new markets. They are providing a public good when they create such markets and sustain the liquidity in them. They need to be further encouraged in this, and also recognized publicly for their contribution to society.

I often encounter resistance to the notion that we should expand our array of derivatives markets, and that we need more active trading of derivatives for such things as consumer prices, GDP, longevity, and real estate risks. The public disgust with financial machinations is enormous right now, and such ideas are met with great skepticism. Many of those who object seem to think that such new markets would only create opportunities for bad behavior. But I find it ironic that no one (that I have ever heard) advocates shutting down trading in the major markets that *already* exist, like the stock market or the bond market. They don't suggest this because the importance of this type of trading in our existing economy is just too great. So how does one draw the line between "good trading" and "bad trading"? If trading of claims on corporate profits (trading stocks) is a good thing, then why isn't trading for claims on GDP likewise good? Corporate profits are, after all, just a (small) component of GDP.

Here is where the impulse for conventionality and familiarity, to be discussed in Chapter 22, is so powerful. People seem to want to return to their moral roots after a crisis, and that seems to imply, to a certain extent, a return to old ways of doing things. We believe that the trading in which we *already* engage is proper—as long as we send those who abuse the system to jail. All financial progress to date—or at least up to just before the start of the current financial crisis—was acceptable, as we have become used to such developments. But progress has to stop there.

Those who express such views do not seem to appreciate that financial trading creates, as we have seen, a reward system, similar to the reward system in the brain, that drives all manner of coordinated human activity. They do not seem to appreciate that the ongoing revolution in information technology is creating massive new opportunities for better-coordinated economic activities, and that financial trading should be expected to evolve with those opportunities. They do not seem to realize that the financial crisis was not primarily caused by a spontaneous outbreak of moral turpitude, but by a failure to appreciate and manage risks (notably real estate risk). They fail to realize that setting up a government committee to guard against financial excesses and bubbles, while probably helpful, cannot really solve the problem—at least not without destroying many of the positive advantages of our market system. They fail to realize that expanding the scope of our financial trading is in its essence a route to democratizing finance—by making financial markets more representative of and responsive to our needs—and thus to advancing the central objective of the Occupy Wall Street movement.

As we have seen, markets—and the people who make them and trade in them—are the vital link that allows financial capitalism to respond to developments in the larger society. It is through markets that we appreciate the value of that which is traded and, in many cases, have a sense of larger trends in our world. We need traders and market makers if we are to transform and improve our system of financial capitalism.

Chapter 7

Insurers

The insurance industry has been extremely important in reducing the impact of both major and minor tragedies on our lives. Most people simply do not appreciate what insurers offer, for the total value of the services they provide can be hard to grasp. In this respect the news media seem to see tragedy in the wrong places. Take for example the 2010 BP oil spill in the Gulf of Mexico, when the *Deepwater Horizon* oil rig exploded and spilled oil into the gulf for three months. The news media described this as a greater tragedy than it was, disregarding that much of the loss was insured. In fact the truest tragedy here was the initial loss of life, including the eleven crewmen who died in the explosion. No insurance policy can bring back life. But the other tragedies of the spill could be—and largely were—dealt with by insurance.

The media described the dislocations to local businesses, the temporary closing of beach resorts, and the loss of local jobs as tourists stayed away, as if they were all uninsured. But to the extent that all risks were insured properly, to the extent that the beach resorts had full insurance against oil spills, that workers and employers had appropriate unemployment insurance or business interruption insurance, then there was no real and lasting suffering. Tourists just went elsewhere until the beaches were cleaned up, and they later returned. To the extent that shares in BP and its insurance companies were held by international investors in well-diversified portfolios, then the losses were spread out worldwide, and then, except for the initial loss of life, the whole event had minuscule effects overall. The truth of a world with insurance is decidedly level and even—a truth that many news reporters would like to ignore in their zeal to write engaging and attention-grabbing stories.

About five million barrels of oil were lost, and at $77 a barrel at the time of the spill that approaches half a billion dollars. That may sound like a lot of money, but it is virtually inconsequential for the world as a whole. If the risks had been fully diversified around the world, major portfolio investors would have been only minimally affected by the lost barrels of oil, to an extent well below the threshold that would provoke any loss of sense of well-being. As regards risks that can be insured, there is no tragedy experienced by individuals—not one that is discernible to any of the individuals involved. This outcome reveals one of the ironies of finance, difficult as it may be to express given our natural emotional response: except for truly planet-wide catastrophes, the amount of total damage hardly matters.

If risks are shared appropriately and comprehensively, then, in the BP example, the clearest economic impact on happiness—on what economists refer to as utility—might come from the ultimate effects on the world economy of the loss of oil. A small part of the world's oil reserves has been wasted, and so the world might run out of oil, say, a few days sooner a century hence. But no—the impact is more abstract than that, as the world will never actually run out of oil. As supplies are depleted, the price of oil will be forced up to encourage economizing and also create an incentive for the development of alternative forms of energy, which will phase in as oil supplies wane. Therefore such an oil spill, in a world with complete insurance, means only incrementally higher prices over the next century—a fact of life that society will certainly learn to tolerate.

The general public should be eager to see fundamental progress in insurance, for all the ways in which it would improve their lives. But for the moment the public does not seem to understand fully the potential benefits of better insurance. The possibilities for future risk management from better insurance seem too abstract and remote. Yet the benefits of insurance—and of expanding insurance to cover many more risks than are covered today—are very substantial and real.

The Democratization of Insurance

The history of insurance in centuries past has been one of gradual extension of coverage to more and more people and to more and more risks. If we are to achieve the good society, we must continue this trend.

Life insurance was invented in the 1600s, but initially only a few financially sophisticated people bought it. The same was true of fire insurance. It was not until the nineteenth and twentieth centuries that these kinds of insurance became widespread in advanced countries. And they *still* have not penetrated to many poorer regions of the world.

The first imperative is to get a far broader segment of the public covered by existing, well-understood policies. For example, the fundamental tragedy of the Haitian earthquake of 2010, even including the loss of life, was that few buildings were insured there. This meant not only that there was no compensation for damage but also that there had been no insurance companies overseeing building codes in years past—a practice that certainly would have reduced damage and loss of life. The Caribbean Catastrophe Risk Insurance Facility had since 2007 tried to establish better property insurance practices in Haiti, as well as other countries in the region, but it had made little headway when the earthquake of 2010 struck. This magnitude 7.0 earthquake caused at least fifty thousand deaths. In contrast, the magnitude 6.7 earthquake in Northridge, California, in 1994—similarly significant in its proximity to an urban center and in its effects—resulted in only thirty-three deaths. The much better developed insurance industry in California as compared to Haiti is a major part of the explanation for this discrepancy.

The World Bank has been launching programs to better protect poor farmers against weather risks that might seriously damage their crops, causing massive hardship or even starvation. It has been estimated that about a billion people in the world have an income of less than one dollar a day, and that three-quarters of them live in rural areas that are heavily dependent on agriculture.[1] For these people the risk of crop failure is paramount, and this risk can be a life-or-death one. Foreign emergency aid tends to reach them too late, after they have already been forced to sell off their meager assets and slaughter their livestock just to survive. Primitive societies try to manage the risk of crop loss by risk sharing within the family.[2] But in practice all members of a family may be affected by the same crop failure, so this approach to risk management is far from ideal.

In the past, insurance companies have tried to help manage this risk by selling crop insurance—insurance directly aimed at crop failure on a given farm. But this kind of policy invites moral hazard: either shirking by the farmer or outright fraud to reduce the apparent yield of the crop. In response, insurers have recently tried to tie their payments not to the crop itself but to the weather conditions that would bring on a bad crop. After all, farmers can't influence the weather. This idea has also met with difficulties, since the kind of weather conditions that bring on a bad crop may be subtle and local or may be very closely dependent on the timing of the bad weather relative to planting and seed germination. But with better information technology and better agricultural science, weather insurance has improved to the point that it is now being actively promoted by the World Bank.[3]

Another problem with weather insurance—and one that underlies the penetration of insurance into less-developed countries generally—has been that poor farmers may not understand the insurance concept and may mistrust the institutions that provide it. They are thus reluctant to pay the premiums that are necessary to make the concept viable. The same problem is encountered with earthquake insurance in poor countries. The solution has to be a better marketing of insurance in such regions and an effort to win the trust of their residents. This is what is meant by humanizing insurance, and it is part of the same process involved in humanizing any area of finance.

Dealing with Long-Term Risks

If the insurance industry is to become more humanized, it has to deal better with the real risks that trouble people, and many of these are long-term risks that reveal themselves only slowly over time. Long-term risks—especially the kinds that reveal themselves slowly instead of catastrophically and suddenly—are still poorly managed.

One of the biggest concerns that people have is about their livelihoods, their ability to earn income. Disability insurance policies cover some of the risks to livelihoods, namely those that occur because of accidents or disease. But in the future insurance can and will do much more.

Livelihood insurance is one possibility.[4] This would be a long-term insurance policy that an individual could purchase on a career, an education, or a particular investment in human capital. One could choose to specialize far more narrowly than is commonly done today—say, on a particularly interesting career direction—developing the expertise for such a career without fear of the consequences if the initiative turned out badly. The insurance policy would pay off with a supplement to one's lifetime income if it turned out years or decades later, based on verifiable data, that there was less of a market, or even no market at all, for people with this career.

Someday there also could be marketplaces, like futures markets, for career incomes by occupation. If the markets were long term, they would entail price discovery for the career decisions individuals made. Promising careers would be indicated by high market prices.

Sometimes when a family member becomes ill, the disability is devastating for the remaining members of the family. Insurance could also be expanded to better cover many of these risks. Long-term care insurance is already privately offered, but the take-up rate for such policies is abysmally low so far.[5] Welfare and unemployment programs will sometimes cover such eventualities, but only on a temporary basis. The illness of a family member can last for many years, even a lifetime. It will take financial innovation to achieve such improvements, to overcome the real barriers to such insurance that we see today.[6]

As another example, hurricane risk in the eastern United States has shown signs of increasing over recent decades, and if weather patterns are changing

so as to make hurricanes much more likely in the future, there may be a devastating impact on property owners in those areas. But hurricane insurance
policies as currently offered are overwhelmingly short term. Thus there is
nothing to insure against the risk that the long-term danger from hurricanes
will increase. A new kind of insurance, long-term catastrophe insurance, which
effectively insures against the risk that risks will increase, is an innovation we
can expect to see in the future.[7]

The Process of Improving Insurance

The process of financial development includes broadening the scope of insurance. And in this area, it is clear that much remains to be done.

Moreover, extending insurance to larger segments of the population is not
exclusively a challenge for the poorest regions of the world. Even in the most
advanced nations, there are still risks crying out to be insured. There is a clear
need for home equity insurance (which insures people against a drop in the
market value of their homes) and, as we have seen, livelihood insurance. These
seem no closer to reality today.[8]

Pushing the concept of insurance to new horizons can be inspiring work.
The intelligent response to stories of human suffering in the BP oil spill or
the Haitian earthquake or agricultural famines around the world is to recognize that the real costs of these disasters could be met by better risk
management—by better insurance. There is certainly a role for those who
wish to enter the field of insurance to make this happen.

Chapter 8

Market Designers and Financial Engineers

$\mathbf{M}$arket designers, sometimes called mechanism designers, start with a problem—the need for a market solution to some real human quandary—and then design a market and associated contracts to solve the problem. They are using financial and economic theory to create "trades" that leave people better off. In so doing they are humanizing finance and making it more relevant to human welfare. Sometimes these people are called financial engineers, since what they do seems analogous to what mechanical or electrical engineers do. At their best, market designers have the same practical common sense and drive to create, and the same grasp of basic science, that successful engineers have.

Alvin Roth is a professor specializing in market design in the Economics Department at Harvard University. One of his most notable achievements was constructing a simple market for kidney transplants. Many thousands of people in need of a transplant die each year for failure to find a suitable donor. The problem has been that few people would volunteer to donate a kidney: the operation is painful and the result may pose complications. The only people willing to donate would usually be close relatives or a spouse. But these people usually do not have the right genetic match.

Roth and his colleagues, inspired by a mathematical model of an ideal housing market devised by mathematical economists Lloyd Shapley and Herbert Scarf, worked out a new market for kidney transplants that solves this problem.[1] They founded the New England Program for Kidney Exchange, which is now operated by the Federal Organ Procurement and Transplantation Network.

The design of the market is incentive compatible. A spouse, brother, or sister of a kidney patient is asked to donate a kidney, not to his or her own relative but to someone who is a genetic match. The market tries to find a trade wherein everyone gets a kidney, though not necessarily from the relative. This process sometimes involves as many as six steps. In the three-step case individual A donates a kidney to the relative of individual B, who donates a kidney to the relative of individual C, who in turn donates a kidney to the relative of individual A. Making this happen requires sorting through a large pool of people to find such a circle of matches. It also effectively requires that all the operations occur simultaneously, lest one person back out after his or her relative has received a kidney. Avoiding that possibility meant putting together a kidney transplant center that could perform many operations simultaneously. Roth's creation of a kidney transplant market is a true step forward in finance, for it deals with risks, incentives, moral hazard, and production by means of a complex contractual arrangement.

Before Roth, people dying for lack of a transplant were almost invisible to society. Since it seemed nothing could be done for them, they simply passed out of our attention. The beauty of creating market solutions to problems is that the markets themselves, once they are up and functioning, steadily generate exactly the right kind of focused attention among people who can actually provide solutions.

Even so, the limits of Roth's kidney transplant market are still apparent today, for such markets have not reached most of the people in need of transplants. The slowness with which financial developments take place again reflects a demand for conventionality and familiarity and an overreliance on tradition, both of which continue to inhibit financial innovation.

The Variety of Market Design Objectives

Market design is becoming a lively field. There are now, for example, mechanisms in place to help reduce the problem of global warming in an efficient manner, internalizing (making the emitters of greenhouse gases pay for) the damage they cause by contributing to global warming. The "cap and trade" system forces producers of CO_2 emissions to buy permits to emit, as measured in certified emission reduction (CER) units, on an open market. Thus a price is set on emissions, and those producers that can most easily sell will do just that, transferring their permits to others who need them more, for a profit. This mechanism ensures that those businesses that can most efficiently make the adjustment to lower CO_2 emissions will be the ones that do so, minimizing the cost of reducing the emissions.

There are now six climate exchanges: the Chicago Climate Exchange, Commodity Exchange Bratislava, the European Climate Exchange, the European Energy Exchange, NASDAQ OMX Commodities Europe, and PowerNext. Analogously, the World Bank has sponsored "cool bonds," which pay out to investors in response to CER units produced.

There have been numerous proposals for other such markets. Michael Kremer and Rachel Glennerster have proposed a solution to the problem of pharmaceutical firms showing little interest in developing drugs for major diseases of the poor like malaria, preferring instead to concentrate on luxury drugs for wealthy people, like wrinkle-reducing creams. Governments would promise to buy and distribute for free drugs for major diseases, thereby creating market forces to motivate private enterprise to find drugs that would cure the diseases.[2] Ronnie Horesh has proposed "social policy bonds," issued by governments, that would pay out more if certain social policy objectives were met, thereby creating a financial incentive for free-market participants to buy the bonds and then figure out how to meet the objectives.[3]

Market-Design Solutions to Even the Most Personal Problems

To appreciate the importance of market design, and how it can really contribute to the good society, it is helpful to think of a very personal problem that creates untold anxiety, yet for which a mechanism can be designed.

Consider finding a mate, someone to live with in a close relationship, usually as husband and wife. It is indeed a sort of market problem, in that the issue is not just finding a satisfactory person but also finding someone, confronted with the same search problem, who is willing to consider *you* as his or her best choice. Finding a match between husband and wife is like finding a trade in a financial market. It entails learning a market price (in the marriage market it is one's attractiveness to certain kinds of potential spouses) and finding the best deal at that price. This analogy is not meant to put a commercial slant on a very personal problem, but instead to start us thinking about how we can design a better solution to the problem.

Finding that special someone is, for most people, essential to the deep meaning of life. The search for a compatible mate is very difficult, as one may have to sort through many different people and it may take months or years to get to know what one has found. One of the most serious problems is confronting disappointment in a relationship, and in many cases having to break off the relationships after "wasted" years together. Help with finding the right person at the start of one's search is essential, but it has not been thought of by economic theorists as a problem for the economic system—until recently.

Even with full information, the problem faced by those who would offer such help, such as dating services or matchmakers, is daunting. The romantic notion of "falling in love at first sight," happening randomly as part of every-day life, cannot be the logical basis for matching people. As far back as 1825, a newspaper article noted the profound importance of the search problem: "Experience proves that thousands lead a life of celibacy, not from choice but prudence, and the reason is obvious: it is because of a limited circle of acquaintance, persons of suitable age, disposition and circumstances cannot be found. We daily hear of unhappy differences after marriage, owing to the great disproportion of age, disposition, & c., which, if there were more facility afforded to become acquainted, would almost invariably be obviated."[4]

Companies that allowed for at least a preliminary search for a potential spouse based on set characteristics (including availability) were early creations of capitalism. For example, a matrimonial plan in England and Wales in 1801 invited persons desiring a spouse to subscribe a sum of money to the plan and send a self-description. The plan offered several suggested examples of what one might include in the self-description. One for a man was "A clergy-man, thirty years of age, dark eyes and hair, robust and healthy, enjoys three curacies, keeps a small school, of which he is heartily tired, and wishes for a more active department, and is of a very affectionate disposition." Another for a woman was "I am tall and thin, auburn hair, one eye rather brighter than the other, active and conversible, having had a good education, and am 24 years old and live with my father, who can give me 1500l. down, if I marry with his approbation."[5] Readers of such short descriptions will certainly find some information worth pondering—even, in the case of the woman, a price. Subscribers to the plan could read a list of such self-descriptions and communicate their interest to the plan. If there was a match, the plan would arrange an interview. This was indeed a sound business idea, one that enabled improved searching for a spouse.

Even these early businesses must have helped people with the market problem of finding a *matched* trade, that is, finding a person who not only is suitable but also thinks *you* suitable in turn. Indeed, finding a coincidence of wants is one of the most painful and difficult aspects of dating. Perhaps the administrators of these plans could have helped people lessen the pain and speed the conclusion if they had used their experience in matching in a way that did not force people to search slowly and sequentially through a list of those who were for the most part uninterested.

Finding a match is an intrinsically difficult market problem. Depending on the relative abundance of those with certain characteristics, people may search for years for a suitable match when their problem is simply not knowing what level of success to expect. They may remain celibate their entire lives not just because, as the newspaper article cited earlier suggests, there is a shortage of available acquaintances, but also because they may have misjudged the available supply of people with the characteristics they desire. That problem might be called, in purely financial terms, a problem of price discovery. Market designers can certainly help with this problem.

But then, once we try to design a technical solution to this problem, and to develop algorithms to provide such a solution, we will discover that there are deeper theoretical issues. For the number of possible matches is very large, and the criteria for sorting through them present some challenges.

Suppose we have a dating service with a hundred male and a hundred female applicants. Even using a computerized database with information about all of them and seeking to assign them to couples, one would find the task daunting. There would be 100 factorial possible pairings of all these people—a number difficult to comprehend, for 100 factorial is approximately 1 followed by 158 zeroes, a number unimaginably in excess of our existing digital storage options. Some of those pairings would undoubtedly be vastly superior to others, but how can we proceed to evaluate them systematically?

The complexity of the marriage problem has been explored by economic theorists. David Gale and Lloyd Shapley defined a particular marriage problem in a 1962 publication in the *American Mathematical Society Monthly*.[6] Let us imagine that each female has given the dating service a ranking (based on her own personal preferences) of all one hundred males and that each male has given a ranking of all one hundred females. How would we write a computer program that chose actual pairings of couples based on these rankings?

The problem, even when so well defined as in Gale and Shapley's terms, presents some complexities. Not only is the total number of possible pairings astronomically large, but it is hard even to decide what should be the objectives of the pairing. Given a candidate for an optimal set of pairings, how would we even decide whether it is in fact optimal?

The first thing that should happen, according to Gale and Shapley, is that the pairings should be "stable." That is, no couple would want to switch places after the fact. There would be no man who wanted to leave his assigned match for a woman who also wanted to leave her assigned match for him. Gale and Shapley provided an algorithm for the dating agency that would find a pairing and ensure that the pairing was stable in this sense. But, as they showed, there are generally many different stable pairings among the hundred men and hundred women. So the dating agency would have to consider which of these was in some sense optimal. They showed a pairing system that could be used to write a computer program for the dating agency that would yield a set of stable pairings that was optimal for the men, and another set that was optimal for the women. But they could not find a system that was in any appropriate sense optimal for everyone.

We need a system to surmount this problem, and that system is not easy to design. Governments that do not encourage entrepreneurial enterprises that actively look for problems to solve won't be very helpful. For example, dating agencies apparently came late to the Soviet Union. For decades, the best help the Soviet economy could provide was the free vacations to Black Sea or Baltic Sea resorts that Soviet enterprises offered their best workers as a reward for achievement. These vacations were intended to help fulfill the narrow objectives of the current five-year plan. Helping people meet others was not part of the plan. Liaisons were nonetheless an unintended by-product—but unfortunately these were mostly short term, as the people one met tended to be from far away.

The central planners of the Soviet Union did not have a reward system in place that focused their attention on the needs of the people. There was no force to allocate capital to enterprises that might provide dating services. Today, in post-Soviet, market-oriented Russia, dating services are well established. This trend reflects the emergence of financial and economic sophistication in that country and illustrates once more the human benefits of financial capitalism.

The point of the dating service example is to provide a real sense of the mathematical and theoretical complexity of even our most intimate problems, and to help us appreciate that financial theory ought to be involved in the future solution of these problems. In the future—thanks to improvements in information technology as well as economic science—we can expect to see more and better mechanisms to help us make all manner of economic decisions.

Financial engineers can help us solve such problems in the future just as mechanical engineers have designed the artificial heart or electrical engineers have designed the mobile phone.

Chapter 9

Derivatives Providers

In recent years, the term *derivatives* has become a dirty word, blamed by many for real evils, including the severe financial crisis that began in 2007. But a derivative is merely a financial product that derives from another market, and it is not inherently good or evil. Those specialists who drive the derivatives market may have gained a bad reputation, but in fact they are involved in some of the most creative and sophisticated aspects of finance.

One example of a derivatives market is a forward market for a commodity, in which one can sign a contract to buy from another a commodity or a property for future delivery at a specified date at a specified price. Another example is a futures market for a commodity, which is the same as a forward market except that it occurs on an organized exchange with established standards for quality, margining, and so forth. There are also markets for options: with an option one can purchase the right to buy something, say a stock or a bond, at a specified future date for a specified future price. Yet another example is a swap market: in a swap, such as a foreign exchange swap, two parties agree to exchange financial instruments (in this example two currencies) at a specified time in the future at a prespecified exchange rate. There is a derivative price in each of these markets: the price of the forward, future, option, or swap.

We have to ask why so many view the people who participate in such markets as evil. Who uses derivatives and why? Does derivatives trading fulfill a constructive purpose? As with other speculative activities, the purchase and sale of derivatives seems to many people to be a form of gambling, or worse, a vehicle for the exploitation by the clever of the less so. Certainly it is gambling to some. But is that all it is?

The Origins of Derivatives

Derivatives go back a long, long way. One of the earliest mentions of derivatives, by Aristotle (384–322 BCE) in his *Politics*, describes the successful trading of the noted Greek philosopher Thales (mid-620s to mid-540s BCE), the man who is sometimes described as the world's first real mathematician for having conceived of mathematics as the practice of formal deduction from stated assumptions with rigorous proofs. Apparently mathematicians were interested in finance from the very beginning!

Aristotle describes Thales as giving earnest money, *arrabon* (ἀρραβών), for the use of olive presses at an agreed rental rate for a later harvest. Earnest money and option premium are really the same thing. The word *arrabon* has taken on a different meaning (that of an engagement to marry) in modern Greek, but in ancient Greek we can say that it referred to a sort of option.

Actually, an engagement to marry *is* a kind of option—and so is marriage itself, as investment theorists Avinash Dixit and Robert Pindyck have argued: both involve nonmonetary commitments that resemble earnest money. As part of their argument that options theory is of ubiquitous importance in everyday life, Dixit and Pindyck offer many examples in which option-like possibilities occur naturally. Consider the exhaustion of natural resources or the destruction of tropical rainforests. Until they are exhausted or destroyed, there is an option to exhaust or destroy them, or to choose not to exhaust or destroy them. The choice itself has option value, before the decision is finalized—something that one must consider before making the choice.[1]

The exact nature of the contract between Thales and the farmers who owned the olive presses is not known. Perhaps the contract gave the presser the right to a fraction of the oil produced in compensation for the costs he incurred in pressing the olives. Thales was buying what we now call options on olives because he could later choose not to buy, and sacrifice his earnest money, if the value of olives fell instead of rising. His contract differs from a typical derivative today in that it appears to be based on total value rather than price, but that distinction is not essential to a discussion of options theory. He was making an asymmetric bet on olive values, benefiting fully if the olives had value above the contract rent but losing only the earnest money if not. That asymmetric bet on prices is the essence of an option.

According to Aristotle's story, the value of olives in fact went up as Thales had predicted. Hence "he gave deposits for the use of all the olive-presses in Chios and Miletus, which he hired at a low price because no one bid against him. When the harvest-time came, he let them out at any rate which he pleased, and made a quantity of money. Thus he showed the world that philosophers can easily be rich if they like."[2] Aristotle's intent in telling this story appears to have been merely to show that scholars can be effective in the real world. The story does not convince us that options markets in and of themselves are a good thing. Indeed it sounds rather like a story of a smart operator taking advantage of the broader public.

But we learn from this story that olive press owners were open to the sale of options. Presumably they had made such trades before. Why were they willing to do this? Clearly the pressers got the worse of the deal in this instance. Were they deceived by Thales?

In fact it is easy to imagine why olive pressers were willing to sell options on use of their presses when Thales came to them with an offer. Here was an offer of money on the table for the chance—which the pressers must have regarded as small—that olive values would increase to a high level. They must have assumed that Thales did not know that olive prices would be higher, so they were trading the "upper tail" of possible performance for a sure thing today. The payment would help them offset their possible losses if olive prices *fell* far below the contracted price. The pressers might have preferred insurance against massive falls in olive prices, if the terms were right—but Thales was apparently not offering that.

Were speculators like Thales, who wished to buy olive options, irrational? Not if they, like Thales, had some way to predict olive values. But we have seen that pressers wouldn't sell to them if they knew that the options purchasers *knew* that olive values would increase. This is a fundamental dilemma for financial theory, one that was discussed previously in connection with the work of Paul Milgrom and Nancy Stokey.[3] It seems from their theory that trade in such markets requires some kind of irrationality, such as overoptimism on the part of the purchaser of a call option or underoptimism on the part of the seller.

On the other hand, trade in olive options markets makes perfect sense if we consider that buyers of options are people who have reason to be concerned about the risk of changes in the price of olives. For example, retail olive oil merchants might wish to sell options on olive values, for if there were a short crop of olives they would expect to have a bad year. Buying the options might offset the damage to their profits. In this case, an options trade between pressers and olive oil merchants would benefit both even in the absence of information about future olive oil prices.

The options market must be working much better today than it did in the time of Thales. Then there was perhaps only one mathematician / option trader in the entire world; with no competition, he could make a fantastic profit. But now such practitioners are so numerous—look at all the graduate programs in mathematical finance, or attend one of the Institute for Quantitative Research in Finance (Q Group) conferences—that they compete heavily against one another, thus bringing options prices closer to their fundamental values.

Justifications for Derivatives Markets

In a classic 1964 article, economic theorist Kenneth Arrow argued that a major source of economic inefficiency is the absence of markets for risks.[4] Financial theorist Stephen Ross made Arrow's theory the raison d'être for options markets. In his 1976 article "Options and Efficiency," he argued that financial options have a central place because an immense variety of useful complex contracts can be " 'built up' as portfolios of simple options."[5]

But in fact only a small fraction of our risks are traded in any derivatives markets. The ancient example of Thales notwithstanding, it is a curious fact that in modern times, until just a few years ago, no olive oil derivatives were traded on any organized markets in the world.[6] More importantly, there are few or no derivatives for such key economic variables as GDP, wage rates, real estate prices, health care expenses, or average lifespans.

Behavioral finance scholars Hersch Shefrin and Myer Statman have argued that much of the demand for options trading is not for the high-minded purpose of managing risks to our livelihoods but is instead irrational. The demand is created by careful framing—by salespeople exploiting the psychological weaknesses of their customers. They argue that the most significant source of interest in options trading is not on the part of people like Thales who think they can predict the market, but from those on the other side of the market who may misunderstand options and see more value in them than really exists. As evidence, Shefrin and Statman quote a manual for options brokers who are seeking out customers willing to take the side of Thales' olive pressers. The manual offers a script for these would-be brokers:

> JOE SALESMAN: You have told me that you have not been too pleased with the results of your stock market investments.
> JOE PROSPECT: That's right. I am dissatisfied with the return, or lack of it, on my stock portfolio.
> JOE SALESMAN: Starting tomorrow, how would you like to have three sources of profit every time you buy a common stock?
> JOE PROSPECT: Three profit sources? What are they?
> JOE SALESMAN: First, you could collect a lot of dollars—maybe hundreds, sometimes thousands—for simply agreeing to sell your just-bought stock at a higher price than you paid. This agreement money is paid to you right away, on the very next business day—money that's yours to keep forever. Your second source of profit could be the cash dividends due you as the owner of the stock. The third source of profit would be in the increase in price of the shares from what you paid, to the agreed selling price.[7]

The argument is apparently effective but ultimately deceptive, for it emphasizes only the number of income sources, but does not suggest a comparison of the price received for the option with the expected loss in those cases when the stock price exceeds the agreement price. If the customer's attention is diverted from consideration of this price, or if the customer has no idea how to price options and thus cannot estimate whether the offered options price is a good one, then the customer could be lured into a bad deal. Others who understand options will be more than happy to take the other side of this deal even if they have no idea where the underlying stock price is going, expecting to make money on average if the prices they pay for the options are low.

Although Aristotle did not suggest it, it seems in fact conceivable that Thales was doing just that, even if he never developed any formal theory of options pricing. He may have had enough intuitive quantitative insight to sense when an option was underpriced, and would buy it just because he thought it was underpriced. He would then do well on average. If this was in fact the case, then Aristotle had a point: mathematicians *will* win when pitted against naïve counterparties.

Fred Schwed Jr., in his 1940 book *Where Are the Customers' Yachts?*, describes other sales tactics of options brokers. One of them is suggesting to clients that they buy out-of-the-money put options (options to sell at a price below the current market price) on stocks that they already hold, thereby putting a floor on their losses:

> There is no denying the fact that the above procedure supplies the speculator with definite insurance, "term" insurance, actually. But like all other forms of insurance it costs money to buy. Thus the simple question is set: is the price of the insurance commensurate with the amount of protection attained? Unfortunately this problem cannot be solved mathematically. It can be attacked empirically, but this method of research is likely to be costly.[8]

It may seem strange that a well-developed options trading industry existed in Schwed's day and yet there was still no theory of options pricing—a prerequisite that would seem essential to trading in that market. Actually a serviceable options pricing theory had been published in 1900 by the French mathematician Louis Bachelier.[9] But there is no evidence that anyone in the options market had even heard of his paper. That did not change until 1964, when the mathematical treatises of A. J. Boness and Case Sprenkle appeared.[10] Boness remarked on the strangeness of this: "Investment analysis is largely in a pre-theoretic stage of development. Security analysis, narrowly defined, consists chiefly of naïve extrapolations from ratios based on accounting data."[11]

Why, if the pricing of options was of such central importance to these markets, did no one care about the mathematical theory behind it? That indeed suggests that these authors are right—that much options selling is fundamentally exploitative. This fact ought to be remembered when we ponder whether markets are really efficient.

There was also, in 1940, no exchange anywhere in the world for the trading of options, so there was no way even to know whether the price a broker quoted was indeed a market price. The first options exchange, the Chicago Board Options Exchange, did not open until 1973.

The lesson is again that our financial system is not nearly a finished product. If traders in 1940 had no mathematical theory whatsoever for options, but were trading them every day nonetheless, it is indeed unlikely that our financial markets have reached perfection today.

The Regulation of Options

Stockbrokers around the world strive to maintain ethical standards against blatantly manipulative practices. In the United States the Financial Industry Regulatory Authority (FINRA) is the self-regulatory organization that represents a variety of investment professionals, including stockbrokers. In preparatory materials for their Series 7 licensing exams, prospective "registered representatives" are warned that in selling options they are constrained from certain unethical practices. But it seems that the Joe Salesman option-selling script is not proscribed. It is difficult for a self-regulatory organization to forbid such subtly misleading arguments, for it is hard to formally define when an argument is misleading.

Firms that value their reputation will avoid having their reps read from the Joe Salesman script, for their savvier clients will see through such a ploy, and they may communicate their dissatisfaction by taking their business elsewhere and telling others. But, in the end, brokers do not really need such a script, for, as Shefrin and Statman argue, many of their clients will fall into this trap of reasoning on their own with no help at all.

The sense of sleaziness associated with options has pervaded the public consciousness, perhaps because of such past bad practices. Most people do not trade options, for they are not on the usual lists of useful financial products recommended in investor advice columns, in the news media, or in investment advice books. Disreputable sales practices for options persist, but by now they have a limited, and declining, audience.

These practices could be reduced further if we could provide the kind of disinterested financial advice to the broad public that is the subject of the next chapter. The fallacy in the Joe Salesman argument is readily apparent to anyone trained in finance. Legal and financial advisers who are committed to serving their customers' interests will easily see through such a sales pitch, and will in fact warn their clients away from it.

If we move to a world in which people have access to better financial advice, then the options market could move closer to the ideal market initially envisioned by theorists like Kenneth Arrow and Stephen Ross. The market might even expand further in its usefulness, by aligning itself more squarely with the real interests of real people. Options could be created that represent genuine, personally significant risks to individuals, like the risks of a decline in home prices or a decline in career incomes. This would make derivatives such as options, even more clearly than they are today, instances of finance in the service of the good society.

Chapter 10

Lawyers and Financial Advisers

Lawyers and financial advisers are fundamental to financial capitalism because they provide information that is tailored to their clients' complex needs. Richard J. Murnane and Frank Levy, whose theory of the role of labor in modern society was discussed in the introduction, chose law as a prime example of an occupation that will not be replaced by computers. They chose it because the practice of law essentially depends on both expert thinking and complex communication. The same is true of financial advisers.

Efforts to create expert-thinking web sites to help people make financial decisions have not entirely succeeded. The mechanization of financial and legal advice with online expert systems is a new and important trend. As our online community continues to expand, as social media take increasing account of the financial community, we may expect to see help with financial problems provided to individuals via this channel. But it will not eliminate the need for more and better human help. The challenge for information technology is to provide an interface to allow people to more readily access both electronic and human help.

Even the celebrated site financialengines.com—created by financial theorists William Sharpe and Joseph Grundfest in 1998, initially to provide financial advice with no human intermediation—has brought human advice back into the loop. Although they do not override its algorithms, the system now provides for human advisers, who help customers determine how best to interact with the site. For the foreseeable future, no computer will fully replace developed human intelligence in helping other humans with their financial needs.

Integrity is still a human force, and even sites that provide automated financial advice, such as financialengines.com, are only as good as the people behind them. If people were ever to rely wholly on machines in making their investment decisions, the shift would open up a huge set of opportunities for investment products lacking in integrity to prey on them.

Quite to the contrary: the value of *human* financial services is so essential that the provision of such services to those of modest incomes needs to be encouraged and subsidized, either by the government or by philanthropic organizations. Certainly financial software will develop further, and it will become an even more important part of an adviser's toolkit. Social media will help advisers disseminate their advice to more and more people. And yet one-on-one human financial counseling will always be an essential prerequisite for satisfactory financial capitalism.

Lawyers

Lawyers are fundamentally involved with finance. Every financial device— including stocks, bonds, futures, and options—is represented by a long and complex legal contract, and typically by multiple legal filings with government regulators as well. In an important sense, the lawyers are the real engineers who construct financial devices.

Yet the boundaries between purely financial and other legal matters may be ill defined; indeed most of the contracts with which lawyers deal have financial elements, including employment agreements, leases, and divorce settlements.

Lawyers who specialize in securities law, corporate law, bankruptcy law, and contract law are rather controversial figures, for they are viewed by many as helping the rich make even more money. Lawyers who help with contracts are, of course, protecting their clients, who represent special interests of one sort or another. And of course their clients are not always rich. When a lawyer writes a bond indenture, the benefit will accrue to anyone who receives income from the security—a group that may include poor people as well as rich.

The role that lawyers play in a society depends on the resources of the people who hire them. If only the rich can afford lawyers, then lawyers will tailor their careers, and their advice, to the needs of the rich. But it does not have to be that way.

The Availability of Lawyers Generally . . .

There are enormous differences across countries in the number of lawyers per capita. Among countries for which data are available, the country with the highest number is Israel, with one lawyer per 169 people. Brazil is second with one lawyer per 255 people, and the United States third with one per 273 people. Next in line are various advanced European countries. At the other extreme are various Asian countries, with Japan at one lawyer per 4,197 people, Korea with one per 5,178 people, and the People's Republic of China with one per 8,082 people.[1] There are nearly fifty times as many lawyers per capita in Israel as there are in China!

Why these huge differences? There does not appear to be a scholarly literature that explains them, but they are no doubt related to complex cultural and institutional differences.

Consider Israel. There are many jokes about Israeli litigiousness. One describes a scene during the Six-Day War, when an Israeli tank and an Egyptian tank accidentally collide in the desert. The Egyptian tank driver jumps out and shouts, "I surrender!" His Israeli counterpart jumps out and shouts, "Whiplash!"

The culture in Israel, which encourages legal action, must certainly be affected by the tradition of Halakhah, the Jewish law. Perhaps it is related to the degree of attention to business issues in that legal tradition, extending back for millennia, and to the focus of that law on the resolution of business disputes.

The presence of a large number of lawyers may also reflect a burdensome legal tradition. For Brazil, writes Belmiro V. J. Castor in his book *Brazil Is Not for Amateurs*, "The judicial system is of limited help, given the unbelievable complexity and formalism of Brazilian laws. Appeals, reviews and suspensions are the delight of lawyers and the despair of plaintiffs. Bringing a lawsuit to right a wrong or repair some damage is invariably complex and expensive. . . . In some cases the situation borders on the absurd."[2]

According to Castor, the complexity of the Brazilian legal system is in turn rooted in deeper aspects of Brazilian culture. There is an aspect of the Brazilian national character, referred to by the word *jeitinho*, which describes a sort of impulse to improvise, to not rely on rules, to find some devious way to get things done in spite of the rules—and hence to make the rules doubly hard to navigate. The resulting atmosphere can be very conducive to lawyers' business.

Explaining differences across countries in the number of lawyers will not be easy. But it is worth noting that in countries such as Israel and the United States in particular, entrepreneurship has flourished in part because the relatively large number of lawyers permits people to undertake much more complex actions, and with more certainty about the outcome.

. . . and for Low- and Middle-Income People

There is an even more serious problem throughout much of the world, in that low- and middle- income people do not have adequate access to lawyers. This dearth affects them in numerous ways, including an inability to readily understand simple financial documents, like home mortgages or credit card contracts. The severe financial crisis that began in 2007 was made worse by the failure of most low- and middle-income people to get anything more than perfunctory legal and financial advice.

Legal advice for low-income people, at least in some minimal form, is subsidized by governments in most countries. Some do this more comprehensively than others. In the United Kingdom a Legal Services Commission provides legal advice to those with low incomes. Its annual budget is £2 billion, and about two million people a year are served, implying an expenditure of about £1,000 per person served, or about £40 per person in the United Kingdom. These services are augmented by the Citizens Advice Bureaus, which give broader-spectrum advice. Questions persist as to whether this is really enough, but the situation is clearly far better in the United Kingdom than in most countries.

In Canada government-sponsored Legal Aid Ontario offers legal services on something like the scale of the United Kingdom's Legal Services Commission.

In most countries a limited amount of free legal advice is offered on a pro bono basis. As such it is surely in short supply. As a result low-income people cannot easily make financial contracts and cannot expect contracts to be honored. The overall effect is to exclude these people from the very financial technology that has brought prosperity to so many.

Financial Advisers

Financial advisers, like lawyers, are very numerous in advanced countries with a tradition of financial sophistication. In the United States, according to the Bureau of Labor Statistics, there were 208,000 personal financial advisers in 2008, or about one for every 1,500 people.[3] But, once again, there are not enough of them.

Government subsidy of financial and legal advice can be justified on the basis of the externality provided by having a society that functions well, without some feeling that they are excluded from the financial world and later finding themselves punished for their mistakes.

In this country we already have *some* government subsidy of legal and financial advice, since these are deductible on personal income taxes. But such a subsidy benefits only those with higher incomes, who are therefore in high tax brackets and who itemize their deductions. We need to democratize the government subsidy of legal and financial advice so that it really benefits everyone, not just the wealthy.

Government subsidy of such advice would be a great democratizer of finance in that it would give people the information they need to make informed financial decisions.

Many countries now support financial literacy programs, and the web sites of government regulatory bodies now often have financial education materials on them. These are cheap and easy to produce.

But individuals need more than just web pages to look at. They need real expert financial advice—advice that is individually tailored and dedicated to their welfare. And this is very costly to provide.

Salespeople for financial products fill an important information-providing role in the modern market economy. But we should not have to rely exclusively on salespeople for financial advice. An adviser, if he or she is to receive any government subsidy, should sign a statement, a code of ethics, agreeing not to collect commissions for steering the client toward financial products that pay such commissions.

In the United States, the commitment required of all members of the National Association of Personal Financial Advisors (NAPFA) can serve as a model:

> NAPFA defines a Fee-Only financial advisor as one who is compensated solely by the client with neither the advisor nor any related party receiving compensation that is contingent on the purchase or sale of a financial product. Neither Members nor Affiliates may receive commissions, rebates, awards, finder's fees, bonuses or other forms of compensation from others as a result of a client's implementation of the individual's planning recommendations. "Fee-offset" arrangements, 12b-1 fees, insurance rebates or renewals and wrap fee arrangements that are transaction based are examples of compensation arrangements that do not meet the NAPFA definition of Fee-Only practice.[4]

But NAPFA advisers are costly to hire: they charge between $75 and $300 an hour, an amount beyond the budgets of many, even those in the middle class. A legitimate case can be made for government subsidy of any financial advice given under a commitment to the client like that required of NAPFA members.

Most people can't afford heart surgeons when they need them either: that is why we have government subsidies of health insurance for low-income people. It is commonplace for governments to subsidize medical advice. We can see—especially in the financial crisis that continues as of this writing, particularly in the United States—that many people have made errors in the purchase of their homes and the selection of their mortgages—errors that could have been prevented had they had proper *financial* advice as well. Avoidance of a financial crisis such as the one in which we now find ourselves offers a perfect example of the kind of externality that justifies government subsidy of financial, as well as legal, advice for everyone.

Legal and Financial Advisers as Key Elements in Financial Capitalism

Increasing access to legal and financial advice—access that affords people a patient and sympathetic adviser—is one of the key factors in developing a truly responsive financial capitalism for the future.

If people have good legal and financial advisers who really *represent* them, who are committed to nothing more than helping them, they will make better decisions. They can sign contracts and take on investments that involve the creative application of financial theory to their individual problems. In evaluating financial products, they will no longer need to fall back on conventionality as an indicator of quality. They will not feel the need to seek safety in numbers by attempting to do whatever they have the impression everyone else is doing. They will be less likely to be victimized by operators who try to appear conventional.

There are some who argue that financial and legal advice would not have prevented some of the errors that led to the current financial crisis. This may be true—most lawyers or financial advisers were not immune to some of the basic errors that led to the crisis. Before cracks in the financial system began to appear in 2007, they probably were victims of the same kind of errors, such as thinking that home prices could never fall and that an AAA rating on a security is a good indicator that it is safe.

But even so, legal and financial advisers who sat down with their clients and patiently talked through the issues would most likely have reduced the extent of the errors that so many made just before the crisis erupted, such as thinking that they should buy the biggest possible house, or even two houses. When one borrows a large sum of money to make an investment, one leverages the risks, as only a small drop in the value of the investment can wipe out the investor—and any competent adviser should know this. Advisers are trained to see the full array of possible investments and to have better knowledge of the risks inherent in leverage.

The further development of legal and financial advisers, including government support of their services to clients with lower incomes, will also create a different culture in our society. It will foster an expanded public discourse that might in turn help change the conventional wisdom, and better connect the knowledge base with the real problems people face, as well as make it more timely and relevant. The more people have access to those with useful knowledge, the more intelligent will be our approach, as a society, to financial capitalism.

Chapter 11

Lobbyists

One of the most troubling aspects of finance in modern society is that it often appears that the financial community now has the ability to take control of the government. They can hire lobbyists to present their case and persuade lawmakers to take their side. The "bailouts" and the favoritism apparently shown to some financial interests during the current financial crisis are widely seen as evidence of this.

The Unbalanced Power of Lobbyists

Arthur Levitt, the chairman of the SEC from 1993 to 2001, wrote about his experiences in a 2003 book, *Take on the Street*. He remarks as follows:

> During my seven and a half years in Washington, I was constantly amazed by what I saw. And nothing astonished me more than witnessing the powerful special interest groups in full swing when they thought a proposed rule or piece of legislation might hurt them, giving nary a thought to how the proposal might help the investing public. With laserlike precision, groups representing Wall Street firms, mutual fund companies, accounting firms, or corporate managers would quickly set about to defeat even minor threats. Individual investors, with no organized lobby or trade association to represent their views in Washington, never knew what hit them.[1]

The financial dealmaking that we have been considering among businesspeople is augmented by dealmaking among businesses and organizations and elected government officials, or among businesses and organizations with the support of government. These deals can be productive, but they tend sometimes to lean toward the sordid. Bribery is illegal, but bribery can take subtle forms. For example, a congressman who supports business interests can often expect to be rewarded with a lucrative private-sector job *after* his term of government service is done.

Levitt details how businesspeople recruited congressmen to battle the regulations imposed by the SEC, and even to threaten him personally for failing to accede to their demands. The appendices of his book contain actual threatening letters to him from congressmen (couched, of course, in idealistic language that disguised their real meaning). He singled out Congressman Billy Tauzin, a Louisiana politician who started out as a Democrat and later became a Republican, as the most no-holds-barred supporter of business interests. Tauzin did not seek reelection in 2004, and he then became head of the Pharmaceutical Research and Manufacturers of America (PhRMA). PhRMA offered him over $2.5 million per year, outbidding the Motion Picture Association of America, which had offered him only $1 million.

There was nothing illegal about what Tauzin did, although it would be illegal today, now that Congress has tightened its own rules regarding lobbying. The Honest Leadership and Open Government Act of 2007 (HLOGA), signed into law by President George W. Bush, specifies that members of the U.S. House of Representatives must now wait one year after leaving their jobs before they can lobby the federal government. Tauzin could still become a lobbyist, but now he would have to accept a slight delay before starting his new job.

Certainly no one can prove that Tauzin wasn't entirely sincere in the causes he took on. Yet it appears that there is at the very least a potential (even with the one-year wait) for abuse when this kind of career path is normal. Ultimately government works as well as it does because people of integrity refrain from actions—or from being coerced into actions—that tarnish their reputations.

This pattern of influence of business on government has changed over decades as financial interests have grown more sophisticated in their lobbying, and reforms like HLOGA can never completely offset that. The amount of money behind special-interest lobbying is now far greater than that behind genuine public interest groups.

For example, Americans for Financial Reform is a lobbying group that represents a coalition of consumer rights, civil rights, investor, retiree, community, labor, religious, and certain business groups. It has an annual budget of $2 million. Its own 2011 analysis of what it is up against, based on public disclosure of lobbying records, shows that the finance industry spends $1.4 million *a day* in the United States to advance its interests.[2]

Lobbying by financial interests is certainly not entirely selfish. Lobbying groups sometimes come to lawmakers with important new ideas. For example, in 1933 the National Association of Real Estate Boards (NAREB, whose successor is the current National Association of Realtors) presented to the U.S. government a proposal for what was in effect to become the Home Owners' Loan Corporation (HOLC).[3] Congress followed this advice almost immediately, passing the legislation to establish the agency that same year.

Undoubtedly NAREB acted out of a degree of self-interest. The HOLC did help the industry with its bad mortgages. But it also helped troubled homeowners who were about to lose their homes, and the latter outcome was extremely important at a time when high unemployment and desperately bad times made home foreclosure a difficult loss for families to bear. Listening to the real estate lobbyists' proposal was certainly a good thing for government to do back then. But was their proposal really biased in favor of the mortgage industry? It is not obvious that it was, and it appears that the "bailouts" the HOLC offered did not cost taxpayers any significant amount of money.[4] Its founding represented a deal whose outcome could not confidently be predicted but that turned out well, for both mortgage lenders and their customers.

Lobbyists do transmit expertise about financial markets to lawmakers, and often enough they help them avoid serious policy mistakes.

But the increasing influence that major financial interests can buy by hiring lobbyists has some troubling consequences. According to the U.S. Congressional Budget Office, for the 1% of the population with the highest income, average real after-tax income grew 275% between 1979 and 2007—quite a dramatic increase. Over the same interval, Americans with income in the bottom 20% of the population saw only an 18% increase.[5] Clearly there has been a dramatic increase in the concentration of income among the most affluent.

Jacob Hacker and Paul Pearson, in their 2010 book *Winner-Take-All Politics*, argue that the increased number and professionalization of lobbyists for financial and business interests since 1979 is a good part of the reason for this increase in the after-tax income of the wealthy. While they do not prove a causal relation between the income increase and the increased number of lobbyists, they offer some compelling circumstantial evidence.

But Hacker and Pearson do not present evidence that a worsening of this situation can be expected in the future. It is not that the increasing sophistication of the financial community will make it better and better over time at exerting control over government regulation. Instead their view is that circumstantial events play a large role in the increasing power of lobbyists. They argue that the increasing number of individuals willing to pay for lobbyists to press cases related to social issues like gay rights or abortion rights has left a vacuum, a shortage of lobbyists willing to argue for the causes important to low-income Americans.

Hacker and Pearson's proposed solution to the problem of the excessive power of financial lobbyists is "the creation of organized, sustained pressure on legislators to make American politics more responsive and open to citizen engagement."[6] Democratic societies have shown a history of legislation to limit the power of wealthy special interest groups. Money does not uniformly buy influence over the government. Indeed studies that try to find an effect of campaign contributions on election outcomes have typically found surprisingly little.[7] It is hard to buy an election because voters will realize what is afoot, if only by observing the number of advertisements thrust in their faces. It does not take a great deal of sophistication to be suspicious of a candidate who is buying massive amounts of advertising. According to Robert Guest, business editor for *The Economist*, "The strongest force shaping politics is not blood or money, but ideas."[8] That is why the wealthy often prefer to sponsor partisan think tanks rather than lobbyists. But even think tanks are successful only insofar as they can make their ideas work in practice.

The history of legislation regarding lobbyists in the United States is full of examples of efforts to curb excessive influence for special interest groups. In particular, the Federal Regulation of Lobbying Act of 1946 required lobbyists to register with the Clerk of the House and the Secretary of the Senate, the Lobbying Disclosure Act of 1995 required lobbyists to write semiannual reports detailing their activities, and in 2007 HLOGA further strengthened disclosure requirements. Congressmen, aware of the potential for scandal, are now far more cautious in accepting any gifts from financial lobbyists. HLOGA has created a web site at which lobbying activity can be monitored by the public. Few other countries have established such extensive lobbying laws. Besides the United States, Australia, Canada, Taiwan, and Ukraine have lobbyist disclosure laws.

Another tactic to control lobbyists is to adopt "clean money" or "voter-owned" election rules that disallow all large campaign contributions. Such campaign finance reform would considerably weaken the power lobbyists could exert on behalf of wealthy vested interests. A number of countries have such laws; indeed in the United Kingdom they date back to the nineteenth century. In the United States several states have them, and a movement is under way to enact them in other states. But vested interests are likely to block such initiatives. In his 2011 book *Republic Lost: How Money Corrupts Congress—and a Plan to Stop It*, Lawrence Lessig, a Harvard Law School professor, suggests tactics that a grass-roots campaign could use to make such a movement a success.[9]

And Yet Lobbyists Can Benefit Society

The problem isn't that financial interests attempt to influence legislators. There is a need for *every* major group in society to help lawmakers reach their decisions, and of course, there is a legitimate reason for forming groups to defend special interests. According to opensecrets.org, financial, insurance, and real estate interests accounted for less than 15% of all lobbying activity in 2011.[10] There are also lobbyists for churches, charity groups, and the helping professions.

Legislators need lobbyists, for there is no way that they can fully assess how their legislation affects various interest groups in society unless informed representatives of these groups convey the appropriate information to them. Ethical lobbyists help make good laws. Lawrence O'Donnell Jr., who served on the U.S. Senate staff from 1988 to 1995, recalled, "There are honorable lobbyists. I dealt with them every day. By honorable lobbyists I do not mean just the ones who did pro-bono lobbying for charities."[11]

What kind of person becomes a lobbyist for an interest group? He or she is per se no less ethical than the general population. Presenting a case for an interest group is not in itself unethical, just as it is not unethical for a lawyer to represent a client in a criminal case, even if that person might be guilty.

Lobbyists tend to be people who are interested in public affairs; they find the profession a way to become involved with issues that interest them and to earn a good income while doing so. It is usually as simple as that. Often a lobbyist is a former lawmaker. Or a lobbyist may be someone who is interested in politics but reluctant to make the sacrifices required by public service. Lobbyists may find the behind-the-scenes action exciting and personally rewarding. One lobbyist, Joseph Miller, who wrote a book about his experiences, *The Wicked Wine of Democracy: A Memoir*, spoke of it this way: "I had experienced big-time politics up close for five years, but I still clung to the notion that my principles had an essential nobility about them and that the real purpose of it all was the betterment of humanity. If that sounds hopelessly naïve, I plead guilty."

But he also described falling for the temptations of a lobbyist: "When I expressed my misgivings to a business-lobbyist friend, he laughed and said: 'Just wait until you make a hundred thousand for getting an innocuous amendment or little clause added to an obscure bill. You'll get hooked. It's like hitting the jackpot. You get addicted.' He was right." Yet the temptations never completely got the better of him. When he was paid to try to influence Stewart Udall, a prominent member of the U.S. House of Representatives, for a less than idealistic cause, Miller ended up changing his mind and refunding the money: "Stewart Udall was my friend, and I was expected to use my influence with him. . . . It turned out that I couldn't. It was just too crass."[12]

Lobbyists are often held in low esteem in modern society, because they are viewed as mercenaries defending wealthy interests. But in fact as a group they are probably more public spirited than most. To function well as a lobbyist in a democratic society one must be fully conversant with the real issues that lawmakers are debating.

To be sure, there was some public anger when it was learned that lobbyists had managed to persuade the U.S. Congress to exempt automobile dealerships from the scrutiny of the Consumer Financial Protection Bureau. And they still manage to win subsidies for farmers that make little sense. But it is not clear that such actions outweigh the benefits of all the information lobbyists convey to government decision makers. The elation that Miller reports on getting a change enacted into law reflects just how hard it is to achieve that goal.

Lobbyists are not all powerful. It used to be thought that there would always be high tariffs protecting domestic producers. It was considered inevitable since the benefits to raising any single tariff rate redound to a small group of producers, while the costs are spread out over all of society. Hence it was believed that lobbying on behalf of tariffs would always be successful. In fact, however, the General Agreement on Tariffs and Trade has reduced most tariffs over most of the world to nearly zero. The same can be expected for financial lobbyists. The level of citizen concern we are seeing today at the excessive influence of financial lobbyists has already set in motion a process to limit this very influence.

Financial lobbyists, if they are properly regulated, are essential, for only the financial community has the expertise to understand the financial marketplace and the ability to evaluate policy regarding it. They must of course be monitored and regulated, but a healthy modern economy will necessarily involve such lobbyists.

Reforming Lobbying and Lobbyists

There is an ongoing process of improving the disclosure of information regarding lobbying and political contributions. Yet more remains to be done; for example, there could be better rules regarding disclosure of the actual force of the lobbying effort. In the United States today, companies can make their political contributions to intermediaries whose actual activities are not disclosed.[13]

Furthermore, if poorer people are not as effectively represented by lobbyists, social inequality will only increase. Indeed there is evidence from voting records that the opinions of the wealthy are taken into account to a disproportionate extent. Political scientist Larry Bartels, in an analysis of data on opinions and incomes collected by the National Election Survey, found that people in the bottom third of the income distribution have virtually no impact on the voting of their representatives in the U.S. Congress, compared with those in the middle and top thirds.[14]

Labor unions have in the past been the most likely lobbyists for lower-income people. But their influence has been waning throughout much of the world.[15] Symbolically important changes came with the aggressive moves of Ronald Reagan, who broke the U.S. air traffic controllers' strike in 1981, and Margaret Thatcher, who broke the U.K. coal miners' strike in 1985. Unions' traditional source of power, collective bargaining, has been weakened by international competition and new labor laws. We as a society must devise other, possibly very different, ways to energize lobbying efforts on behalf of neglected interests.

We need lobbyists as representatives for *all* groups in our society, including the "other 99%" with which the Occupy Wall Street protesters identify. The laws that provide for disclosure of lobbyists' activities do not themselves restore balance to lobbying efforts.

We need somehow to encourage lobbying activities on behalf of under-served groups. And subsidizing public interest lobbying on behalf of the currently voiceless is a good cause for philanthropists, as many of them already know.

Chapter 12

Regulators

Regulators as people with vision and purpose are typically omitted from discussions of financial markets. We hear a lot about energetic and effective entrepreneurs, but rarely about the people who work for regulatory agencies, whether they regulate government or industry. But in fact regulators and their intellect are fundamentally important to the financial system. It is they who make and interpret the all-important rules of the game.

Just as in sports, people in business want referees who will enforce the rules. Everyone has an interest in the game being fair. The fact that players try to push the limits of the rules or argue with referees doesn't mean they don't want them. In the same way, businesspeople very much want regulators, for regulations imposed on all players do not generally work to their individual disadvantage—quite to the contrary, they typically work to the advantage of all. Without effective rules one is forced to do things that one finds personally questionable to stay in business. That is why businesses set up their own self-regulatory organizations, which impose rules that are usually (though, to be sure, not always) in the public interest.

But there are some who think that regulators are not doing anything of the sort. Milton Friedman, following his 1954 study with Simon Kuznets of occupational incomes and regulation, made a strongly worded argument against regulation, particularly occupational licensing, in his 1962 book *Capitalism and Freedom*.[1] He thought regulation was little more than a cynical ploy to limit the supply of services so as to keep their prices high. Friedman's book turned out to be very influential, creating a measure of public distaste for regulation.

His University of Chicago colleague George Stigler carried the theme forward, writing in 1971 that "as a rule, regulation is acquired by the industry and is designed and operated primarily for its benefit."[2] Stigler believed that the principal goal of regulation, whether government regulation of an industry or self-regulation by the industry itself, is to deny entry to competitors.

Despite Friedman's and Stigler's arguments, the scope and extent of regulation have only grown in the United States. Morris Kleiner and Alan Krueger find that the purview of occupational licensing has grown dramatically in the United States, from only 5% of the labor force licensed in the 1950s to 29% in 2008. The increase in the percentage of the labor force that is licensed more than fully offsets the decline in the percentage of the labor force that is unionized.[3] That same trend may not be observed elsewhere in the world, and of course the trend around the less-developed world has been toward greater reliance on free markets. For example, a major part of the Indian economic reforms in the 1990s was a massive cutback in industrial and trade licensing.[4]

The Friedman complaint was taken up again by other University of Chicago economists, Raghuram Rajan and Luigi Zingales, in their 2003 book *Saving Capitalism from the Capitalists*. But now the argument is more nuanced. Rajan and Zingales recognize the need for appropriate regulation in many places and also believe that society can exert oversight over regulators to help prevent their capture by private interests. It isn't that we need "more" or "less" regulation, but that regulation must not be commandeered by selfish special interests, and that it needs to be done right.[5]

Indeed, whereas there should be some prudent concern lest regulators be captured by the industries they regulate, we need not take that as a foregone conclusion. At least in today's developed countries, regulation has not been totally captured by business interests. In the United States, we have had a civil service since 1872 (copying many other countries going all the way back to China in the Han Dynasty), which prevents hack political appointees from taking control. Regulators are now trained professionals. Although an elected politician could in theory try to divert civil servants from their responsibilities, it would be much harder to order them to formulate regulations designed to create monopoly power on behalf of some special interest. In today's climate of media alertness, such behavior would soon be revealed and lead to a scandal.

In his 2010 book *No One Would Listen*, stock market analyst Harry Markopolos argued that government regulators can be deaf to evidence of financial excess, even fraud, if the culprit appears to have legitimacy and prestige. The regulators quickly go after small-time crooks, Markopolos argued, but when it comes to large companies, they are "captive to the companies they are supposed to regulate." Markopolos uncovered substantial evidence that the massive hedge fund run by the respected Wall Street figure Bernard Madoff was nothing more than a Ponzi scheme, a fraudulent investment scheme built on a plan for social contagion of enthusiasm among investors. The fund was eventually exposed in 2008. But Markopolos had complained about Madoff's scheme to the SEC as early as 2000. In 2005, three years before the ultimate collapse of the scheme, Markopolos presented a twenty-one-page document to SEC New York Branch Chief Meaghan Cheung and explained his findings. According to his account of their meeting, she told him she had read his report, but she did not have a single question for him. "The strongest impression that I got from her was that I was bothering her. There was no excitement, no enthusiasm, no recognition that I had just put in her hands the biggest case she would ever have in her career."[6]

Ms. Cheung, in an interview with the *New York Post* after the book was published, responded that she was not at liberty to discuss the SEC's deliberations regarding Madoff, but that she was distressed by the Markopolos accusations: "I was not influenced, and I don't believe anyone in the New York office was influenced, by any other desire than to find out the truth. . . . There is no other reason to work there for so long, except that I love what I do. No one in my office had any incentive to miss something like this."[7]

Of course there is no way we can reconstruct exactly what happened, but I am inclined for the most part to believe Ms. Cheung. What influence could Madoff have had to induce the SEC to cover up a massive fraud that, according to Markopolos, would eventually be discovered and create a national scandal? If influence by Madoff was indeed a factor, it must have operated at a subtle, interpersonal level, in much the same way that confidence men influence their sometimes-too-credulous victims.

People are quick to blame regulators. The mistake of not prosecuting Madoff earlier can probably be traced largely to mistakes by overworked regulators or to faulty administrative procedures. A significant error will naturally occur in any system from time to time, and the major sources of that error can be corrected. Despite the arguments of critics like Markopolos, regulators—at least in the United States, both those appointed by industry itself and those in the government—are much more often well meaning and substantially more effective than is commonly acknowledged.

Self-Regulatory Organizations

In the United States, as we have seen, FINRA is a nongovernmental self-regulatory organization funded by the securities industry that works to set professional standards and encourage ethical behavior among practitioners. Originally it was called the National Association of Securities Dealers (NASD), and it launched the NASDAQ trading system and stock price index. The NASD merged with the member regulation, enforcement, and arbitration functions of the New York Stock Exchange in 2007. Today FINRA regulates some 630,000 registered representatives in nearly five thousand brokerage firms.

Other countries have similar agencies, such as the Investment Industry Regulatory Organization of Canada and the Securities Investment Institute in the United Kingdom.

To become a registered representative in the United States—that is, to be licensed to sell securities and have the power to act as an agent—FINRA dictates that one must pass the Series 7, Series 24, and Series 63 examinations, which heavily emphasize standards of ethical dealing, and also demonstrate a level of general knowledge about securities. In the preparatory materials for these difficult exams, prospective stockbrokers, or registered representatives, are warned against using deliberately misleading sales tactics, such as "selling dividends," that is, pressuring a client to buy a stock so as not to miss a dividend check, without pointing out that the price of a share generally falls after a dividend is paid. They are forbidden from "front running," that is, buying shares on their own account just before filling a large customer order, to profit personally from the price rise the large order will create. They are warned against "churning," deliberately advising a client to make many purchases and sales merely to generate commissions. Registered representatives are at all times required to communicate with their supervisors, who are expected to uphold an even higher standard of conduct.

FINRA also requires registered representatives and their supervisors to participate in regular continuing education programs. During some of these, the reps are shown video clips of actors portraying real-world situations in which temptations can arise.

It is hard not to come to the conclusion that the activities of FINRA are fundamentally well meaning and effective in improving the climate of the financial industry.

Government Regulators

The "bureaucrats" who run government regulatory agencies are rarely appreciated publicly. There is no room in our public imagination to view them as of any interest, let alone as heroes. We hear about pitched battles among elected officials, and about the often dramatic activities of lobbyists and powerful corporate interests, but little or nothing about the everyday activities of the final arbiters who actually deal with all the details.

It is hard for most of us to know with certainty whether these regulators are doing a good job for the citizens who depend on them. Of course we can count the number of regulations they promulgate, but we cannot say with any certainty how our society would be different if they weren't in place. The rules they make have numerous effects on our lives, but it is difficult to quantify or summarize these effects. We are left for the most part with only vague impressions of what regulators do.

In 2002 I visited the SEC with my colleagues at a firm I had co-founded, MacroMarkets LLC. Going there on business was unusual for me, for I was (and still remain) a full-time professor devoted mostly to education and research. We went to the SEC to gain approval for a new and unusual security that we wanted to launch: MacroShares, which were intended to make previously untradable risks tradable, and in so doing to provide price discovery for basic economic values for which there was at the time no such discovery. In truth I did not have particularly high expectations for the kinds of people we would meet at the SEC.

We were accompanied by representatives from the American Stock Exchange and our lawyers from Skadden, Arps, Slate, Meagher & Flom. I was impressed by the team we had assembled on our side. But I remember sitting there thinking that many of those representing the SEC were equally impressive—knowledgeable, enlightened, sympathetic. It seemed to me, as an outsider to such things, that together both sides represented a community of intelligent, public-spirited, sincere people.

The sense I got of the SEC that day is another reason why I am inclined to believe Meaghan Cheung when she denies being influenced in the Madoff case.

On another occasion, when I was visiting a second U.S. government regulatory body, the Federal Deposit Insurance Corporation, I asked some of the regulators at lunch: Why do you do it? What drives you to take a job like this? Many of them feel that a stint as a government regulator is an important part of a career in finance. Individually they seemed to have a well-thought-out sense of their own careers, of their places in the financial community, and of a broader mission. Collectively there seemed to be a sense not only of self-advancement but also of social purpose.

I invited Laura Cha, former vice chair of the China Securities Regulatory Commission and a member of the Executive Council of Hong Kong, now non-executive deputy chairman of the Hong Kong and Shanghai Banking Corporation, to talk to my Financial Markets class about her experiences as a regulator. She reflected as follows:

> So, I had a total of 14 years of experience as a regulator. And I have to say that it has been hugely gratifying, because as a regulator and a policy setter I was able to facilitate the development of markets in Hong Kong. In the early days— I mean in the '70s and the '80s—Hong Kong was largely a local market. The international players like Goldman Sachs and Morgan Stanley, they came and they went, they took a look and decided the Hong Kong market was too small for them. All that took a change in 1992, when the Chinese government decided that they wanted to use the Hong Kong market as a way to help transform or reform the state-owned enterprises.[8]

I believe she is speaking honestly here—a career as a regulator can be highly gratifying, quite apart from any personal financial profit. To effect changes in a market as she did is to be part of history—in her case, part of the historic advance of the Chinese civilization.

Of course, things don't always go so swimmingly well in negotiations with regulators, and I am told that many of the people who pay visits to the SEC can be manipulative and adversarial. There is also, among those who work at the SEC and at other regulatory agencies, a degree of frustration with political interference, inadequate budgets, and overwork. Because it is the regulators who make and enforce the rules that govern financial capitalism, they must be given adequate resources to do so, as well as the respect and appreciation that they deserve.

Chapter 13

Accountants and Auditors

For an economic organization to function, it must have its own memories and its own way of storing, accessing, and communicating those memories. Accountants manage the repositories of financial memories, whether of an organization or of an individual client. Auditors evaluate and interpret their work. Accountants—particularly those who are chief financial officers of companies—are essential to finance because they preserve the integrity of essential financial structures.

People who are actively involved in managing and running a business will typically have fine short-term memories, but, like most of us, they may not always be able to remember details over time. They are best at remembering the specifics of their *own* employment contracts, their own options, their own incentive compensation. More typically, their memories become fuzzy when it comes to remembering promises made to *others* in their organizations, or to dealing with the minutiae imposed by tax authorities or regulators. CEOs have loftier goals in mind, and they can't be expected to know all the details.

We have compared CEOs to the prefrontal cortex of the brain. In the same way, we could compare accountants or chief financial officers to the hippocampus, which converts short-term memory into long-term memory and connects different memories in the brain. An organization draws inspiration from its CEO in terms of vision and goals, but it also needs a different kind of inspiration, no less lofty than that expected of a CEO: a drive for orderliness and consistency.

Accountants have to determine what is important to remember, to document, to publish. The term *bookkeeper*—with its suggestion of dusting off old documents in a basement archive—gives a misleading impression of what they do. Their responsibilities are far more central, for they are essential to the stewardship that should be the central mission of our financial institutions.

Responsible for storing essential information, accountants are upholders of consistent moral standards, since consistency of standards is a prerequisite for remembering commitments and details. They must have a strong sense of their own standards. They tend to be hired by those who want or need to prove to others that they are honest—but who sometimes behave as dishonestly as possible within that constraint. This fact creates a moral challenge for accountants, a major theme in their everyday lives. But the best, and over time the most successful, in the accounting profession are those who embrace this moral challenge.

In her book *Confessions of a Tax Accountant*, Noelle Allen reveals a long list of dishonest tax dodges that her clients have asked her to approve. Reading her account reminds one of the deceptive side of human nature. She tells a story: "I was called for jury duty recently. As a part of the process of jury selection, the prosecuting attorney in the case asked me if I thought I could tell when someone was lying. I replied 'Sir, I'm a tax accountant. People lie to me all the time.' His response: 'Ms. Allen, you're excused.'"[1]

An accountant has to keep an emotional distance from the people and organizations he or she serves, so as not to be drawn into any of their machinations. Of particular importance, a corporate accountant must feel a general sense of sympathy for the various claimants to the organization's purse, so as to remember all of them and treat them all fairly.

A CEO cannot double as the accountant or chief financial officer of an organization. Human impulses to be manipulative and self-dealing are too strong. There is necessarily a degree of conflict of interest between the CEO and the accountant—a conflict that is built into the very model of the modern organization. The CEO is supposed to be a visionary, looking to the future. The accountant remembers commitments and resource limits, with an eye to the promises of the past and the realities of the present.

There are a large number of self-regulatory organizations in the accounting profession. The International Accounting Standards Board (IASB) (a successor to the International Accounting Standards Committee) traces its history back to 1973, when it was created by a number of accounting organizations: the American Institute of Certified Public Accountants (AICPA), the Canadian Institute of Chartered Accountants, the Ordre des Experts-Comptables et des Comptables Agréés in France, the Institut der Wirtschaftsprüfer in Germany, the Institute of Chartered Accountants in Australia, the Institute of Chartered Accountants in England and Wales, the Japanese Institute of Certified Public Accountants, the Instituto Mexicano de Contadores Públicos in Mexico, and the Nederlands Instituut van Registeraccountants in the Netherlands. Many other countries' groups representing accountants have become involved since then. The U.S. Financial Accounting Standards Board signed a memorandum of understanding with the IASB in 2002, with the goal of converging accounting standards around the world.

These professional organizations set and enforce standards for the activity of their accountant members, notably their practice in auditing corporate books. They discipline members who do not meet these standards. And they serve as lobbyists for accountants' interests.

Some of these organizations have come under criticism during the current severe financial crisis. In the United States, AICPA's performance has been the subject of some dispute. AICPA performs a number of important regulatory functions that are essential to maintaining an honorable profession. It administers the Uniform Certified Public Accountants Examination for licensing accountants, and the exam includes detailed questions on ethics and responsibilities. But AICPA was chastised for doing nothing to prevent Arthur Anderson & Co., then one of the so-called Big Five accounting firms in the United States, and the auditor for Enron Corporation, from conspiring to manipulate that company's earnings statements. Arthur Anderson was convicted on criminal charges in 2002 and went out of the accounting business.

Arthur Levitt, the former chairman of the SEC, pointed out in 2003 that AICPA has disciplined few accountants and that no Big Five firm had ever failed a peer review. He was annoyed by what he saw as the institute's aggressive lobbying on behalf of its members, to the exclusion of the interests of ordinary investors. He concluded that "AICPA has fallen down on the job."[2]

And yet examples like the Arthur Anderson fiasco are rare. The accounting industry does have a reliable sense of professional ethics, which it imparts to its members and which forms the backbone of our system of financial capitalism. Accountants are responsible for ensuring that financial appearance matches reality, and it is ultimately through their efforts that we trust our businesses enough to find it motivating and even inspiring to work for them or invest in them.

Chapter 14

Educators

A t this point we have discussed the most central roles and responsibilities in the financial world, and we now move to some of those on its periphery. But peripheral does not mean less important, merely less involved in day-to-day operations. Educators are of central importance to the functioning of the financial system. Delicate as the proper functioning of the system is, it requires some understanding of the origins of its institutions, its practices, and their purpose, and a sense of how one's own career can fit into that picture.

Errors by educators in recent decades seem to have played an important role in the severe financial crisis that began in 2007. In particular, the efficient markets theory was oversold to students, and this helped contribute to the formation of speculative bubbles. Many teachers seemed to inculcate the extreme view that markets are perfectly efficient. From this view many of their students drew the conclusion that it hardly matters ethically what one does in business, since nothing one could do would ever disturb this magnificent equilibrium.

But educators are also responsible for the rapid expansion of financial sophistication in the financial markets in recent decades and for teaching the method and mission of financial stewardship. These roles will continue to be fundamental to financial institutions in the future.

The Historical Mission of Business Education

There has long been tension about teaching finance and business in colleges and universities. There has been a sense on the part of some in academe that these disciplines are somehow beneath other areas of study in the arts and sciences curriculum that has dominated higher education. Many colleges have long resisted starting an undergraduate business major and may offer very few business-related courses. Business education tends to occur only in separate business and law schools, which tend to be viewed by some as "vocational" schools which are not quite as intellectually strong. These attitudes are by no means new; they relate to the negative attitudes about those in business and finance that have characterized our society for centuries.

The fight against these negative prejudices has been most evident in the United States, which has always placed great emphasis on practical education. This practical focus is a long-standing trait of the United States. Benjamin Franklin, in a 1787 article for Europeans thinking of moving to the United States, described it thus:

> According to these opinions of the Americans, one of them would think himself more obliged to a genealogist, who could prove for him that his ancestors and relations for ten generations had been ploughmen, smiths, carpenters, tanners, or shoemakers, and consequently that they were useful members of society; than if he could only prove they were gentlemen doing nothing of value. . . . There [in America] they may be taught and practice mechanic arts, without incurring disgrace on that account; but on the contrary acquiring respect by their abilities.[1]

Even so, even in America, it would not be for another hundred years that a college business school would open its doors. The first such school was founded at the University of Pennsylvania in 1881, and the first graduate school of business (offering a master of science in commerce, essentially today's masters of business administration or MBA) at Dartmouth College in 1900. No other country followed suit until Canada's University of Western Ontario did so in 1951, half a century later.

Joseph Wharton—who made a fortune with the Bethlehem Steel Company, was the author of scholarly papers on metallurgy and other scientific topics, and later became a philanthropist—founded the business school at the University of Pennsylvania. It was at first called the Wharton School of Finance and Economy, a name that has since been shortened to the Wharton School. It was dedicated to teaching business as a noble calling. According to an 1881 summary of its prospectus, its purpose was "to inculcate, among other things, the immorality of acquiring wealth by winning it from others rather than by earning it through service to others."[2] Here Wharton was on to a fundamental truth about finance: it is not, and should not be, merely a zero-sum game, but rather an adjunct to, and a means toward, a productive life.

Wharton's was not the first business school in the United States, but its predecessors were not university-affiliated and were strictly vocational, teaching only basic business skills. An even older example of a business school was Bryant and Stratton College, founded in 1854 and incorporating the earlier

Folsom Business College. It claimed some prestige in its day and later included among its illustrious students John D. Rockefeller Sr. and Henry Ford. The college still exists today, offering associate of applied science degrees in accounting and other business fields, bachelor of science degrees in financial services and other fields, and preparation for certification examinations for financial planners, registered representatives, and others. The difference between Wharton and Bryant and Stratton remains the same today as it was at their founding: Wharton is more broadly intellectual while Bryant and Stratton is focused on teaching important basic business skills.

In 1890 Joseph Wharton gave a speech about education at the Wharton School in which he described his motives in founding the school within a college. He made it clear that one of the measures of a college should be the marketable skills its students receive. The speech was received with a chorus of negative comment from the presidents of the elite universities of his day. Francis Amasa Walker, the president of the Massachusetts Institute of Technology, declared, "I exceedingly dislike to see the question of college education put upon such low ground. A young man who would allow his decision between going to college or staying away to be determined wholly or mainly by the prospect of pecuniary return is unworthy of the benefit of a liberal education." Franklin Carter, the president of Williams College, said, "I have believed that the business men of the future are to come from the colleges. But then they must be trained men, disciplined and developed in all mental directions, not overfed mollusks."[3]

The same views, only slightly transformed, were still in evidence a hundred years later. In his 1991 book *Creating Academic Settings*, the economist John Perry Miller detailed the arguments he had to make for founding a management school at Yale University while he was dean of the graduate school there. Yale did not get its management school until 1976 because of the objections of many alumni who thought such an addition too vocational. Miller on the other hand believed that management and finance are indeed intellectual disciplines, which potentially offer their own intrinsic rewards to everyone in the intellectual community:

> Equally important is the impact of such a program on the life and vision of the faculty and students in other parts of the University. The horizons of faculty members and their educational programs are affected significantly by the various professional schools which surround the central Faculty of Arts and Sciences. Yale's faculty members are different and, I believe, better for living in an environment of colleagues pursuing research and education in the various professions. The effects are subtle but real. The perspective of faculty and students is broader, their vision of man and woman and their ways richer.[4]

By the time Miller wrote, the field of finance had become transformed from a discipline of description and rote memorization into a mathematical and empirical science considered by many worthy of becoming part of a true liberal education.

Our colleges and universities are where finance starts, where the people who make the decisions are first exposed to the theory and philosophy of business. They need to understand both the abstract theory and the practical applications and issues of morality that underlie a life in business.

Economic Education and Morality

It is in school—starting with the education of children and teenagers, and leading next to undergraduate programs and MBA, JD, and PhD programs— that young people have their only real, unhurried opportunity to examine the underpinnings of their future professions, to talk to others unhampered by nondisclosure requirements and professional loyalties. This is where the moral decisions that will guide later life are really made, and educators have a responsibility to see that they are made well. There is unfortunately a so-called agency problem, particularly in our colleges and graduate schools, where academic faculty often see themselves as having no purpose other than to train scholars like themselves. Their teaching may become too focused on the frontiers of research and on research methods, rather than on preparing their students to be participants in the real-world practice of financial capitalism.

Business education must to some degree be vocational: it should not avoid teaching basic skills. But it should also integrate this knowledge into a broader intellectual framework. This is particularly important for those students who will become business leaders. Our educational institutions have an obligation to present a view of the true workings of financial capitalism, and to cover both the mathematics of finance and its human, practical, and moral side.

Chapter 15

Public Goods Financiers

Public finance, the financing of public goods and causes, is curiously considered a very different profession from "straight" finance. Courses in public finance at the university level are generally offered in the economics department, not the business school, and it appears that the professors in the two fields rarely talk to one another. Communications between the fields seem to be improving, and recognition is growing that they are, or at least ought to be, closely related. They deal with essentially similar problems, differentiated by the fact that public finance confronts a special "public goods" problem. Yet there still remains an unfortunate division between the fields, one that adversely affects their intellectual content.

The fundamental problem for public finance is that public goods are not naturally provided in a free-market system. A public good is an economic activity that automatically benefits the public, including all those who choose not to pay for the activity. Roads and scientific knowledge are public goods, as are clean air and cities free from crime. If one thinks the air is not clean enough, or that the streets are still too dangerous, one cannot go to a store and buy these things for oneself. The provision of these goods has to be public, the result of a collective decision to embark on certain costly activities. Individual and corporate philanthropy is usually inadequate to deal with the full range of public goods opportunities that present themselves. Indeed the primary justification for having a government is that it provides public goods.

A problem with public goods provision is that information about what can be done is neither visible nor comprehensible to most voters. A candidate for public office extolling some new plan to clean the air or reduce crime will be met with incomprehension by most individuals. They might know how much cleaner they would like the air to be and how much they would pay for that, but such awareness does not translate for them into specific knowledge of how they should vote on the issues.

Most individuals do not have the imagination to conceive of what might possibly be done. They tend to have some understanding of public goods *already provided*, for they observe their benefits. But they are unlikely to have any sense of what to do next.

General-mail postal services, provided on a mass scale for the public, have a public goods aspect since they furnish an economic infrastructure— something like an older version of what the Internet does today. This infra-structure, when it was introduced long ago, changed the playing field for everyone and made possible whole new lines of business activities that people could not even have imagined until the infrastructure was in place. Postal services may not be provided adequately by the private sector, without gov-ernment support, because private markets do not take into account the value of the public good and because of the monopolistic pricing problems that may be associated with the natural monopoly of a massive delivery system.

Before effective and economical postal service was provided extensively in the nineteenth century, most people probably did not regret its absence. They knew that they could get something delivered, at considerable expense, through private couriers or through an expensive government mail service, and they probably did not imagine that they would ever find much reason to want to have something delivered cheaply by mail. They could not have known that the development of an infrastructure for cheap and efficient delivery would launch a million other economic activities. They could not have known that creation of a national postal service with post offices in every town would change the economic layout of the nation, creating jobs and opportunities, improving land use, and resolving congestion problems.

It was not until after a persuasive 1837 pamphlet was published by Rowland Hill in London that there came to be an extensive and effective postal network in England, a "Penny Post" with the rule "for every letter a penny." Hill argued that the British government was charging too much for postal services in an effort to maximize government revenue. Considering the cost of delivering mail, the government was, he argued, in effect putting a tax of at least 200% on postal services. This tax came at the expense of (though he did not use the term) an important public good:

> When it is considered how much the religious, moral, and intellectual progress of the people, would be accelerated by the unobstructed circulation of letters and of the many cheap and excellent non-political publications of the present day, the Post Office assumes the new and important character of a powerful engine of civilization; capable of performing a distinguished part in the great

work of National education, but rendered feeble and inefficient by erroneous financial arrangements.[1]

Even after the Penny Post was fully implemented, it would have been hard to *prove* quantitatively that it had become a "powerful engine of civilization"— but people believed just that. It was soon copied all over the world. Nevertheless it is something of a miracle that, thanks to the calculation of public financiers like Hill, extensive postal networks got started in the first place.

The provision of public goods is essentially a deep financial problem. It is subject to the same constraints seen in the provision of private goods. We need to encourage organizations of people who together can be productive in providing public goods. We need to identify genuine public goods and to assign a priority ranking to them. We need to see that the people charged with providing them are appropriately incentivized and not corrupted. We need to deal with the fact that information about what might ideally be provided as public goods is dispersed among many people and somehow has to be pooled. And so the financial technology that we have put in place for providing private goods carries over to the provision of public goods.

There have been several major milestones in the provision of public goods— milestones that are significant for the spur they gave to creativity in this area.

In 1932, in the depths of the Great Depression, President Herbert Hoover created the Reconstruction Finance Corporation. A key idea underlying effective public goods finance is that it does not have to be the government that comes up with ideas for public goods through a political process, and it does not have to be candidates for national office who dream up such ideas. The Reconstruction Finance Corporation listened to ideas from the private sector and actively sought private-sector advice. And the strategy worked: even in the midst of the Great Depression, almost all of the loans it made to private businesses were repaid.

Another key idea is that the government can finance organizations of individuals rather than hire single individuals as employees of the government. In that way, expenditure on public goods is entirely analogous to expenditure on private goods, except that the customer is the government.

In 1950, at the suggestion of Vannevar Bush, former dean of engineering at the Massachusetts Institute of Technology, the United States created the National Science Foundation. Bush had written a short book in 1945, *Science, the Endless Frontier*, and presented it to President Franklin D. Roosevelt. The book argued that scientific research was a profoundly important public good, which up until then had been supported primarily by private benefactors and private universities. Bush had clear ideas about how government should facilitate the advancement of science. Grants should be made to organizations outside the federal government, which should never operate its own laboratories. Decisions to award funds would be made not by bureaucrats but by real scientists, outside the government, who would volunteer to evaluate research proposals.[2]

The National Science Foundation would thus operate more like an investor in a venture capital firm, specializing in science, than a typical agency of the government. The foundation would provide the funds that would enable risk management and incentivization, but beyond that, market forces would be allowed to operate. Bush's model has been a spectacular success, and it has been copied by virtually every developed country in the world.

Public finance will always need arrangements like this, to stimulate public creativity in the realm of public works, just as the private sector stimulates creativity through commercial enterprises.

There is widespread public concern about the continued provision of public goods and a tendency to think apathetically, to believe that nothing can be done. Popular singer-songwriter Joni Mitchell's song "Big Yellow Taxi" had the famous refrain, "They paved paradise and put up a parking lot." The song offers no ray of hope. But what are the concrete complaints that she aired in that song? She mentions the unnecessary cutting down of trees to make way for "a pink hotel, a boutique, and a swinging hot spot" and the destruction of birds and bees by farmers' insecticides. It is the job of public financiers to provide the resources to enable projects to protect the trees, birds, and bees and to manage land use.

Fortunately, we do have public works, and we do have environmental protection agencies that fund specific environmental projects. Problems like those in Mitchell's song are being addressed—albeit not as creatively, extensively, or quickly as we might like. The challenge is to create more effective strategies for public finance to allow us to continue to achieve such goals in the future.

Chapter 16

Policy Makers in Charge of Stabilizing the Economy

Financial capitalism is far from a perfect system, and one of its fundamental problems is that it is vulnerable to booms and busts, recessions and depressions. These events have happened so many times in the past that one can predict with certainty they will happen again. So it is widely appreciated that we need policy makers whose duty is to counteract such instabilities and reduce their impact.

But preventing these episodes presents a difficult problem: the reasons for them have never been well understood. The causes of economic booms or busts are multifaceted, and understanding them requires human judgment—judgment of people's motives, of their patterns of thinking, and of the changing political climate.

There has long been hope that forecasting and stabilization of the economy can be reduced to a science. To a significant extent this hope has been fulfilled: there *is* a science of economic forecasting. My own research with Ray Fair, the author of FairModel, an econometric model of the world economy, confirms that his and other prominent models of the economy do have some ability to forecast. The model makers have learned how to extrapolate economic data, and moreover their models do more than just extrapolate plots of data: their underlying economic theory appears to be sound as well.[1]

But the value of these models is limited. The forecasters are somewhat good at predicting the time path of run-of-the-mill recessions, the kind of relatively short-run fluctuations that they have seen many times. But they are not at all good at predicting the kind of rare and severe economic crisis that started in

2007—a crisis of a severity that has not been seen since the Great Depression of the 1930s. It is no surprise that the forecasters are not so good at predicting events that come along very rarely and that fracture key financial institutions. And yet it is these severe economic crises about which we care the most.

For the foreseeable future, economic stabilization will require dedicated people to use their intuitive judgment, as well as formal models. These policy makers often resemble politicians more than scientists, for the kind of judgments they must make not only are constrained by politics but also depend on social and political forces. The success of expert judgment in the social and political sphere has been notoriously hard to verify and quantify, and that problem is very much with us in evaluating the efforts of policy makers tasked with economic stabilization.[2]

Monetary Policy Makers

Central bankers have been the first line of defense against economic instabilities ever since the Bank of England evolved from a private bank into the world's first central bank. As we have seen, it was founded, initially with no clear economic-stabilization responsibilities, in 1694. Though it was initially a private bank, over the centuries it gradually assumed a stabilizing function for the broader economy. It became the primary issuer of paper money in Britain, and it could use its power of credit to lean against excessive booms and to support the economy when it was flagging. The success of the Bank of England was noticed all over the world, and it became the model for many other central banks, including, in 1913, the Federal Reserve System of the United States.[3]

Central bankers' role is substantially to try to manage the major driving force of the economy, business confidence, or its close analogue, credit. As Walter Bagehot, then the editor of The Economist, put it in the 1896 edition of his book Lombard Street: A Description of the Money Market: "Credit—the disposition of one man to trust another—is singularly varying. In England, after a great calamity, everybody is suspicious of everybody; as soon as that calamity is forgotten, everybody again confides in everybody. . . . The Bank of England is bound, according to our system, not only to keep a good reserve against a time of panic, but to use that reserve effectually when that time of panic comes."[4] The job of trying to manage such things as suspicions and panics is inherently difficult for anyone—more akin to the work of a psychotherapist than a scientist or an engineer. It is a fundamentally human task—so much so that it is very difficult to conclude in hindsight whether the task has been done well or to draw really useful lessons for future interventions.

In a best-selling biography by Bob Woodward published in 2001, Alan Greenspan, the chairman of the Federal Reserve System from 1987 to 2006, was nicknamed "Maestro" for his ability to guide the U.S. economy. The book appeared near the very end of the spectacular stock market rise and economic boom of the 1990s.[5] Greenspan was widely admired, even considered a genius. But it turns out that he was presiding over an unsustainable boom, one that devolved into a severe financial crisis soon after he left his post in 2006. Suddenly he was no longer a genius.

The financial meltdown tested the stabilization abilities of the world's central banks, and they were forced to improvise and try altogether new policies. Yet even these were not adequate to prevent a precipitate world financial crisis. The interconnectedness of the world financial system caused an initial crisis in the housing market and the market for subprime mortgages in the United States to set off a chain reaction around the world.

At the root of the difficulties central bankers face is the difficulty of anticipating crises or preparing for them. In its May 10, 2006, statement, the Federal Open Market Committee of the U.S. Federal Reserve System—which is the committee of the U.S. central bank that is most directly in charge of stabilization of the economy, through its control of interest rates and credit—had no clue of the coming crisis: "The Committee sees growth as likely to moderate to a more sustainable pace, partly reflecting a gradual cooling of the housing market and the lagged effects of increases in interest rates and energy prices. . . . The Committee judges that some further policy firming may yet be needed to address inflation risks."[6]

In his July 26, 2006, introductory statement to the European Central Bank's interest rate announcement, bank head Jean-Claude Trichet wrote, "Global economic activity remains strong, providing support for euro area exports. Investment is expected to pick up, benefiting from an extended period of very favourable financing conditions, balance sheet restructuring and accumulated and ongoing gains in earnings and business efficiency."[7]

The International Monetary Fund, an international agency that works closely with central banks, also saw little of the problems that would bring on the crisis. In its April 2006 *World Economic Outlook* the fund said: "Notwithstanding higher oil prices and natural disasters, global growth has continued to exceed expectations, aided by benign financial market conditions and continued accommodative macroeconomic policies. Looking forward, the baseline forecast is for continued strong growth, although . . . risks remain slanted to the downside, the more so since key vulnerabilities—notably global imbalances—continue to increase."[8]

Concern with "global imbalances" is a long-standing refrain of the fund's, describing such things as the U.S. trade deficit and the Chinese trade surplus, having nothing fundamentally to do with the severe financial crisis that began in 2007. There was a brief mention later in the report of a "key uncertainty" for the United States in its inflated housing market.[9] But the reader of this summary surely came away expecting "continued strong growth" thanks to "benign financial market conditions."

The Bank for International Settlements in Switzerland, which also works closely with central banks, in its June 2006 *Quarterly Review,* would say only that there were "hints of trouble ahead" in highly priced asset markets.[10]

The fact is that *no* central bank saw the crisis coming, even on its very eve. A 2006 study by Martin Čihák of the International Monetary Fund of the then-most-recent financial stability reports issued by forty-seven central banks around the world concluded that "virtually all (96 percent) have started off with a positive assessment of soundness of the domestic system, characterizing the health of the system as being, e.g., 'in good shape,' 'solid,' or at least 'improving.'"[11]

This total failure of central bankers to anticipate the crisis is related to the politically involved nature of their jobs, the importance of political judgment to their jobs, and the difficulty political forecasters have always faced. The bankers, being professionals, no doubt wanted to avoid sounding any alarms until they had objective evidence—but what evidence there was of a coming crisis required personal intuition to judge, and there was no politically correct consensus that would have encouraged them to use such intuition publicly.

Forecasting the crisis would have required making judgments about such things as the wishful-thinking bias that led to the housing bubble, the moral lapses that many leaders showed in failing to criticize the bubble, the political reasons for the failure of regulatory authorities or securities raters to confront the bubble, and the convenient opportunity the bubble gave to politicians to make use of the "let them eat credit" strategy (to use a term coined by Raghuram Rajan after the collapse of the economy) to deal with worldwide rumblings of discontent resulting from increasing social inequality.[12]

Reforms in the wake of the financial crisis have included the creation of new government agencies charged with learning more about financial instabilities and recommending policies to deal with them. In the United States the Dodd-Frank Act of 2010 created the Financial Stability Oversight Council, and in the European Union the European Parliament created the European Systemic Risk Board, initially under the auspices of the European Central Bank.

But these agencies face difficult tasks going forward. Somehow they must figure out in advance that trouble is coming so that they can take action to deal with it—action which itself is politically difficult. Given that central bankers already had prodigious research departments at their disposal and regularly attended international conferences, yet had hardly any clue about the present crisis, there is plenty of room for skepticism that they will succeed.

The severity of the world crisis suggests that the efforts of the central banks, though rather late in coming, were nevertheless helpful in staving off real disaster. But they alone are not enough to prevent severe dislocations arising from economic contractions. The other main tool for stabilization of the modern economy is fiscal policy, the tax and expenditure policy of the government.

Fiscal Policy Makers

Starting with the Great Depression in the 1930s, the idea took hold that government policy makers need to stimulate the economy from time to time, when central bank policy has proven inadequate, by means of appropriate fiscal policies, that is, by cutting taxes, raising government expenditures, or both. Such policies were called "pump priming" during the Great Depression, the analogy expressing a wish that a little fiscal stimulus might make a big difference to the economy.

The problem with this notion—discovered during the Great Depression and again in the economic crisis of the 2000s—has been that while it seems easy to cut taxes, cutting taxes without cutting expenditures increases the national debt. If the depression continues for a number of years, the burgeoning national debt becomes a concern, and the public is likely to call for a period of fiscal austerity—a possibly premature reversal of the stimulus.

In theory the economy may be boosted by a balanced-budget stimulus, increasing both taxes and expenditures by the same amount, so as not to increase the national debt. Economists in the 1940s asserted that the "balanced budget multiplier" was equal to one, at least when interest rates were stuck at rock bottom, as they were in the Great Depression and are in the United States today. That means that GDP goes up dollar-for-dollar with the increase in government expenditures.

But the problem here is that the tax increases weaken the impact of the fiscal stimulus, so that the policy effect is not so much "pump priming" as it is "commandeering." If one wants to boost the economy with balanced-budget expenditures, one has to use a lot of such expenditures.

Then there comes the problem of finding suitable causes on which to spend the government money. It is very difficult to come up on short notice with quality government expenditure projects on a large scale—projects that can also be fairly quickly shut down if the economy improves.

This difficulty limited the ability of government policy makers to stimulate the economy in the Great Depression as well as in the economic crisis of the 2000s. If the projects are not well chosen, there may be extensive public complaints that they benefited only special interest groups, and public support of the stimulus program may not last. That is indeed what we saw in the later years of the Great Depression and also, at the time of this writing, in the current financial crisis.

During World War II there was talk in the United States about this problem, since many people feared another Great Depression once the economic stimulus of wartime expenditures was removed. In 1941 the U.S. government formed the Public Work Reserve, which was to create a "shelf" of high-quality, turnkey public works projects that could be started any time the economy faltered.

According to a 1943 analysis of its operations by Benjamin Higgins, the control of that organization was divided between several agencies, and "a struggle for control developed in which the agency that established jurisdictional rights turned out to be the agency which had no funds to continue the project."[13] The operations of that agency were also inhibited by the distractions of the war itself, and it was disbanded in 1942, its responsibilities distributed among other agencies, and soon forgotten.

The short life of the Public Work Reserve does not necessarily prove that such a program could not be a success. We need agencies that are more forward looking, as the National Science Foundation has been. Martin Shubik has proposed re-creating something like the Public Work Reserve in a new form that he calls the Federal Employment Reserve Authority.[14]

It is likely that fiscal policy will need to be deployed in future economic contractions, and one way or another we should develop a system of more responsive fiscal policies, to prevent the implementation problems encountered in the past.

Developing Financial Institutions to Reduce Economic Fluctuations

We have seen that stabilization policy makers are essential to the success of modern financial capitalism, and that their job is inherently difficult. We can, however, make their job easier if we develop better financial institutions to manage the risks of these largely unpredictable crises. Financial markets, despite their vulnerability to excesses and speculative bubbles, at least have the advantage that their activities are not overly influenced by political correctness: the markets attract independent-minded people who are not shy about taking action depending on their intuitive—and perhaps unprovable—theories.

We ultimately cannot completely prevent major economic fluctuations with monetary or fiscal policy, but we can still lessen the impact of those fluctuations on individuals by setting up appropriate financial institutions. These are known as automatic stabilizers—institutions that relieve the policy makers of the burden of making politically difficult stabilization moves.

Unemployment insurance, as government policy, dates back to 1911 in the United Kingdom. It lessens the impact of economic fluctuations on vulnerable individuals. A progressive income tax is another automatic stabilizer, since tax collections automatically decrease in an economic downturn and increase in a boom, thus dampening the fluctuations.

In the future, such automatic stabilizers should, and probably will, take many new forms. There could be insurance policies against declines in home prices or home equity, which would protect homeowners against declines in the value of their homes, or there could be risk-managing forms of mortgages like the continuous-workout mortgages that I have proposed.[15]

Governments should issue shares in the nation's GDP or other similar measures of its economic success.[16] This would be like issuing equity—shares in the nation's economy—rather than debt. Thus debts would be made more flexible, and the repayment of debts would become more contingent on economic outcomes. For example, the GDP-linked bonds would automatically become less onerous to the government in an economic crisis. Countries could issue shares in their GDPs to investors around the world. If one share was equal to one-trillionth of total GDP, these might be called "trills."[17]

Perhaps governments should issue *leveraged* shares in their GDPs to international investors, shares that go up and down by more than one-for-one with GDP. Think of the collapse of the Greek national debt that the world has been expecting since 2009. Had the Greek government, whose debt nearly collapsed in 2010–11, substantially financed its borrowing before the crisis with such debt, its indebtedness would have dropped sharply with the crisis—and in fact there might not have been a crisis at all.[18]

Stabilization in the Future

Our ability to insulate people from the vagaries of booms and depressions still seems to be one of the most imperfect aspects of our financial system. A good part of the reason why we have found it so difficult to manage such instabilities is that they arise from a higher-order system, a complex system that involves people and their emotions. People must be incentivized to do good work, but such incentivization, by reason of its emotional component, becomes hard to design to perfection. One cannot do controlled experiments with national economies to learn their dynamics. But we must do the best we can, developing a better understanding of the instabilities in a modern financial economy and being as creative as possible in our application of this understanding.

The current major tools of stabilization policy—tax and expenditure policies by the government and monetary policy by the central bank—have been standards around the world since the middle of the twentieth century, and their significance surely increased with the financial crisis of 2007. But a changing environment will see these policy tools evolve in the future, and they may one day even be obsolete and largely forgotten, like the clearing house loan certificates, the nineteenth-century technology for dealing with bank failures.

The information technology revolution, coupled with innovations in financial technology, is even now changing policy. Central bank policy, traditionally focused on managing the money supply, is already relying on tools that were unknown a short while ago, such as large-scale asset purchases, currency swaps, and quantitative easing. The scope and complexity of the financial system are fundamentally changing.

And even more fundamental changes are in the offing, like the elimination of money in favor of electronic units. The change could be the occasion for a new system of economic units of measurement, like the *baskets* described in Chapter 22 of this book. It is likely that there will be a fundamental change in the nature of our central banks in coming decades—if they are even called central banks anymore. Central banks are an invention that served its purpose at a certain time in history, in a certain kind of environment. Their time may have passed.

Stabilization policies around the world are being reinvented right before our eyes, in response to the current financial crisis, and they will continue to be reinvented. Yet their defining purpose—the stabilization of a naturally unstable economy—is likely to remain unchanged. The real story of the central banks is not their current array of tools and procedures but their lasting commitment to real-world application of sophisticated financial tools for this purpose.

Chapter 17

Trustees and Nonprofit Managers

Trustees manage portfolios to support others' causes—causes that tend to out-live their clients, the people who defined them. Nonprofit organizations make grants or undertake activities in support of a cause. They enable people to see to it that their purposes are carried forward on a large scale and over a long time frame, though not always as perfectly as they might have wished. Defining such institutions is a difficult financial problem, but one with which we, at this point in history, have had some success.

Trustees Make Long-Term Purposes Achievable

Most human goals have an implicit time frame, and many goals cannot be achieved without consistent activity over a long period of time.

Trust companies, and trust departments in banks, outlive individuals and so make it possible for people to manage causes for the ages. To take a familiar example, parents with a special-needs child may set up a trust to support that child. They will do this since they expect the child to outlive them, and they need someone to help manage their child's future life. In so doing, they can extend their activities in support of the child far beyond their own lifetimes. Trusts are a remarkable invention of modern finance, allowing people to extend their lives of purpose and even, under certain circumstances, making them "immortal."

The system works well in many ways, though there is a difficult agency problem: the world changes, the nature of the cause changes, and the people who finance the trust find it difficult to define how future trustees should respond to such changes.

The Shakers, officially called the United Society of Believers in Christ's Second Appearing, is a religious sect originating in North America that was founded by Ann Lee in the eighteenth century, based on the concept that celibacy is the route to salvation. Since members had no children, the community could not grow through reproduction, and they hoped to prevail by recruitment, partly through orphanages they ran. But their hopes were in vain, as U.S. laws began to look askance at church-run orphanages and recruitment success fell, and the Shakers exist now primarily as a financial legacy, only because of the trusts they set up. The Shaker Trust with the state of Maine now maintains a Shaker community at Sabbathday Lake Shaker Village in that state, but today the people there are almost entirely non-Shakers. As of this writing, only three living Shakers remain in the village.

And yet the Shaker tradition lives on through their financial arrangements. The United Society of Shakers, Sabbathday Lake, Inc., is a nonprofit corporation, devoted to promoting the Shakers' beliefs—but now run by non-Shakers. The board of a nonprofit is constrained by its corporate charter to fulfill its stated mission as they see fit, and to hire and pay appropriate salaries to the people who do so (including themselves). Since there are no longer any young Shakers to fill that role, the board members must interpret their mission in light of present-day conditions as best they can. Perhaps the board members are not overly sympathetic to the aims of the trust, and they may not be doing all they can to reestablish the religion. But the religion lives on in the financial sphere, long after the ecstatic spiritual motivation for it has faded. Hope for a rebirth of the active religion may not run very high, but with the help of the nonprofit it survives financially. We can imagine that the founders of the religion would not be entirely pleased with this outcome, given the intensity with which they apparently held their religious beliefs. But a good society has limited ability to make everyone's dreams a reality—and finance is all about reality.

The financial arrangements that trusts make possible are the best device that society has yet come up with to make life's goals and purposes immortal. They are not perfect institutions. But they far surpass any other institution for allowing us individually to fulfill our personal goals over a long time frame. The alternative—lobbying the government specifically for funding for our goals—can work, but only if those goals are "politically correct" and have at least some legitimacy among the majority of the population. The Shakers certainly could not pass that test, and there are myriad other people with causes that would fall into the same category.

Nonprofit Organizations

A nonprofit organization, as the name implies, distributes no profits. It has no stockholders who can expect dividends. In some cases a nonprofit may be nothing more than a charitable trust. But it often runs a business, such as a nonprofit hospital or university. Some nonprofits even engage in controversial business practices, in competition with the for-profit sector. For example, according to a study by Total Compensation Solutions, a human resources consulting firm, in 2007–8, 42% of nonprofits in the United States have put formal executive bonus plans in place to incentivize their top managers, and the percentage is increasing.[1]

A nonprofit differs from a for-profit organization in that it does what it does on behalf of some cause rather than to achieve a return for investors. The nonprofits represent an important "third sector" of the economy (after government and for-profits).

U.S. law is unusually focused on the concept of for-profit companies as existing solely for the benefit of shareholders. Ever since Adolf Berle and Gardiner Means wrote their classic *The Modern Corporation and Private Property* in 1932, U.S. law has emphasized protecting shareholders (who are too dispersed to oversee the companies in which they have share ownership) from selfish boards of directors and giving them rights to sue directors if they do not uphold the shareholders' interests.[2] U.S. corporate law, through a sequence of state court decisions, has evolved the concept of "duty of loyalty" of board members into a duty of loyalty to shareholders.

In contrast, in Europe (where share ownership has traditionally been less dispersed), corporate boards have less to fear if they interpret their duties more broadly than making money for shareholders.[3] Institutional structures encourage less focus on shareholder value. In Germany, for example, the supervisory board (*Aufsichtsrat*) of a corporation must by law, in most kinds of companies, have members representing labor, and boards often include representatives of labor unions.[4] Surely such boards will be less focused on maximizing shareholder value.

There is of late a movement under way in the United States to persuade state governments to create what is envisioned as a "fourth sector," comprising a new kind of corporation—called a benefit corporation—that includes in its charter acknowledgment of some broader cause, beyond simply making a profit. A benefit corporation is not legally obligated to maximize return to shareholders and so does not need to worry about lawsuits from those shareholders if it does not single-mindedly pursue profits. The articles of a benefit corporation may stipulate a specific public purpose, which would make these corporations more clearly publicly oriented than are European corporations. A benefit corporation does not enjoy the tax advantages of a nonprofit.

To date seven U.S. states have passed legislation to make possible these corporations. Maryland was the first, in April 2010, followed by Vermont, New Jersey, Virginia, Hawaii, California, and New York. Still more states have legislation pending to enable them.[5] This seems a healthy development, for many investors in private companies really do not want them to pursue profits single-mindedly. So-called ethical investing has a clientele, and the odds are that this clientele will be growing and that they are likely to be interested in investing in benefit corporations. In Chapter 28 I argue that there could be still another kind of corporation—one that I call the participation nonprofit, different from a benefit corporation—that might enable social purposes even further.

Benefit corporations are still a new concept and remain inconsequential to the financial system as a whole, but true nonprofits are already very important. It is remarkable that we have as many nonprofits as we do. In the United States in 2010 there were 1.6 million of them.[6] Why have so many people set these organizations up when they derive no profit from them? The answer is that people really do have purposes other than making money for themselves.

Of course, one can still make money from helping set up a nonprofit or working for one, for nonprofits pay salaries to their employees. The difference is that these salaries are expected to be in line with market salaries for comparable jobs in the for-profit sector. By creating a nonprofit one can create jobs for oneself and others. One is just not supposed to get rich doing so.[7]

This is not to say that a nonprofit does not *make* profits. It simply does not *distribute* them; it keeps them in its endowment for the furtherance of its causes. Many nonprofits find themselves really *trying* to make a profit as they compete alongside often similar for-profit organizations. They may even start to look very much like the for-profits. But they are fundamentally different because they exist to serve an institutional cause rather than the individual causes of their owners, and so their organizational identity can have a stronger element of corporate idealism.

The economist Joseph Schumpeter wrote about these organizations in his classic *Capitalism, Socialism, and Democracy* in 1950. He gave the example of a nonprofit hospital, an important institution in a capitalist society but one that is in a sense not capitalist since it does not have the profit motive. He wrote, "It is nonetheless the product of capitalism not only, to repeat, because the capitalist process supplies the means and the will, but much more fundamentally because capitalist rationality supplied the habits of mind that evolved the methods used in these hospitals."[8] Indeed, nonprofit hospitals have financial arrangements as complex as those of any for-profit entity— with their donors, with their employees, with their creditors, and with the government.

Institutional Accumulators

Many nonprofit institutions accumulate money over many years, with little thought as to what will eventually be done with the accumulated wealth. Universities typically grow their endowments with no plan to spend them down, living only off part of the income. This seems irrational: if the money is never to be spent, then why have it?

There is evidence that nonprofit hospital corporations do not respond as well to declining demand for their services as do the owners of for-profit hospitals. They continue to plow their profits back into new hospitals even when this does not represent a wise allocation of resources. In a sense, the profits are converted to "trapped capital" that continues to stay allocated to the same purpose even after it is no longer needed.[9]

Universities sometimes amass huge endowments from their activities. To what purpose do they put them if they never spend them down? One argument is that the endowment is a buffer, to be used in emergency situations. But, as economist Henry Hansmann has stressed, most universities typically have not drawn down their endowments—not in any historically known contingency.[10] The severe financial crisis that began in 2007 did not cause universities to spend any substantial amounts of capital from their endowments; instead they tended to curtail activities.

This accumulation of endowments for no apparent purpose is the institutional counterpart of individuals accumulating wealth far beyond their ability to benefit from it. Indeed it seems at least in part driven by some sense of immortality. By maintaining a large endowment in perpetuity, a university is able to appeal to alumni donors, who see their own mortality and look to the university as a means of transcending it.

The Future for Trusts and Nonprofits

The jobs performed by trustees and nonprofit managers are fundamental to financial capitalism because they extend our economic powers beyond the promotion of immediate consumption and direct them to our nobler purposes—and do so in an individualistic and democratic way. In the future, the structure of our nonprofits might be improved to help deal better with the problems discussed in this chapter, including loss of focus among trustees and trapped capital in nonprofit entities. I discuss some specific remedies later in this book.

That structure can and should be improved, to allow trustees and nonprofit managers to be more effective in achieving their ultimate goals. As our understanding of human psychology and of behavioral economics improves, we can expect to see further refinements in the structure and management of nonprofit institutions.

But even as they stand today, trusts and nonprofits have emerged as important vehicles that allow many to fulfill the purposes that give meaning to—and in some cases transcend—their lives.

Chapter 18

Philanthropists

Philanthropists are essential to the market economy. Indeed there is only so much a purely selfish individual can do with the large amounts of wealth that our financial system can bestow on successful people. One can drive (or be driven in) only one car at a time. One can eat only so much food, or wear only one set of clothes at a time. Virtually all of the things one can buy are based on products that are made available to the great mass of people, and hence are not that dissimilar from the products everyone else consumes. One can buy the finest wine, but in truth it is only incrementally different from other wines produced for the multitudes. Certainly some wealthy people do strive to own multiple large homes, expensive cars, and other luxury items, but we must assume there is diminishing satisfaction in amassing such possessions.

This fact was noted by Adam Smith in his *Theory of Moral Sentiments:*

> It is to no purpose, that the proud and unfeeling landlord views his extensive fields, without a thought for the wants of his brethren, in imagination consumes himself the whole harvest that grows upon them. The homely and vulgar proverb, that the eye is larger than the belly, never was more fully verified than with regard to him. The capacity of his stomach bears no proportion to the immensity of his desires, and will receive no more than that of the meanest peasant. The rest he is obliged to distribute among those, who prepare, in the nicest manner, that little which he himself makes use of.[1]

The Little Prince (in Antoine de Saint-Exupéry's classic 1943 children's book of the same name) met, in his space travels from asteroid to asteroid, a businessman who claimed he owned the stars. The man was scrutinizing a large sheet of paper that had them all listed, all 501,622,731 of them. But, the Little Prince asks, "What good does owning the stars do you?" The businessman answers, "It does me the good of being rich. . . . It lets me buy other stars, if someone discovers them."[2] Ownership of most other things is just as meaningless—a bit of basic wisdom that Saint-Exupéry felt the need to instill in children.

Seeing the futility of amassing large fortunes, most people choose not even to try. Many choose another kind of benevolent behavior that is akin to philanthropy: they enter occupations that are relatively low paying but that give them the satisfaction of helping people and seeing the results directly. Teachers and nurses are obvious examples, but one might argue that *most* people's jobs are philanthropic in this sense.

The Fundamental Economic Role of Philanthropists

The philanthropists that are the subject of this chapter are those who do their work with the objective of making money and then giving it away in support of causes; charitable, religious, artistic, scientific, environmental, educational, and so on. Because they spend much of their lives focused on making money, they may, as they live their lives, miss the opportunity to see directly the good that they are doing and enjoy the gratitude of their beneficiaries—but they may also be able to multiply the amount of good they are doing. For people of considerable managerial or financial talents, and possessed of an ability to think ahead to the future benefit to others, there is a moral obligation to do just that.

People who amass large fortunes *have* to plan to give it away, whether to their children, to friends or relatives, or to philanthropic causes. There is no other sensible end to their story. But that ultimate disposal of the fortune should not be just an afterthought for them. There is a natural mission for a person who amasses great wealth. The kind of person who is able to earn a fortune in business is also most likely well suited for managing philanthropic endeavors.

Andrew Carnegie argued this in his article "Wealth," published in the *North American Review* in 1889 and soon renamed "The Gospel of Wealth."[3] The article immediately attracted great attention and controversy, and there has been a revival of interest in the article in recent years, over a century later.

It is not that those successful in business are necessarily smarter than other people. In fact they may be relatively insensitive to the real needs of the poor and, because of their specialization in business, to many intellectual pursuits as well. It is rather that they are specialized in a particular kind of intelligence: the ability to put human talents and business opportunities together. This same talent can and should be used for human benefit.

Carnegie wrote in his article that "men possessed of this peculiar talent for affairs, under the free play of economic forces, must, of necessity, soon be in receipt of more revenue than can be judiciously expended upon themselves; and this law is as beneficial for the race as the others."[4]

Carnegie's article was a theory of capitalism as an arena for competition: the business world is a stage for "survival of the fittest."[5] Those who are most fit in practical managerial skills will tend to rise to the top and become wealthy. But for Carnegie it is not simply a vicious Darwinian competition, for a moral duty stands over it. The moral duty of the winners in the economic struggle is to retire from their business careers when they are still young enough to retain the skills that got them where they are, and to begin managing the disposal of their wealth for the public good.

His own life embodied this ideal. His philanthropic endeavors began, seven years after the publication of "Wealth," with the founding in 1896 of the Carnegie Museum of Natural History, an institution that led numerous pale-ontological expeditions. He did this at age sixty-one. He founded the Carnegie Institute of Technology (now Carnegie-Mellon University) in 1900. He sold Carnegie Steel to J. P. Morgan in 1901 and retired, at the age of sixty-five, to embark in full on his life of philanthropy. There followed the Carnegie Institution (dedicated to scientific research) in 1902 at age sixty-seven, the Carnegie Endowment for World Peace in 1910 at age seventy-five, and the Carnegie Corporation of New York (to advance education) in 1911 at age seventy-six. He died at the age of eighty-three.

In our own time, perhaps inspired by Carnegie, Bill Gates and Warren Buffett, currently the two richest men in the United States according to the Forbes 400 survey, have begun advocating what they call the "giving pledge."[6] Wealthy people are asked to pledge half of their wealth to philanthropy before they die. In 2010 they both traveled to China and invited fifty of the wealthiest people in that country to meet with them to hear about the pledge.

The Bill and Melinda Gates Foundation gives to a number of international causes. It does this in a different way than governments, which are often hampered by having to justify their activities as being in the national interest. For example, the foundation gave a grant to the Liverpool School of Tropical Medicine to find a cure for river blindness, a disease that is a scourge in poorer regions of Africa and Asia. Government support for such a cause is too weak, for there is little political capital to be gained by helping poor people in foreign countries—and there would certainly be political difficulty were the U.S. government to propose funding a U.K. university to benefit people in far-off countries. Yet a private foundation can simply sweep past all such obstacles to make it happen.

Egotism and Philanthropy

Philanthropy often seems to be egotistical—but of course much of it is. There is a generous side to human nature, but it is not the only side. Yet it is still philanthropy even if the donors insist on putting their names on it and enjoy-ing the rewards of earning a reputation for generosity.

One comes to the realization that the satisfaction great wealth might bring lies almost entirely in enhancing one's own self-respect, and hardly at all in either the consumption of wealth or the gratitude or admiration of others. A newly wealthy person has most likely already received praise for his or her many achievements, from a distance, from relatives and associates, and the actual making of the money is only the last in the long string of those achievements. These same relatives and associates are unlikely to know much about, let alone praise, the individual's philanthropic contributions. After the initial thrill, wealth provides at best a lonely pleasure, and each discovers for him- or herself that it brings neither fame nor friendship. Contemplating one's wealth may in fact lead to an empty feeling.

Reflecting on what to do with one's fortune becomes at once a realization of the limits of property. One can win in the capitalist game and indeed own something very substantial, but one soon realizes that this ownership is merely a set of specific rights that are limited by law, and ultimately even more starkly limited by one's own frailty and mortality. Wealth enables one to obtain others' help in tasks one has deemed significant. But one is left wondering what tasks one really wants done—and whether one can in fact use the wealth to persuade others to do those tasks constructively, and not end up spending the money on something very different from what one wanted.

In the end, for all of us who strive to achieve, whether in business or in other walks of life, the end of life is a disappointment. The personal pleasure over a lifetime was mostly in the striving and in one's friendships and interactions. The pinnacle of achievement does not bring happiness, but at best the reflection that the striving achieved some benefit for others, unappreciative and unrelated though those others may be.

The quandary that people feel when they contemplate giving away most of what they have accumulated over their lifetimes is an important example of the discontents experienced under financial capitalism. Our satisfaction with our lives—under whatever economic system we live—can never be perfect. We have an instinct for heroism and a yearning for the eternal achievement of fundamental goals, and yet we find that realistically we have to live out most of our lives at best as minor specialists in specific occupations—not unlike those we have considered in this part of the book.

In the next part of the book we will focus in on a number of these discontents and their relation to principles of human psychology. We will then be able to consider how—even if the simple psychological reality is that we can never be fully happy—we *can* find a meaningful place in one of the occupations supported by financial capitalism. We *can* improve the system so that it makes such meaning more genuine for us. We *can* contribute to a financial system that better enables whatever long-term goals we may decide upon in our most focused contemplation.

Part Two

Finance and Its Discontents

In his 1930 book *Civilization and Its Discontents*, Sigmund Freud described a "profound long-standing discontent with the existing state of civilization" and a widespread popular view that "civilization itself is to blame for a great part of our misery, and we should be much happier if we were to give it up and go back to primitive conditions." He attributed the popular appeal of traditional communism to such a view: "By abolishing private property one deprives the human love of aggression of one of its instruments."[1] But Freud ultimately concluded that civilization, with its complex psychology, is not so easily improved.

Our discontents reflect fundamental human nature and are refractory. The human spirit is not just aggressive; it yearns for something more. Eliminating private property under traditional communism was like treating anxiety with a lobotomy.

Indeed we cannot go back to a simpler, older, kind of civilization. We can only move forward. And to be successful at that, we have to come to a better understanding of these discontents. We must also ask: What are our inspirations? What kinds of innovations, financial or otherwise, should we focus on developing?

The next phase of our civilization—with an expanded scope of our financial markets and an information technology vastly superior to the one we have today—will cause the financial roles and responsibilities that were discussed in Part One to evolve into something perhaps very different. Yet there is no clear roadmap to this future. Any proposed remedies for our discontents are not obvious or without their own risks.

Chapter 19

Finance, Mathematics, and Beauty

Financial theory, as well as economic theory more generally, can be beautiful. I was struck by remarks to this effect at a retirement dinner for my colleague Herbert Scarf, a distinguished mathematical economist. A number of speakers at the dinner noted that his lectures were "elegant." They of course meant that the field itself had an inherent beauty, and that Herb was a master at expressing it.

The fact that the real world of financial capitalism is so often messy and inhuman, and that it involves so much hypocrisy and manipulation, may detract from this sense of beauty. But the same is true of nature: for all its beauty, it produces ugly things as well.

Symmetry

"Beauty is bound up with symmetry," wrote mathematician Hermann Weyl in his assessment of beauty in mathematics and other fields.[1] He thought that the sense of beauty we find in mathematics was related to the sense of beauty we derive from art, and he analyzed works of art and architecture to reveal an underlying similarity in the achievements of fields that at first seem completely different.

That symmetry is perceived as beautiful has been proven experimentally. Psychologists have shown, in experiments in which subjects are asked to judge the beauty of human faces from photographs, that people respond more favorably to photographs that have been digitally altered to be more perfectly bilaterally symmetrical than to the originals, and yet they seldom realize that they are so affected by symmetry.[2]

But the reaction to symmetry goes far beyond the mere assessment of balance. It is about the *discovery* of hidden and important symmetries. "Comprehending the universe means understanding its symmetries," wrote physicist Leon Lederman.[3] Symmetry in physics goes beyond the obvious things such as particle-antiparticle pairs. Conservation laws in physics are one example of the broader application of the symmetry principle in that field. And mathematics is the language of conservation laws. What is conserved is namable and reflects a deeper reality. Though the word *energy* is ancient in its origin, it had only a vague meaning until mathematical physicists gave it a precise definition. With that definition, we see that energy takes many different forms—forms which can be seen as expressions of the same fundamental reality only if we understand the language of mathematical physics.

There is a fundamental concept of symmetry implicit in the concept of market efficiency. This is the idea, fundamental to financial theory, that prices in different markets are just different manifestations of a deep underlying truth. The apparently meaningless jiggles in financial market prices are reflective of powerful forces. The accumulation through time of these small price changes amounts to a result that is not random but that instead provides discovery of true economic value—a value that is highly useful in the allocation of economic resources and in generating our livelihoods.

The discovery of a mathematical law to describe the price of a stock option in terms of the price of the underlying stock (as exemplified by the famous mathematical formula derived by Fischer Black and Myron Scholes) is an example of a conservation law in finance.[4] The option price is driven by exactly the same shocks as affect the price of the underlying stock, but with a nonlinear transformation of effect, a transformation that is at first challenging to comprehend but that, upon sufficient reflection, seems almost obvious. The same kind of conservation laws can be found throughout the field of financial derivatives pricing.

The so-called Modigliani-Miller theorems reveal another fundamental conservation law in finance. The theorems showed, at least for an idealized world in which we abstract from the intricacies of tax law, that there is a fundamental irrelevance to a firm's dividend payouts or to the choices firms make between financing through equity and financing through debt.[5] Once again a scholar has to learn how some values and returns are transformed by financial decisions, so that total value is exactly conserved.

The impulse toward perfection in framing any theory has been behind the widespread acceptance of efficient markets theory, the theory that financial markets efficiently incorporate all publicly available information, so that their price movements are not the result of any human error but, on the contrary, of some grander design that is essentially perfect. Implicit in much efficient-markets theorizing by economists is the notion that those who trade in markets are perfect rational calculators. Such a belief gives economic thinking a solid core.

Yet our belief in the perfect applicability of the efficient markets theory goes even further than that, to an impulse to simplify the mission we expect businesspeople to pursue, and hence to moral implications. For example, consider the theory that corporate executives should take as their sole goal the maximization of shareholder value. If that is what executives do, it greatly simplifies the theory. One single objective, measured by the price of a share, becomes the driver of everything, just as energy in physics is the driver of everything, and this objective manifests itself, subject to mathematical trans-formations, in every other financial variable.

As another example, our faith in efficient markets seems to have given rise to the notion of Ricardian equivalence, as expounded most notably by Harvard economist Robert Barro, refining the work of nineteenth-century economist David Ricardo, who had suggested the concept over a century earlier.[6] The principle is that government deficit spending to stimulate the economy is in a sense a trick, for savvy taxpayers will know that any such expenditure needs to be followed by increased taxes to pay back the debt. A simple mathematical expression called the present value relation equates the future tax increases to the present stimulus. Here again there is a conservation law at work, and one of some value—though of considerably less practical value than many economists perceive.

There is a very human tendency to be a bit too attracted—perhaps distracted —by the symmetrical and the beautiful. The conservation laws of finance are only as valid as their underlying assumptions, and their applicability to real-world phenomena has been overrated. And yet the sense of beauty pervading the theory, tempered with reality, remains part of the satisfaction for practi-tioners of this or any other science.

The Beauty of the Economic Activity Supported by Finance

Beyond the beauty of the theory, there is even more beauty in finance for what it *creates*. For finance is about human desires and human possibili-ties, and it facilitates all the day-to-day activities that constitute our work-ing lives. These purposeful activities are themselves beautiful, and one can stand back and marvel at them, as did Walt Whitman in his 1892 *Leaves of Grass:*

A Song for Occupations!
In the labor of engines and trades and the labor of fields I find
    the developments,
And find the eternal meanings.
Workmen and Workwomen![7]

It is in the facilitation of the full variety of human activities—of an active human society with a richness and diversity shared and appreciated by all people—that finance manifests its most genuine beauty.

Chapter 20

Categorizing People:
Financiers versus Artists and Other Idealists

One of our feelings about economic inequality is that high incomes in our society seem often to reward selfishness and narrow-mindedness rather than idealism and humanity. People naturally categorize other people, and we place them into groupings that take on exaggerated significance in our imaginations. We tend to think that those in careers other than our own are fundamentally different kinds of people. Personality and character differences are indeed somewhat associated with occupations. But this overly strong tendency to categorize people is related to what psychologists have dubbed "the fundamental attribution error."[1] It is a known fact that we tend to attribute the behavior of others to personality differences far more often than is warranted.

We tend to think of the philosopher, artist, or poet as the polar opposite of the CEO, banker, or businessperson. But it is not really so. The idea that businesspeople have personalities fundamentally different from those in other walks of life is belied by the fact that people often combine or switch careers. Let's consider a few examples.

Walt Whitman is one of our most revered poets, and his poetry is among the most spiritual. How did he achieve his success? He wrote notable poems, of course. But first he had to free himself from the economic necessity that forced him to write his first major work, *Franklin Evans, or, The Inebriate: A Tale of the Times,* a mass-market novel that made money but was an embarrassment to him. The first edition of his classic work *Leaves of Grass* in 1855 was self-published. That means he had somehow managed to convince a printer to support the idealistic endeavor. Whitman offered to set his own type as part of his deal with the printer. He himself arranged for booksellers to take a chance on his book. Although the book gradually gained acceptance, each subsequent edition of *Leaves of Grass* was not published without additional business struggles, and getting his poetry into the hands of readers became a lifelong passion for Whitman. His third edition was long delayed, and then the publisher's bankruptcy caused the printing plates to be put up at auction, so that Whitman lost profits that could have helped finance his further writing. Such are the financial travails of a successful poet, but they are not something that we hear much about.

Charles Ives, thought by some to be America's greatest symphonic composer, was first a highly successful insurance executive. He graduated from Yale in 1898, and in 1909 he and a partner founded a life insurance agency, Ives & Myrick. Ives wrote a finance book, *Life Insurance with Relation to Inheritance Tax*. Ives & Myrick, which by 1929 had grown to be the biggest life insurance agency in the United States, made him a fortune of over $20 million.[2] His wealth gave him the ability to produce, and subsidize the performance of, his idiosyncratic and not immediately popular music. We do not know exactly how such a fortune enabled him to persist over a lifetime with genuinely important but mostly still unpopular compositions, but we can take some clues from a biographer, in a discussion of the making of one of Ives's phonograph recordings: "Once again, probably with a sigh or a curse, Ives pulled out his checkbook and tried to make everybody happy. He would pay for another conductor for Ruggles but insisted on Slonimsky for his own pieces, and he would pay Nicolas the same as if he had done both sides."[3] Surely, aided by his fortune, Ives was better able to produce only the kind of music in which he truly believed. He did not have to take hack composing assignments just to support himself. The composer Arnold Schoenberg said of Ives, "There is a great man in this country who solved the problem of how to be true to oneself. His name is Charles Ives."

Two of the most highly regarded—and highly priced—contemporary artists, Jeff Koons and Damian Hirst, both sometimes sell their works for over $10 million apiece. Koons once held the world's record auction price for a living artist: $25,752,059 for his sculpture *Balloon Flower (Magenta)* when it was auctioned at Christie's in 2008. Koons and Hirst are not just solitary artists; they are both financial sophisticates. Both run businesses with numerous employees, and both are aggressive marketers of their own works. Koons started out as a commodities trader at Smith Barney and used his profits there to finance his art.

Christie's, on its web page for *Balloon Flower (Magenta)*, includes a disclaimer that reveals just how tight has become the nexus between art and finance:

> Special Notice: On occasion, Christie's has a direct financial interest in lots consigned for sale which may include guaranteeing a minimum price or making an advance to the consignor that is secured solely by consigned property. This is

such a lot. This indicates both in cases where Christie's holds the financial interest on its own, and in cases where Christie's has financed all or a part of such interest through a third party. Such third parties generally benefit financially if a guaranteed lot is sold successfully and may incur a loss if the sale is not successful.[4]

It would appear that the lawyers had a hand in writing this disclaimer, in anticipation of the possibility of litigation by other financial interests. The image of a struggling artist devoted exclusively to art for art's sake, waiting to be discovered by an influential art critic, thus to achieve success, hardly describes Koons—or many other artists, for that matter.

Even those in the most spiritually minded professions—in the church, in the arts, or in philanthropy, for example—find themselves routinely involved in managing financial resources and executing financial contracts that immerse them in calculations and dealmaking.

Even revolutionaries have to involve themselves in finance. In *Walden: Or Life in the Woods*, Henry David Thoreau described how he spent the years 1845–47 completely apart from modern society in the woods at Walden Pond, contemplating nature and spirituality. But he was not really an advocate of dropping out, and in fact in his own life he did not do so. Throughout most of his life he was actually involved in managing his family's pencil company and even invented a new way of making pencil leads. So he was actually a businessman; he just thought that making money should never be the overriding purpose of his life. "To have done anything by which you earned money merely is to have been truly idle or worse." The key word in this sentence is *merely*.[5]

The *British Quarterly Review* wrote of Thoreau in 1874, "Still it is a vital error to lead in any way to the idea that Thoreau was a hermit, or that he permanently banished himself to Walden Wood to study trees, and beasts and fishes, and to map out the land like a surveyor. . . . And yet with us in England he is too much conceived of in this light."[6] In fact, Thoreau was able to take his time off at Walden because the income from his family business gave him the leisure to do so. It was in reality a well-earned vacation to a beautiful spot. Today he would likely be posting his vacation photos on the Internet. Moreover, the Harvard education his family had purchased for him probably helped him conceive and execute the wonderful book about his vacation that has come down to us today.

We can even add political revolutionaries to this list. Jerry Rubin was an antiestablishment political radical, author of *Do It! Scenarios of the Revolution*, who was sentenced to four years in prison for inciting protesters to riot at the 1968 Democratic National Convention in Chicago. Sometime after the sentence was overturned by an appeals court, he joined Wall Street to work as a market analyst for the brokerage firm John Muir & Co. The press thought his two careers, "from yippie to yuppie," a fundamental contradiction, but Rubin himself insisted there was no contradiction. In 1980 he said, "The fact is money has always been power. But in the 1960s a picket line made a difference. The Eighties are much more hierarchical. Picket lines don't get much attention. Accountants have more power. Money is more the pressing social issue of our day."[7] The point here is not whether Rubin has a coherent moral philosophy. Rather it is that the very same person could be either on the picket line or on Wall Street, depending on personal proclivity or historical circumstance.

This may not be the world about which young artists, philosophers, and poets fantasize, but it is reality—and a reality we must learn to accept. Self-promotion and the acquisition of wealth, whether by financial or other means, is no crime. In fact, some of our greatest human achievements have their origins in just such behavior.

Chapter 21

An Impulse for Risk Taking

Economic theory presents people as sub-stantially risk averse, rationally avoid-ing uncertainty. And yet there is a side to people that impels them to do just the opposite—to put themselves in risky situations. This natural impulse, which is connected with our sense of adventure as well as our self-esteem, is part of what drives entrepreneurship, what drives animal spirits in the real world. It is also part of what causes speculative bubbles and ultimately crashes.[1]

This side of human nature has not been adequately recognized in much of financial research—even in much of the work of behavioral finance researchers, who often measure risk preferences by asking people to choose between hypothetical risky prospects on paper, in situations where well-defined probabilities are laid out. When we consider the real functioning—and malfunctioning—of the financial system, we need to keep in mind the visceral impulse for risk taking that shows up in real-life experiences.

Wolfram Schultz, whose classic experiments with the dopamine reward system in the brain were described in Chapter 6 on traders in Part One, has shown that the reward signals from dopamine neurons respond to uncertainty. He found that uncertainty that takes the form of a chance of a future reward is itself stimulative.[2] Nature has built into our brains a tendency to savor the *possibility* of future rewards, and to put ourselves in a position where such a possibility is real.

Apparently there has been some evolutionary advantage to such deliberate risk taking. Schultz and his colleagues speculate that the dopamine signals in a time of uncertainty trigger attention and learning responses in the brain that are appropriate to the situation. But there is a side effect of these signals. The mere presence of uncertainty in a positive direction creates a pleasurable sensation, and so the reward system creates an incentive to take on risky positive bets. Maybe that side effect is also advantageous from an evolutionary point of view. It helps people not just to focus on the predictable and the known but to be visionaries.

This human tendency helps explain why people like to gamble, and why many people will return every day to bet a small sum in a lottery. It also helps explain why people are willing to speculate aggressively on investments.

Not everyone is the same in his or her attunement to risks. Psychologists have identified a personality trait—which differs measurably across people—called sensation seeking. Psychological testing can reveal those who have more of a sensation-seeking personality.[3] A substantial psychological literature on sensation seekers exists. High sensation seekers are restless people, those who want excitement in their lives. They seek excitement per se rather than pleasure. They want novelty for novelty's sake. They are more prone to alcoholism and drug abuse, to having multiple sexual partners, and to engaging in unsafe sex. They may also be useful to society, more likely to be entrepreneurs.

Neuroscience is just beginning to explore the neural origins of sensation seeking.[4] Neuroscientist Sarah Martin and her colleagues have found that high sensation seekers tend to have larger hippocampus regions in their brains.[5] Jane Joseph and her colleagues found that when subjects were subjected to sensation-arousing stimuli while under observation with functional magnetic resonance imaging, high sensation seekers showed more activity in the insula region, while low sensation seekers showed quicker responses in the anterior cingulate cortex.[6] Thus sensation seeking appears to reflect physical properties of the brain, something that we cannot change by the mere exercise of "free will."

Risk Taking Becomes a Calling

Human culture has also evolved to respect and admire risk taking, within limits. Adam Smith recounts an ancient story of a man whose highly spirited horse became uncontrollable and accidentally killed a slave. But, Smith notes, the rider was not criticized for keeping and riding such a horse: "That timid circumspection which is afraid of every thing, is never regarded as a virtue, but as a quality which more than any other incapacitates for action and business."[7] Indeed for some, risky pursuits are a moral imperative.

We instinctively respect people who take risks, so long as they are not antisocial in so doing. One result of this is our tolerance for social inequality. Despite all the anger that inequality can generate, it actually does so only when it is thought of as ill gotten; great wealth is even admired. All our financial arrangements are focused on eliminating ill-gotten and fortuitous inequality, leaving the respect for the real winners.

Inequality is not in and of itself a bad thing, so long as it is not accompanied by crushing poverty and resentment.[8] Correcting inequality will have economic costs, and doing so may make it harder for us as a society to achieve other ends. Most of us value many of the achievements of our admittedly unequal society, such as those in the arts and sciences and in sports. We are fascinated by thinking of the wonderful things the future will bring. But such things come about only with a vibrant economy—which seems to necessitate a degree of inequality.

Beginning in the past few centuries, the idea has gradually taken hold in human thinking, or at least in western thinking, that finance, among other occupations, can be pursued as a calling—a noble call to duty. Max Weber argued that the concept of a calling—meaning a life's purpose defined by participating in any of a wide array of occupations—initially took form with Martin Luther and the protestant Reformation and continued to have great influence in the evolution of capitalism.[9]

Disquiet and Inequality

The problem with a life in business is the focus it gives to attention to serious risks—risks that can be disquieting—rather than to spiritual fulfillment. Yet a sense that one is fulfilling a calling in life—a calling to take on certain challenges—can be deeply rewarding, even if the challenges are disquieting.

A career that involves one with financial risks, like a career in the military, has at its heart a sense of the uncertainty created by adversaries who would do you harm. The need to take measures against them can be an everyday event, and in some people that can lead to a feeling of stress and emptiness. In others, it can lead to a sense of calling, a sense of satisfaction in having met risks and dealt with them in a masterly way.

People have to find out who they are—whether they are sensation seekers, and whether or not they can find meaning in a life that is filled with risks. Modern society allows us to sort ourselves into occupations according to our self-assessments, and this self-sorting is one of the reasons for the success of financial capitalism.

The economic inequality that we tend to observe is in part a consequence of this sensation seeking. In this respect, inequality that is the outcome of constructive risk taking, as long as it does not become excessive, is not altogether a bad thing: it is a consequence of some of our natural proclivities.

But sensation seeking is not directly a desire to make one's lifetime well-being uncertain, though it can have that consequence. A well-designed financial capitalism should allow outlets for sensation seekers, in the form of stimulating opportunities, while at the same time making it possible for people to avoid meaningless uncertainty. Risk management needs to be a fundamental principle in our financial system, even though many people will ignore or try to circumvent it.

Chapter 22

An Impulse for Conventionality and Familiarity

Standing in opposition to the impulse for risk taking described in the preceding chapter is a nearly opposite impulse for conventionality and familiarity. This impulse can take many forms, but for our broad purposes here it is important to consider how it can push people toward reliance on old-fashioned financial institutions and outdated economic structures.

Financial concepts, as abstract as they are, are difficult for most people to comprehend. They fear being manipulated or cheated by others who are more facile with these concepts. And yet people readily understand that financial arrangements are terribly important to their lifetime well-being, as individuals, or for the long-run success of their enterprises, as managers. They fear surprises, years or decades down the road, that may do real harm.

There is thus a tendency to rely slavishly on traditional financial forms, to want to copy time-honored institutions, and often to do so based on outward appearances. People are naturally drawn to financial forms that appear to be steeped in long tradition and that are thought of as characteristic of the successful. These forms even become viewed as elements of a system of justice: the traditional financial arrangements are associated in our minds with the eternal rights of mankind.

There are a number of reasons for this impulse for conventionality and familiarity. Partly it is just habit. If one looks at newsstands, one will find that they are for the most part selling the same brands of candy bars they were thirty or fifty years ago. We just tend to grab for the familiar.

Partly it is because of concerns about liquidity: we do not want to get into an unconventional financial instrument because we think we might have difficulty selling it, for other investors would not be familiar with it. Partly it is because we fail to take into account the often-subtle special factors (e.g., legal restrictions, the state of information technology) that once made older forms of finance necessary, factors that may no longer be relevant in modern times; thus we tend to conclude, incorrectly, that those older forms have a still-relevant essential wisdom behind them.

Partly it is because we think that it is always risky to experiment with new things (such as new medicines) because their problems will be revealed only with time. Partly it is a problem with government financial regulators, who may feel restricted by bureaucratic structures and the perceived need to respect past law, created in an earlier environment that did not anticipate a particular financial innovation. Partly it is because of a free-rider problem: there is little incentive for the provider of a new financial instrument or service to expend resources to educate the public on its value if that value will just go to other providers who will hop onto the bandwagon after its worth has been proven.

For whatever reason, conventionality is a major factor inhibiting the application of financial principles to the design of new financial institutions. Financial modernization has been a very slow process, and the latitude for financial innovation is circumscribed. Often important new financial ideas are adopted by only a small fraction of the population who have better understanding—or who are more trusting of others who understand. Thus the democratization of these innovations proceeds at a snail's pace, often over centuries. Progress in finance can seem excruciatingly slow.

The invention of corporate shares, as we have noted, dates to ancient Rome. But the shares were used only for certain limited purposes then, and corporations did not reappear until the seventeenth century. The invention of insurance, in its simplest forms, likewise goes far back into ancient times, but the first modern forms of insurance did not recur until the seventeenth century. Even so, well into the twentieth century most people in developed countries still did not have either life insurance or fire insurance. Most people in less-developed countries are still not adequately insured.

The amortizing mortgage—in which the borrower pays the same amount each month, and, after a specified number of months, is done paying and has no more principal to repay—sounds like a very simple, commonsense concept. Such mortgages have an advantage in that the borrower does not have to have the foresight and self-discipline to accumulate the money to pay off the principal when it comes due. But amortizing mortgages did not become well established in the United States until the government stepped in to encourage them, well into the twentieth century.[1]

Inflation-indexed bonds were invented in the eighteenth century, but there were virtually no issues of them until the second half of the twentieth century.[2]

Even today most people do not appear interested in replacing their fixed-income investments with inflation-indexed ones, let alone in adopting some more complex investment vehicle that is tailored to their particular risks and designed to share these risks effectively.[3]

The first mutual fund—an investment vehicle that treats all participants equally and that is transparent about its methods of investing—was set up in the 1920s. But mutual funds did not become a significant part of the market until the late twentieth century.

Progress is certainly made, but fundamental progress in finance seems to be measured in lifetimes rather than years.

People seem to want to persist in using the same tried and true financial technology that was used by their grandparents—even though there may be memories of major economic dislocations in their grandparents' times. We are very happy to adopt the newest automotive technology, or the newest kind of computer or smart phone, and so we see rapid progress in those areas. But progress in financial technology is another matter altogether.

This slowness to innovate has to do with our difficulties in handling basic financial concepts, which are unfamiliar abstractions, and our reliance instead on the familiar concepts that are already built into our thinking.

Taking Words for Things

The philosopher John Locke, in his 1690 work *An Essay Concerning Human Understanding*, discerned a human tendency to err in "taking words for things." He noticed that we tend to imbue concepts that are associated with words in our language with an objective reality that causes us to exaggerate their importance. When concepts are dignified by a word, they start to seem "so suited to the nature of things that they perfectly correspond with their real existence."[4] Opinions, once given names, seem more than opinions; they seem to take on an objective and tangible reality, so much so that they make our thinking more rigid. This human tendency, Locke believed, encourages schools of thought, which in turn encourage an obstinacy in thinking that is related to the language of the particular schools of thought.

The names of political parties or approaches to philosophy seem to reflect an objective, not just a transient human, reality. But the names and slogans of political parties in other countries seem baffling to us. So too do the names of financial instruments. Innovative financial instruments often seem to be tied to the culture of one country; thus we have securitized mortgages in the United States and, in a somewhat different form, covered bonds in Europe. From the U.S. perspective, covered bonds seem inscrutable—in the same way securitized mortgages do to those in Europe.

Psychologist Paul Bloom refers to such a tendency as "bad essentialism."[5] The brain categorizes things by their presumed essentials, and concepts are filed away with these essentials as filenames—making it very difficult for the mind to avoid taking these presumed filing categories as essentials in every respect. The dominance of word and metaphor in our thinking has been an important object of inquiry for the field of linguistics.[6]

It appears that neuroscientists are just beginning to find a physical basis for this practice of "taking words for things." Neuroscientist Friedemann Pulvermüller has studied the neuronal architecture that represents individual words—arrays of neurons that he calls "word webs" because they are not located in a specific isolated region of the brain but consist of webs of neurons scattered around the brain. He finds that these webs are hardwired into regions of the brain associated with the meaning of the particular word: "If the referent is an object usually perceived through the visual modality, neurons in the temporo-occipital areas should be included in the web. If a word refers to actions or objects that are manipulated frequently, neurons in fronto-central action-related areas are assumed to be wired into the cortical representations."[7]

There is still no agreement among neuroscientists on just how words are processed in the brain.[8] But the evidence for word webs in the brain does seem to enliven the idea, due to the linguistic philosopher Ludwig Wittgenstein, that words stand for family resemblances—series of overlapping similarities in which no one similarity is common to all the meanings of the word.[9] With such complex neural circuitry corresponding to individual words, it is inevitable that cognitive errors will be made that have the effect of "taking words for things."

The highly familiar words we have for money and currency impose a structure on our thinking.

The scientist Simon Newcomb noted the confusions related to the word (or metaphor) *money* in 1879. Remarking that people tend to measure wealth in terms of currency units, such as dollars, even when the buying power of the currency unit in terms of commodities swings wildly, he noted that "Even when the facts are understood, the idea that the change is in the value of the commodities measured, and not in that of the dollar itself, is so natural that a long and severe course of mental discipline is necessary to get rid of it."[10]

As a result, people seem to strongly prefer contracts denominated in currency, and thus lay themselves open to financial disaster should the value of the currency swing widely. They show relatively little interest in inflation-indexed bonds, wherever they are offered, substantially because of the "taking words for things" phenomenon and the resulting belief in currency as a standard of value.[11] Throughout history hyperinflations have repeatedly wiped out the value of bonds into which people put their life savings, and yet most of them never learn, at least not for more than a generation. The 1923 hyper-inflation in Germany—which virtually wiped out the real value of all bonds and contributed to the social unrest that brought Hitler to power—left a generation or so of Germans strongly opposed to inflation, but by now that resistance is fading among younger Germans.[12]

Financial innovation is never going to be just a technical challenge, for part of the innovation must lie in the reframing or re-marketing of familiar concepts. We correct or reposition such concepts by inventing new words for them—words that, once they gain a foothold in our language, gradually grow in familiarity. Thus, for example, following the failure of investment funds after the bubble years of the 1920s, we needed to invent a whole new word for such vehicles, and out of that need came the mutual fund. The word *mutual* lent the necessary democratic and benign quality to the name.

We can correct the aforementioned problems with inflation by devising a system of economic units of measurement that provides new words for essential concepts. In some countries, such new words have already been invented to help people correct their thinking. In fact, ancient Rome had the *denarius communis:* a unit of account, not represented by any physical coin, whose exchange rate with the silver denarius coin was announced periodically by the government. Wages and prices were set in terms of this unit, whose real value could instantly be adjusted by the Roman government.

More to our point, Chile has since 1967 had a *unidad de fomento* (UF), a non-monetary unit of account indexed to inflation. In Chile money is often no longer used for specifications in contracts and quoted prices. Prices are quoted in UFs, though transactions are executed in Chilean pesos, according to a published exchange rate.[13] For example, the rent on one's apartment is likely to be quoted in UFs, and so there are no fluctuations in its real value. Every month one pays a different amount in pesos. It makes sense to do this, but in most countries of the world apartment rents are quoted in currency units, and so the real value of rents declines steadily with inflation for a while until the landlord takes the painful step of announcing a rent increase in currency units. Thus, in most countries, the real value of apartment rents describes a sawtooth pattern through time, an absurdity that reflects problems with our language.

I have argued that something like the UF should be adopted all over the world, and with a simpler name.[14] I would call consumer price index units of account *baskets* to refer to the market basket of consumer goods and services that statisticians price each month to produce the consumer price index that is used to measure inflation. People would then understand that, for example, when their rent is quoted in baskets, they are in essence paying with a fixed number of real baskets of goods and services that matter to them, and not in terms of some arbitrary and unstable unit. With modern electronic technology, it ought to be possible to make payments directly in baskets without even bothering to look up the exchange rate. There could also be other kinds of units of economic measurement, representing consumer prices for subgroups of the population (such as the elderly), or representing income flows, or for the special purpose of wage setting.

Simple financial words like *debt* have profound implications in our language. If it is government debt, it seems to be associated with our patriotic faith in our government. But if it is our own debt, then the word is immediately, reflexively, judged as aversive, even though debt plays a fundamental role in the modern economy. Renaming the debt incurred to buy a home as a *mortgage* changes the whole frame of thinking, for now the debt is thought of as in some sense part of the home, and therefore acceptable to people who would never otherwise think of going into debt. Those who approach debt in that way are likely to want the terms of their mortgages to correspond to traditional forms.

Debts are a traditional contract, almost always fixed in terms of currency units. Experimentation with alternatives tends to fizzle out. For example, in the late 1970s, when inflation in the United States reached double-digit levels, mortgage lenders began introducing price-level-adjusted mortgages (PLAMs). But after the inflation rate started coming down in the 1980s, public interest in these faded. And yet, even today, PLAMs would be a great idea, since mortgages tend to be long term, often up to thirty years, and the uncertainty about inflation over a period that long remains very high. But—having experimented in recent years with alternative forms of home financing, often to unhappy effect—people now seem to be drifting back to the familiar conventional mortgage.

One would think that debts should be tied to a variety of economic outcomes, not just the inflation rate, from the start. Debt should be flexible, should respond to economic circumstances. For example, mortgage borrowers should have, in the initial debt contract, a preplanned workout. The continuous-workout mortgage that I have proposed would specify changes in the terms of the mortgage in the event of an economic contraction or a fall in home prices.[15] We would probably not have experienced the financial crisis of 2007 if such mortgages had been the norm. But few attempts have been made to implement anything like them. One reason is that people have a strong cultural tie to the simple notion that one should promise to repay another in the simplest possible terms when viewed from the perspective of our existing language.

Regulators and lawmakers find themselves attached to traditional forms, such as nonindexed straight debt, even if they are presented with logical arguments that it is not ideal. They may fear that their reputations might be harmed by backing a new product that looks a little odd. They are fearful that new forms will not be liquid—that is, will not have a ready market—if others are unfamiliar with them. Tradition in financial contracts is a surprisingly powerful force.

Declarations for change by the government tend to come only during an emergency—a war or a depression, for example. Financial progress can happen at such times—although it is then unfortunately hampered by the distractions of the crisis itself, which discourage thinking about how to implement the innovations in the best possible way for the long term.

Part of the reason for this rigidity of thought is that people maintain in their minds certain stereotypes, or personas, of how one should behave. Becoming part of the financial profession is a profound choice, one that in turn cuts off other choices, and it seems to require hewing to a conventional standard of behavior that has at least some superficial acceptability.

Yet all of these biases can be reduced if we introduce new words, and new units of measurement, to help shift patterns of thinking. Such seemingly inconsequential matters as changes in wording must actually be part of how effective financial innovation proceeds.

Entitlements

There are ancient traditions behind the framing of our ideas of the *rights* of humankind, and while these ideas have enormous positive force in our world, the traditions behind them sometimes conflict with financial reality. That is, the rights of man are set down in financially inconsistent ways that are the result of arbitrary or traditional framing of concepts, rather than in terms of some sensible philosophy. The word *right* is of great force in human discourse, and it can trump any other words of societal advantage or compromise.

The Universal Declaration of Human Rights adopted by the United Nations in 1948 provides some examples. It says in Article 25 that "Everyone has the right to a standard of living adequate for the health and well-being of himself and of his family, including food, clothing, housing and medical care and necessary social services." Article 26 proclaims that "Everyone has the right to education. Education shall be free, at least in the elementary and fundamental stages."[16]

The declaration is well intentioned. But it neglects to consider how these activities will be financed: who will pay for them and what should be the economic situation of those who pay. The declaration does not build in any flexibility or compromise. The rights that people have ought instead to be defined in terms that respect the well-being of *all* people, in terms more carefully crafted to represent the concerns of *all* segments of the population.

Social security systems around the world defend the rights of the elderly—usually without regard to the situation of the working people who must pay for those entitlements. The right to a standard of living in old age is framed in an absolute manner, and so the provision of pension benefits becomes stuck in an ancient system. Government pensions should instead be indexed to some indicator of taxpayer ability to pay, such as GDP, but this is rarely done. This and similar policies would promote intergenerational risk sharing, allowing people of all ages to share the major risks to our society, without piling those risks onto any one generation.[17] But reliance on conventional entitlements works against such risk sharing.

The "living wage" that many reformers have been advocating, often for government employees, is again described in absolute terms—as if it were a right to dignity and respect that somehow has become incarnated in a fixed amount, the living wage, without regard to the situation of those who will pay for it.

We need to reframe the wording of "universal human rights" so that they represent the rights of *all* people to a fair compromise—to financial arrangements that share burdens and benefits effectively.

In the future of financial capitalism, we ought to see better development of our covenants regarding these "rights," as financial contracts that are more democratic and nuanced, with the rights of mankind redefined in more basic terms.

This means that our business world should be less constrained by pre-written, standardized financial contracts and be more imaginative in its definition of such agreements. As we have seen at various places in this book, the process of improving our financial arrangements will involve new concepts, new language, and new information technology—inviting conflicts but at the same time laying a path to their resolution.

Chapter 23

Debt and Leverage

The impulses described in the preceding two chapters can interact to create a dangerous situation regarding debt and leverage. The impulse toward risk taking can cause people to disregard danger signals and run with crowds and bet on bubbles, taking on too much debt to do so. The impulse toward conventionality and familiarity can mean that they take no steps to protect themselves from the risks they assume. When the calamity comes, they are in serious trouble. It is no surprise that people have done such things repeatedly throughout history, given the primacy of these basic impulses.

When one has borrowed a considerable sum, using conventional debt, any slight decline in one's economic fortunes can lead to disaster, for the decline is leveraged against the existing debt, which does not decline. Moreover, when there is less inflation in consumer prices than expected, as tends to happen in an economic crisis, the real value of the fixed debt actually goes up, making the situation even worse.

Such mistakes have happened readily throughout history because the institution of debt, in some form, is such a simple and natural one. Every modern society has mechanisms for borrowing and lending. These institutions reflect the fundamental purpose that these markets serve. People have special needs when they are young and have not yet accumulated assets: children must be educated and young adults may wish to buy a house. So they borrow, they become indebted one way or another. And in so doing, with conventional debt, they become leveraged—that is, they begin to suffer the problems of life as a debtor.

Their best earning years tend to come rather late in life. This presents a fundamental economic problem that has been solved since time immemorial through family relations, not by means of formal borrowing and lending. Because of instincts to care for their young, parents naturally provide for their children and even help them to purchase homes, thus keeping some indebtedness within the family.

In a modern economy, we recognize that this primordial system of transferring resources from old to young is imperfect. Some parents—and some children—are irresponsible. Even if they are responsible, their means vary. Children typically do not want to borrow from their parents these days because of the conflicts that may result from such an arrangement. But the children will likely need to borrow from someone. So they become indebted, and their indebtedness and the associated leverage become a public policy problem.

Businesses likewise have needs when they are young or have expansion plans, and just as with individuals their best earning years tend to be later, when they are mature. Businesses cannot get started without funds. This problem has also been solved since ancient times by the family, which may lend the resources to start a family business—but the family is even less well suited to providing funds to launch such a substantial enterprise. In modern times, businesses have acquired the ability to raise funds by selling shares in themselves. But even this method of raising funds has its limits. Simple borrowing by businesses, and the financial institutions to support that process, have appeared in parallel with the issuance of shares. But indebtedness creates a danger for the firm, leaving open the risk that a going concern could be forced into liquidation by its creditors.

Governments also have need to borrow, notably when they too are young and at other times as well, when they foresee greater needs ahead. For example, a new city may need to build roads and a sewage system in expectation of a later population influx, since putting the whole system in place at once is the most efficient approach. It would be sensible for the city government to finance these infrastructure needs by borrowing: the current population of the city cannot afford them, and they ought to be paid for by the subsequent residents, who will actually use them and be resident in the city when the debt comes due. Governments may also need to borrow during an economic crisis, again in expectation of better times ahead. Yet the indebted government may run into problems, for example if the anticipated future population does not arrive or if the economic crisis lasts longer than expected.

Human Errors Regarding Debt

People and businesses have trouble living up to the standards of rationality presupposed by the economic theorists who model and quantify these fundamental economic issues.

First of all, as discussed in the previous chapter, people—individuals and to a significant extent those in corporations and governments as well—seem to blandly accept the kinds of credit vehicles that are put before them by salespeople, and that have been sanctified by conventional wisdom or popular opinion. As discussed in Chapter 10 on lawyers and financial advisers, most individuals do not usually have experts available to help them with such decisions. Financial engineers—who might help reduce the problems associated with leverage—are by and large not listened to in public policy discussions. So people often find themselves faced with serious leverage problems.

To behave rationally, in accordance with theory, those involved in financial decision making must keep in mind the long-term wealth management problem: initially borrowing, then eventually tapering off their borrowing and saving enough wealth, given interest rates, to provide a good long-term outcome.

Yet individuals, as well as businesses and governments, often have difficulty in fully understanding—at least before a crisis develops—that when they borrow heavily they become leveraged, so that any otherwise small problem becomes magnified by the debt. If debt becomes too large relative to resources, there is a "debt overhang," which inhibits any form of positive action. People, and firms and governments as well, feel pinned down by their debt. Few of the individuals presented with this problem have the quantitative skills to understand and resolve the underlying issues without the help of financial advisers.

Lenders may step into this situation, hoping to make a profit, and sometimes with little regard for the real interests of the borrowers. The extent to which they can advertise and the kind of lending schemes that regulators allow differ significantly from one country to another. Hence there are massive differences across countries in average levels of indebtedness, and in propensity to save and build wealth.

Leverage in the U.S. Financial Crisis of 2007

During the boom in the United States just prior to the severe financial crisis, between 2001 and 2007, household debt, including mortgage debt and credit card debt, doubled from $7 trillion to $14 trillion. Household debt as a fraction of income rose to a level not seen since the onset of the Great Depression. After the decline in home prices began, strapped households began to curtail their consumption, setting a course toward a severe recession.

The United States has in recent decades had a low savings rate, and in the years just before the crisis the personal savings rate was just about zero. At the same time the personal savings rate in China was approaching 25%. This enormous difference cannot be justified in terms of different economic fundamentals; it is concrete evidence of a failure of our financial institutions to reliably address fundamental economic problems. It is a sure sign that our financial institutions remain imperfect.

In the years leading up to the crisis, U.S. mortgage loan-to-value ratios soared. The boom in home prices that preceded the financial crisis was intimately tied up with increasing leverage. Mortgage lenders, caught up in the same psychology as the home buyers, were willing to accept lower and lower down payments as the boom progressed. The lower down payments made it possible for people to afford increasingly expensive housing.[1] When the boom came to an abrupt end, mortgage lenders became worried and started demanding higher and higher down payments, making it impossible for home buyers to buy homes, even at reduced prices, and thus contributing to a downward cycle. The contraction led to a large number of foreclosures on houses, and the states with the strictest laws enabling foreclosures tended to have the steepest economic declines.[2]

In the United States in 2008, on the eve of the crisis, there were five credit cards per person, while in China there were thirty-three persons per credit card. Credit cards in the United States were, until the financial crisis, widely advertised, even sent out unsolicited to households, accompanied by glossy, flattering advertisements informing the recipient that the card was an honor and a recognition of achievement, thus overcoming natural skepticism about borrowing. Relatively few people in China received such a credit card or advertisement.

Overreliance on credit cards has been a serious problem. Those U.S. counties which had shown the greatest increase in credit card debt before the crisis likewise showed the sharpest contraction afterward.[3]

There has in recent years been recognition of the problem of aggressive credit card promotions leading to overburdening debt. In the United States, this recognition is behind the development of the Consumer Financial Protection Bureau, created by the 2010 Dodd-Frank Act, which has jurisdiction over lending services, including credit cards. If these beginnings set a path for further discussion about changing our patterns of leverage, we can start reformulating our debt institutions to work more effectively in the public interest.

Leverage and the European Debt Crisis

The European debt crisis that came to widespread attention in 2010 has occurred substantially because of similar problems, related ultimately to the impulses toward risk taking and conventionality. The political process does not naturally bring to the public's attention financial advisers and economic theorists who might present sound advice about the quantity and form of debts. During a time of complacency, as before the crisis, there is a natural tendency to underestimate the risks of indebtedness. At such times politicians do not generally want to focus on the issue, for fear of being accused of harming public confidence in business. They do not find it advantageous even to raise the issue of overindebtedness, so few citizens give it any thought.

In Europe the problem of excessive government debt in some countries was compounded by European bank regulators, who imposed zero capital requirements on banks' holdings of euro-denominated government debt. This regulatory decision meant that government defaults could also bring down banks. Why did the regulators decide that government debt was riskless? Probably they did not really believe that, but they did not want to disturb confidence by signaling their concerns through capital requirements. It was a case of burning the bridges behind us to force ourselves to keep marching ahead: a sense that they did not want to destroy confidence by calling attention to risks. Moreover, almost no one was paying attention to the problem, and, given the social basis for human attention, it was natural that most people would simply not think about debt overhang.

These are powerful psychological motivations *not* to fix the fundamental problem, and as of this writing European banks still have zero capital requirements against euro-denominated government debt, although a new temporary capital buffer has been imposed, and a European Banking Authority was created in 2010 to impose new procedures to evaluate banks.

The European Systemic Risk Board was also created in 2010, to provide oversight intended to minimize the risk of another such crisis. Creating such a board does not in itself alter the political impulses that brought on the crisis, but it begins a cycle of research and dialogue that may ameliorate the problem.

The outcome of the crisis is still not apparent as of this writing, but it is clear that it has had the potential for major repercussions. The crisis may result in the fragmentation or loss of the euro, the very name of which had come to symbolize European unity. The loss of that symbol may indeed be disastrous in the long run, given the human tendency to take words for things.

The Leverage Cycle

There is a leverage cycle that extends over the whole world. The cycle is not of fixed length, and there may be a long interval between crises. But everywhere one looks, overindebtedness seems naturally to develop during boom times, and it leads to collapse after the booms are over.

The same pattern is seen when one compares countries. In a study of sixteen countries, those that saw larger increases in leverage from 1997 to 2007 tended also to show larger increases in home prices. Moreover, the countries with larger increases in leverage during the interval 1997–2007 tended to show larger drops in consumption expenditure in the depths of the crisis, the years

2008–9.[4] Clearly a leverage cycle was at work on a global scale in producing this financial crisis.

In such cycles the overindebtedness can be individual, corporate, or governmental—or a combination of all three. The idea that such a cycle is fundamental to economic fluctuations has received only limited attention from economic theorists, perhaps because economists tend to focus on the relatively small fluctuations—the recessions that occur frequently and that provide a great deal of data—rather than the infrequent major depressions or near-depressions.

The economist Irving Fisher wrote in 1933 that a cycle involving leverage was the major factor leading to the Great Depression of the 1930s.[5] When prices fell after 1929, the real values of all debts were magnified. This change benefited creditors at the expense of debtors, but the net effect was negative. The augmented debt overhang led to cutbacks in expenditure that persisted as long as did the overhang problem.

Recently economic theorist John Geanakoplos has expanded on Fisher's theory; he argues that although there has not been significant deflation during the severe financial crisis that began in 2007, the crisis is indeed well thought of as a debt overhang problem.[6] When people's debts exceed their assets, many problems are created for the economy: Geanakoplos lists nine troubling "externalities" caused by the debt overhang. These include troubles in the construction industry, setbacks for small business, rising inequality, loss of productivity, and damage to collateral.[7] Thus there is a clear role for government regulation of leverage.

A boom period tends to be a period of overoptimism and complacency. There is a sense that "the government" will fix any problems that might occur, and a feeling of safety in numbers as millions of people increase their indebtedness. After the boom, during a time of severe debt overhang, there is still a tendency to regard the government as the ultimate savior, and to circle in a holding pattern, hoping for help. The holding pattern itself generates economic distress.

The debt overhang problem is remarkably refractory. People, corporations, and governments who have accepted higher leverage in boom times may be unable to rid themselves of its adverse effects for years to come.

Evidence for the persistence of a debt overhang problem can be seen in the events that typically follow a change of government in a country. When there is such a change, one might think that the new government would readily disavow the debts to foreigners incurred by its predecessors. In fact there are only limited circumstances under which international law allows such repudiation of debt.

Not only are new governments often unwilling to cancel financial debts incurred by previous governments, they may sometimes even restore indebtedness that was repudiated by an earlier government. Hitler repudiated

Germany's World War I reparation debt when he took power in 1933, but part of that debt was recognized again after World War II by the German government, wishing to reestablish trust after the atrocities of the war. A final payment of $94 million was made in October 2010—over ninety years after the debt was first incurred.

The nations of the world are more aware of such problems in the current financial crisis, but they still have not found a reliable way to fix them. As we have noted, new government regulators have been created, including the Financial Stability Oversight Council in the United States and the European Systemic Risk Board. The Financial Stability Board in Basel and the Basel Committee on Banking Supervision are involved in studying leverage problems on a global scale. But regulatory organizations have in the past not done enough to prevent the problem of the leverage cycle from recurring. The truly effective actions lie not with regulators alone, but also in the development of better financial procedures and instruments—instruments that do not rely on our current rigid mindsets and traditions but change the fundamental ways in which we do things.

Lasting solutions to the problems of the leverage cycle and the debt overhang have to balance the benefits of freely available credit against the cyclical and systemic problems that debt can create. Designing these solutions will be a challenge to the development of new financial institutions and techniques—a task for many minds and for the most creative financial innovators.

Odious and Salubrious Debt

The idea that there is something evil about money lenders extends back to ancient times. The Catholic Church took a clear stand against the charging of interest with the First Council of Nicaea in 325, and that prohibition lasted until the time of John Calvin and Henry the Eighth in the sixteenth century. The Koran contains passages that appear to condemn the charging of interest, and Sharia, the religious law of Islam, effectively blocked Muslim banking until the 1960s. Halakhah, the Jewish law, has forbidden money lending by Jews to other Jews, and orthodox Jews today continue to condemn the practice.

There is a legal concept according to which not all debt is evil, only so-called odious debt: debt that does not originate in free and informed contracting between the parties, or debt that is not managed in a humane way. For example, in the United States in the years leading up to the crisis that began in 2007, excessive mortgage debt was cynically issued to low-income, ill-informed families, who were not told of its consequences. This debt may be considered odious, and it may therefore give the debtors some later moral claim to help with their predicament. If a country with a dictatorial government borrows money without any implied consent by its public, and does not use the money to benefit the public, then a subsequent government can disavow that debt as fraudulent and not binding on the new government. Unfortunately there is as of now no international body that defines in an orderly manner which debt is to be considered odious.

More attention must be paid to the problem of odious debt, and that attention must be paid early, before massive problems appear. Economists Seema Jayachandran and Michael Kremer have argued that an international authority like the United Nations should declare the future debt of certain governments—governments that it might wish to punish for unacceptable behavior—as odious. These measures would make it harder for them to borrow, even from lenders who themselves had no scruples, since the lenders would have no moral authority to demand repayment from a successor government. Such sanctions will be less easily evaded, Jayachandran and Kremer argue, than the conventional trade sanctions typically used today to influence rogue governments.[8]

The opposite of odious debt—let us call it salubrious debt—is debt that is designed by the lender to have a salutary effect in terms of social welfare. Such debt has conditions, either as part of its covenants or in associated agreements and understandings, that are designed to provide healthy incentives to borrowers or other relevant parties.

An example of such salubrious debt is the loans (along with grants) that the United States made to various European countries after World War II through the Marshall Plan (officially the Economic Recovery Program). As argued by economic historians Helge Berger and Albrecht Ritschl, these loans stipulated conditions to correct a dangerous tendency in Europe at that time.[9] They came as European countries were demanding heavy reparation payments from Germany—demands that were being met by the dismantling and exporting of much of the German capital stock, demands based on deep-seated anger and antagonistic feelings that were hard to set aside. The Marshall Plan envisioned an open European marketplace, including a Germany restored to its traditional industrial prowess. Of course, U.S. motives were not entirely selfless, for America had an interest in a stable and prosperous Europe. But the ultimate outcome—a reunited Europe with a once-again-prosperous Germany—certainly benefited all.

In ensuring that more debt is salubrious rather than odious, and that debt is used to solve basic human problems, financial regulators face a long road ahead. Achieving this state of affairs will mean encouraging financial innovation that allows debts to be defined more flexibly, as in the continuous-workout mortgage or the GDP-indexed national debt described earlier, or other indexation schemes that really work in the interest of the borrower. Achieving better management of debt and leverage—more enlightened debt—will require a change not only in the lending institutions themselves, but also in the way they hedge, securitize, and bundle debt.

Chapter 24

Some Unfortunate Incentives to Sleaziness Inherent in Finance

There is a widespread sense that there is something sleazy about the business of finance, or the people who populate it. This impression is probably behind the commonly voiced opinion that it is a shame so many young people today are going into finance-related occupations, when they could be doing something more high-minded in other fields.

Many people in business do seem to feel rewarded, for the short run at least, in putting salesmanship ahead of purpose, in cutting corners on the law or the intent of the law; they seem to be focused on the money above all else and to have little moral purpose in their business affairs. Yet if one lives in the real world one has to work with, or even for, such people. They are a reality. There may be a slippery slope, as one is obligated to carry out their orders, wrong though they may seem.

The reality is that battling against the slippery slope is an ongoing challenge, a part of living in all walks of life. Certain finance-related fields are among those that often put people in positions offering more than the usual temptation to be manipulative or less than honest. Some of them are aware at some level that they are doing this, and cognitive dissonance (as we shall see below) may push them to develop a mechanism to defend their self-esteem and justify such behavior. Their perceived self-righteousness may in particular rankle those who have dropped out of a similar life situation.

Finance may seem to have more than its fair share of sleazy practitioners because it is a profession that offers, at least to the lucky few, astronomically high incomes. On occasion we may even ask: why would anyone with a sense of personal morality go into finance?

Finance may also seem corrupt because the management of information is so central to success in the field—and that immediately means that there are opportunities for providing misinformation to others. To make the best deal in a financial transaction, there is always the temptation to withhold information.

What other occupation offers such temptations to manipulate others' thinking by selective release of information? A schoolteacher's neglect of students, a sin of omission rather than commission, can evoke negative emotions in parents—but emotions not nearly as anger-producing as those in response to deliberate financial deception. Not only is the latter case viewed as outright theft, it is also ego-wounding to those who have lost money, challenging their sense of self-worth as they feel foolish to have been duped.

A Comparison with Gambling Casinos

Gambling casinos offer a revealing example of the commercial exploitation of patterns of recurring errors in judgment. How is it that casinos, considered by some to be the epitome of sleaziness, are able to induce many people to make investments (in the form of bets) that have a negative expected return—and to do so repeatedly, so that, by the law of averages, losses become a virtual certainty?

The "gaming industry," as it styles itself, defends its activities as a form of entertainment. Certainly it is that, but it is unique among entertainment forms in that it cultivates and amplifies to a considerable extent human risk-taking impulses, sometimes with disastrous consequences.

The puzzle comes down to why one would be willing to place even one single bet at a casino. Research by psychologists Daniel Kahneman and Amos Tversky has shown that people exhibit a tendency toward loss aversion.[1] They are pathologically avoidant of even small losses. If offered an asymmetrical bet on a coin toss—to win $20 if it comes up heads, to lose $10 if it comes up tails—most people will turn down the bet, even though it has a positive expected return of $5. How then are gambling casinos able to induce people to place bets with a negative expected return, and to do so again and again despite having experienced repeated losses?

Part of the answer has to relate to the impulse for risk taking described earlier, which is context specific. The casino context is expressly designed to deflect attention from the reality of the actual gamble and to place that gamble in a context that encourages risk taking. Casino operators are usually not psychologists, but they experiment with different settings, and they replicate anything that works for them. They tinker with many seemingly minor details of the gambling environment—things that one might not even consciously notice, but that affect the willingness to gamble. Survival of the fittest among casinos has resulted in casino environments that are exquisitely designed to overtake risk aversion.

Casinos arrange their environments in certain particular ways, some of them very obvious, to lower inhibitions. They freely serve alcohol. They also cultivate the notion that those who frequent the casinos are rich and successful. This confuses some people, who lose sight of the reality of their repeated losses at the tables.

Psychologists Joseph Simmons and Nathan Novemsky have noted that casino gambling differs from the psychological laboratory settings of Kahneman and Tversky in a number of subtle ways.[2] In casinos people see others making large gambles, which makes their own potential losses less salient. When there are maximum wager amounts, the amounts are set at a high level, which makes the bet actually placed seem small. People are asked to generate their own wager amounts while subject to a minimum allowable wager. Simmons and Novemsky replicated some of these features in their psychological laboratory setting, and they found that such factors indeed encourage risk taking.

Left to unregulated market forces, many brokerage services would closely resemble gambling casinos. We know this from observing the nature of securities establishments before regulation was effective. The "bucket shops" of the late nineteenth and early twentieth centuries, where customers bet on commodities and prices, were not that different from casinos. They allowed patrons to make many very small bets, in a social atmosphere and while watching others bet—not unlike a casino of today. One patron described a bucket shop in the financial district of New York in 1879 in these terms: "The bucket shop always reminded me of a horse-pool room—in fact, there is very little difference—and I would never be surprised to hear dead and gone 'Doc' Underwood's resonant voice crying, 'Now gentlemen, Falladeen has gone as the favorite for six hundred dollars; what am I offered for second choice?'"[3] (The horse-pool room was a place for an early form of parimutuel betting, and Doc Underwood was a well-known promoter of such betting.)

It is hard to see how people could make good investment decisions in such an atmosphere. For quite a while, reports of police raids on illegal bucket shops were regular newspaper fare. In the progressive era in the United States, in the first two decades of the twentieth century, these bucket shops were eliminated by state regulators.

But outside these casino-like establishments, sleazy brokerage practices persisted. In the 1940 book *Where Are the Customers' Yachts?* stockbroker Fred Schwed Jr. vividly called attention to this problem, with enough amusing accounts of the tricks and hypocrisy at brokerage houses to gain his book a wide readership. He focused on the showmanship of these brokers, who were attempting to project an impression of wealth (with many rich customers) and confidence (with carefully crafted but largely phony advice), all the while surely knowing that their investment advice was practically worthless. Schwed describes a typical stockbroker or adviser:

> And, if you ask Mr. Big on what he predicates his fifteen-year opinion, he will give you so many reasons you will wish you had not asked. But he ought to know better. If he should ever lift his nose out of the minutiae of his fascinating business and view its history whole, he would be forced to admit the sad truth that pitifully few financial experts have ever known for two years (much less fifteen) what was going to happen to any class of securities—and that the majority are usually spectacularly wrong in a much shorter time than that.[4]

Although Schwed's book was anecdotal and presented no statistical evidence, it was an early and effective statement of the efficient markets theory.

Cognitive Dissonance and Hypocrisy

Cognitive dissonance, a term coined by social psychologist Leon Festinger, is a negative emotional response, a feeling of psychological pain, when something conflicts with one's stated beliefs—an emotional response that may lead to something other than a rational updating of the beliefs.[5] In particular, when a person's own actions are revealed to be inconsistent with certain beliefs, he or she often just conveniently changes those beliefs. Hypocrisy is one particular manifestation of cognitive dissonance, in which a person espouses opinions out of convenience and to justify certain actions, while often at some level actually believing them.

The evidence that Festinger and his successors presented is solid: cognitive dissonance is a genuine phenomenon and leads with some regularity to human error—or at times to what we would label sleaziness. And yet there remains skepticism about cognitive dissonance in many quarters, particularly among people who feel committed to the fully rational model of human behavior.

Recently a new form of evidence has appeared in support of Festinger's theory. It has been found that brain structure is fundamentally tied to cognitive dissonance. Neuroscientist Vincent van Veen and his colleagues put human subjects in an experimental situation in which they were paid or otherwise incentivized to lie about their true beliefs as they were observed by functional magnetic resonance imaging. The researchers found that certain regions of the brain, the dorsal anterior cingulate cortex and the anterior insula, were stimulated during this experience. These are regions of the brain that are known to be stimulated when people lie. When van Veen and his coworkers measured the extent of stimulation in these regions, they found that some subjects showed more stimulation in these regions than did others. Importantly, those subjects with more activity in these regions showed a stronger tendency to change their *actual* beliefs to be consonant with the beliefs they were made to espouse.[6] We thus have evidence of a physical structure in the brain whose actions are correlated with the outcome of cognitive dissonance, and that thus appears to be part of a brain mechanism that produces the phenomenon Festinger described based solely on his observations of human behavior.

If hypocrisy is built into the brain, then there is a potential for human error that can be of great economic significance. A whole economic system can take as given certain assumptions, such as, for example, the belief in the years before the current financial crisis that "home prices can never fall." That theory was adopted by millions of people who would have experienced cognitive dissonance had they not done so, either because they were involved one way or another in a system that was overselling real estate or because they themselves had invested in real estate.

For another example, there may even have been an element of cognitive dissonance behind the decision of European bank regulators years ago to put zero capital requirements on euro-denominated government debt. The decision had already been made, and widely affirmed, that an end to the euro was unthinkable; hence any later decisions that recognized the risk of failure would have created dissonance. So European regulators adopted what in retrospect seems a hypocritical stance—that euro-denominated debt was completely safe—thus setting the scene for a potential disaster in the banking sector.

This kind of psychological problem is perennial and fundamental. But the finance professions also attract people who are relatively invulnerable to hypocrisy. It attracts those who become traders or investment managers, who delight in the truth that is ultimately revealed in those markets. They are often people who are troubled by hypocrisy. They seek vindication by being proven right, not by sounding right.

A financial system that lets them take a stab at doing just that will generate some economic inequality. But they do collectively offer a benefit to society in leaning against conventional and politically correct thinking. The presence of people who will respond in this way to financial opportunities is part of the success story—poorly understood by most of the public—of modern financial institutions.

For financial theorists, it is often difficult to comprehend the real reasons we have the financial institutions that we do and the reasons that they contribute so well to a good society. Many theorists have tried to represent people as merely profit maximizers, perfectly selfish and perfectly rational about it. But people really do care about their own self-esteem, and profit maximization is at best only a part of that self-esteem.

Moral Purpose

It might appear that the sleaziness constantly pursued by the regulators is a real taint on the entire profession of finance. But in fact the practice of finance does not universally incline its practitioners to such behavior. It also seems to reward people with a certain kind of moral purpose—one that may be visible to outsiders only intermittently. Even high-minded financial professionals may appear superficially sleazy because of those with whom they associate, and whose orders they may be required to carry out.

The moral purpose inherent in helping one's clients is hard to see on a day-to-day basis, and it is easy to conclude that such moral purpose does not even exist among those in finance. But in fact the human spirit, among most people, naturally projects such purpose onto the day-to-day routine. It appears that most people need such moral purpose, such a spiritual direction, in order to carry out all the activities that define a job. Most of us instinctively want to be helpful and good, within certain limits, to those around us.

The moral calculus of accumulating large sums of money over a lifetime and dispensing them near the end of that life is extremely opaque for most of that period, since one cannot appreciate the purpose of such accumulation until it is over. We will for the most part never have a true reckoning of our own moral purpose, let alone the moral purposes of others, as no one is keeping score; not many here on earth are ranking people after their deaths with an accounting of the moral purposes that drove their lives.

One makes a moral decision knowing that there is virtually no one evaluating whether one has made the right decision, for no one is really paying attention except superficially. The news media like to gossip about the rich, but the stories they love the best are those that depict their moral lapses. The general public has very little interest in the good deeds of the wealthy.

We have an inherent desire to think of ourselves as good people and to live up to this self-image. But the desire, if followed through logically, seems to put us in a lifelong loop in which we do that which often does not appear inspiring, with no clear moral vindication, no clear end, no final judgment.

John D. Rockefeller Sr., himself the son of a small-time huckster and bigamist, was a ruthless, take-no-prisoners aggressor in his business life. In her 1904 book *The History of the Standard Oil Company*, Ida Tarbell made a scandal of his business practices.[7] But in his later life he became a philanthropist in the mold of Andrew Carnegie. His actions in business may have appeared sleazy, but his life had a noble conclusion, including his founding of the Rockefeller Foundation, the University of Chicago, and Rockefeller University. Moreover he bequeathed much of his fortune to his son John D. Rockefeller Jr., who continued his philanthropy and in turn trained his six children, five sons and a daughter, in the ways of public service. All of them played important public and philanthropic roles. One of them, Nelson Rockefeller, became vice president of the United States. The fourth generation includes John D. Rockefeller IV, who is a U.S. senator from West Virginia and has been in that position for over a quarter of a century.

So what ultimately motivated the Rockefellers? Was it mere ego gratification and the drive to found and perpetuate a family dynasty? Or did their philanthropy serve some deeper moral purpose? It was most likely a little of both. Some will see inspiration in the century-long philanthropic tradition carried on by members of a family that emerged from controversial business origins and matured into a positive social force, each generation picking up the torch from the previous one. Such a story indeed suggests to some a model for living. Unfortunately, stories like that of the Rockefellers are rare, for the intergenerational transmission of purpose and values is usually far from perfect.

I have sometimes been struck, when talking with wealthy people who have family foundations, how important the foundation appears to be to their sense of self. They can become genuinely emotional in discussing it. It gives them a sort of moral superiority. Something like this sense may also come, for example, from having donated to a college and having a building named after oneself. The behavior appears to be at once egotistical and altruistic, both motivations coexisting in the mind.

And yet the rest of the world generally takes little note of family foundations or the names on campus buildings. We all would probably acknowledge, if our attention were ever drawn to the people behind the foundations or the buildings, that they are good people for having made these gifts. But we almost never meet these people and so do not think about them. Thus they are able to achieve a sense of public praiseworthiness, and achieve their own moral purposes, without inciting direct envy or hostility.

Being Mistaken for the Sleazy

One problem with the attractiveness of financial dealings for the genuinely sleazy has been that they discredit the entire profession, even those who are scrupulously honest. At one extreme is the inherent risk, even for the most ethical, that they will be indicted for crimes and misdemeanors they did not commit and thus suffer a permanent loss of reputation.

Those in finance and business management acquire genuine power—power to make things happen that perhaps only *they* individually *want* to have happen. Even a top elected official with a budget in the billions has less power because, at least in democratic countries, he or she is subject to checks and balances and holds power for only a limited time. The essentially unlimited power achieved by the very successful in business (and their heirs) is almost unknown in other walks of life.

For males (and most financiers are male) this also means power over women, and this is a source of resentment among both women and other men. In parts of the world today, their status brings with it the power to command multiple wives, at the expense of other men who will have no wives—a situation sure to cause resentment among those men. Some women in these polygamous marriages might be even more resentful. In much of western society, ever since ancient Greece and Rome, polygamy has been illegal or at least widely opposed. But even with those conventions, wealthy men find it much easier to have affairs outside their marriages or to hire the most sought-after prostitutes.

More concretely, the power that the rich obtain is the power to engage in what the economist Thorstein Veblen termed conspicuous consumption, which, when indulged in by men, is instinctively recognized by the general public as a possible ploy to attract the opposite sex—even if the plan is never consummated. Underlying the desire for wealth is a sexual and social-status impulse. This applies as well to women, whose desire for wealth may arise from somewhat different, though equally strong, motives.

The hostility that is felt against the rich is partly in recognition of that power. Even if people plan to give away all their wealth eventually, no one else knows for certain what their ultimate intentions may be, and thus others are naturally suspicious of those intentions. Such suspicion may express itself in a tendency to brand all of the rich as sleazy.

People Are Certainly Conscious of Sleaziness

As we have just discussed, attitudes toward top businesspeople are often negative. Yet quantitative research suggests that such negative stereotypes are pervasive but not universal.

In 1990 Maxim Boycko, a Russian economist, Vladimir Korobov, a Ukrainian economist, and I did a questionnaire survey comparing American (specifically New Yorkers') and Russian (Muscovites') attitudes toward business.[8] We asked, "Do you think that those who try to make a lot of money will often turn out to be not very honest people?" In both countries many people answered yes. But more felt that way in Russia: 59% of the Muscovites said yes, compared with only 39% of the New Yorkers.

We then asked a more personal question: "Do you think that it is likely to be difficult to make friends with people who have their own business (individual or small corporation) and are trying to make a profit?" In Moscow 51% of the respondents said yes, compared with only 20% in New York.

It is significant that the perceptions of sleaziness were higher in the country that had had no experience with *legal* businesspeople. It would appear that part of any country's process of becoming financially advanced involves getting over exaggerated perceptions of sleaziness. And, with some 20–40% of Americans perhaps still holding a low opinion of businesspeople, there is clearly still work to do in dealing with the problem in our own country.

Avoiding Overreaction to Sleazy Behavior

The further success of financial capitalism once again depends on people adopting a more nuanced view of human nature as it is expressed in a financial environment. We have to accept that some less-than-high-minded behavior may be the product of an economic system that is essentially good overall.

Financial speculation, the subject of the next chapter, is associated in many people's minds with sleazy behavior, since it takes place in an economic environment that brings out the selfish and manipulative. It is hard to judge the role of speculative markets in the good society without thinking of this less-than-inspiring behavior. But we must take a careful look at just what constitutes that behavior, and what its overall consequences are.

Chapter 25

The Significance of
Financial Speculation

There has long been a negative feeling among the general public about speculation in markets. To them, the activity doesn't seem to contribute to society. It seems to many to be a form of recreation for the rich or for those who really just want to be rich, an activity that is fundamentally selfish and egotistical— and, on top of that, often delusional. In a 1904 essay Charles Conant observed that

> One of the most persistent of the hallucinations which prevail among people otherwise apparently lucid and well informed is the conception that operations on the stock and produce exchanges are pure gambling. A moment's reflection, it would seem, might convince such persons that a function which occupies so important a place in the mechanism of modern business must be a useful and necessary part of that mechanism; but reflection seems to have little part in the intellectual equipment of the assailants of organized markets.[1]

Certainly, Conant was right about public opinion. Many thought leaders have said as much. He must have known that Karl Marx thought speculation was akin to gambling: "Since property here exists in the form of stock, its movement and transfer become purely a result of gambling on the stock exchange, where the little fish are swallowed by the sharks and the lambs by the stock exchange wolves."[2] And among the critics of speculation we have also to count the most important and influential economist of the twentieth century, John Maynard Keynes: "It is generally agreed that casinos should, in the public interest, be inaccessible and expensive. And perhaps the same is true of Stock Exchanges."[3]

The controversy between those like Conant on the one side, who think that speculation is an essential economic activity, and those like Marx and Keynes on the other, who have grave doubts, has continued for more than a century and remains unresolved to this day. The reason it has not been resolved is that there is an element of truth to both sides—or perhaps both sides are speaking half-truths. Moreover, the extent to which speculation lives up to Conant's ideal depends on our financial institutions—which can either encourage or discourage healthy and productive speculation, and can either attract or repel the kinds of people who are naturally and productively speculative.

Speculation Contributes to Market Efficiency

The term *efficient markets* has long been used with various meanings, but it was given its specific modern meaning by University of Chicago economist Eugene Fama in 1965:

> In an efficient market, competition among the many intelligent participants leads to a situation where, at any point in time, actual prices of individual securities already reflect the effects of information based both on events that have already occurred and on events which, as of now, the market expects to take place in the future. In other words, in an efficient market at any point in time the actual price of a security will be a good estimate of its intrinsic value.[4]

The "competition among the many intelligent participants" clearly refers to speculators, for if the intelligent advice were to *avoid* speculation, and just diversify broadly, then there would be no force pushing prices to the right, "efficient," level.

Long before Fama, many besides Charles Conant had expressed similar ideas about the perfection of financial prices. The difficulty in forecasting changes in prices (as we noted in quoting Fred Schwed Jr. in the previous chapter) has often been interpreted as attesting to their perfection. Moreover, statistical research—as in the work of Holbrook Working in 1934 and Maurice Kendall in 1953—had already found evidence, years before Fama, that short-run changes in prices in speculative markets are hard to forecast.[5] But Fama raised this theory to the status of a broad new scientific paradigm and likened to astrologers the old-fashioned analysts who looked to patterns in stock market data for trading opportunities. Fama believed that market prices were too perfect to be predictable, to show any pattern other than a random walk.

Fama used a data set that had recently been compiled by the Center for Research in Security Prices (CRSP) at the University of Chicago, founded in 1960 with a $50,000 grant from Merrill Lynch. The center's initial purpose was to put a huge set of monthly (later daily) stock prices, and associated information about capital changes and dividends that would allow accurate computation of returns, on magnetic tape so that the data could be analyzed with a UNIVAC computer. The CRSP directors obtained the cooperation of the New York Stock Exchange. But they soon found that the exchange had never organized these data and was in no position to get the data ready quickly and accurately. The extent of their unexpected woes revealed that no one else had ever organized such a data set before, in the United States or anywhere else in the world. When the information was finally prepared, the tapes mounted on the computer, and the data processed, the authority of the idea that speculation makes for perfect market prices was much enhanced.

That same "CRSP tape," considerably updated, is still the major source for daily prices of individual stocks going back to 1926. By bringing financial analysis into the computer age, the efficient markets hypothesis gained the status of an icon, and as a result it led people to infer much—in fact too much—about the perfection of markets.

The discovery that day-to-day fluctuations in stock prices are difficult to forecast should have come as no big surprise: if there were a simple trading strategy that consistently offered a profit of as little as a tenth of a percent a day, it would yield annual returns of over 30%. Clearly someone would already have been onto such a trading strategy, and its adherents, competing against each other, would have the effect of eliminating the opportunity in the market. That would have to be the effect, since we can't all get rich by trading with each other. Having daily data on the CRSP tape made it possible to produce voluminous studies confirming the obvious: that it is not very easy to get really rich really quickly through short-run trading.

A great deal of the horsepower of academic research was focused on testing one aspect of the efficient markets hypothesis: whether it is easy for smart traders to beat the market. Another aspect of the hypothesis—whether prices behave the way they ought to if markets are indeed working so well—is much harder to test.

As the enthusiasm for the efficient markets hypothesis after Fama's watershed 1965 paper reached excessive levels, it brought forth an unhealthy degree of credulity in people trusting their money to financial markets. Investors lost the sense that markets are a matter of opinion and that their fluctuations represent, in substantial part, changing public moods.

In fact, when one considers the aggregate stock market, it appears that price changes in the United States have been *mostly* due merely to changes in moods or attitudes or something else unrelated to the actual changes in real underlying value to which the changes are constantly ascribed. In my 1981 paper "Do Stock Prices Move Too Much to Be Justified by Subsequent Changes in Dividends?" I presented evidence, using stock market data for the United States since 1871, that the fundamentals corresponding to the aggregate stock market just never changed very much from year to year.[6] If people had known the future perfectly and priced appropriately, then the stock market should have behaved pretty much like a stable upward trend. So it doesn't make sense to think that all those fluctuations up and down around the trend could be attributed to "new information" about the future. Instead there is excess volatility in the stock market.

Thus, for example, the stock market crash of 1929 was not justified by the depression that followed. Even if people in 1929 had known that an economic collapse was imminent, even if they had had a perfect crystal ball, they still should not have marked down the price of the U.S. stock market by very much. For in fact U.S. companies fared much better in the Great Depression than is commonly suggested by our embellished stories. Not a single company of the thirty in the Dow Jones Industrial Average went bankrupt. In fact large U.S. corporations generally did quite well overall. They lowered their dividend payments for just a few years, and then they were back on trend. The value of a share in a company ought to be related to the present value of all future dividends, and not just the next few years' dividends. So if the 1929 crash was a reaction to information about the future, it was an egregious overreaction.

For a more recent example, consider the market reaction when a conference of European Union leaders in Brussels announced, on October 27, 2011, a broad package of measures to deal with the ongoing financial crisis. They said they would increase their bailout fund, recapitalize the banks, and reduce Greece's debt load. The German DAX stock price index rose 5.3% in one day. The news media suggested, by the way they quoted people and referred to economic "facts," that the price changes made some basic sense. On subsequent days the volatile price changes were interpreted as reevaluations of the news about the European economy. Suggestions that all the aggregate price changes are, at their core, psychological in origin are usually omitted from news stories—as if there were a common and unquestioned consensus that markets are efficient.

Most financial writers have apparently never heard of excess volatility, and they continue to write their stories about the day-to-day fluctuations in the stock market as if the market were dominated by traders with razor-sharp minds and fast computers who have a deep understanding of the economy and grasp the import of every nuance in today's economic news. Writing in this way flatters their readers, and most of these writers are not in the business of challenging comfortable conventional wisdom.

Many traders do indeed have sharp minds, but the game they are playing is not generally to involve themselves in macroeconomic forecasting. They are instead playing a game against each other—a game of guessing each other's psychology.

This excess volatility of the aggregate U.S. stock market, despite some controversy about it, is, in my opinion, an established fact.[7] This does not mean that the fluctuations in the Chinese or Indian stock markets, where underlying fundamentals are changing much more rapidly, are as irrational. This does not mean that all speculative markets are as crazy as the aggregate stock markets. In the next chapter we shall see that fluctuations in *individual firm* stock prices make somewhat more sense. If the efficient markets controversy teaches us anything, it is that we have to consider more carefully what *really* drives aggregate markets.

Animal Spirits

The success of our financial markets in producing prosperity has much to do with the way in which they guide animal spirits—our inner stimulus to action, something John Maynard Keynes described as "a spontaneous urge to action" rather than careful and deliberate calculation. He believed that real business decisions are emotional, not "the outcome of a weighted average of quantitative benefits multiplied by quantitative probabilities. . . . Thus if the animal spirits are dimmed and the spontaneous optimism falters, leaving us to depend on nothing but a mathematical expectation, enterprise will fade and die;—though fears of loss may have a basis no more reasonable than hopes of profit had before."[8]

My colleague George Akerlof and I were so convinced of the importance of these fluctuations in animal spirits, and of their importance in the world economic crisis, that we wrote a book about it, entitled *Animal Spirits*.[9] Fluctuations in animal spirits that are shared by large numbers of people are, we argued, social phenomena, the result of epidemic social contagion, which makes these fluctuations very hard to comprehend and predict.

Some of the inherent fragility of our decision-making process can be appreciated if we look introspectively, as we consider our own decisions about whether to launch some risky and time-consuming endeavor. There is a distinct emotional flavor to any such decisions.

Ultimately human judgments are driven by emotions, and their origin is largely subconscious. Marcel Proust, an introspective novelist, gives, through the voice of his protagonist, a sense of these inner storms. He reflects on the mystery of his own fluctuations in animal spirits: "And I begin asking myself again what could it be, this unknown state which brought with it no logical proof, but only the evidence of its felicity, in reality, and in whose presence the other states of consciousness faded away?"[10]

A decision not just to tell friends about an interesting investment whose fundamentals can't be verified but to actually raid one's life savings and put them at risk to make the investment is an emotional decision that cannot be taken lightly. It must be influenced by the social milieu and by the psychology of others.

Looking back on Eugene Fama's original formulation of the efficient markets theory, as discussed earlier in this chapter, it seems from our vantage point a little glib to take it for granted that "intelligent participants" know how to reflect new information, as it arrives, in financial prices, and that they are perfectly logical and ready to stake their fortunes on this knowledge. Such a world view presumes that they have a solid economic model that tells them just how much prices should change due to any new information. In reality it is not always easy to say in which direction a bit of business news should move a stock price; beyond that, it is nearly always extremely difficult to know by how much the price should move and, even more confounding, whether the price was even anywhere near right *before* the news came. Any model of stock values is really just a matter of opinion, and the model must be subject to change. Moreover, the structure of the world and the economy is always changing in new and different ways, and so past statistical analyses of stock prices are of questionable relevance. Thus no one really knows how to do the reflection that Fama presumes. There is no escaping the role of animal spirits in driving prices and financial activity.

Selection and Speculative Behavior

Countries and cities that seem to be highly successful in generating healthy animal spirits and entrepreneurship are the objects of imitation around the world. Less successful places wonder how to achieve the same results—a problem of the greatest importance.

A realistic assessment of the situation, however, suggests that such animal spirits will never be successfully exported, in fullest form, everywhere in the world. For in fact those regions of the world where such spirits are predominant may have gotten that way by in effect selecting the kinds of people who will go there to live.

John Gartner, a psychiatrist at the Johns Hopkins University Medical School, alleges that countries with a significant share of self-selected immigrants in their populations have attracted a large number of manic as well as "hypomanic" (a subdued version of manic) people.[11] The United States, Canada, and New Zealand, he points out, are, according to studies published in psychiatric and medical journals, the three countries with the highest proportion of people who have mental illnesses that fit the medical definition of bipolar disorder. Hence they probably have a high proportion of hypomanic people as well. They are all nations of self-selected immigrants who had to overcome hurdles to reach their shores. I would think that other centers of business, like Dubai or Hong Kong or Singapore, have been favored by similar selection. People who emigrate from the comfortable environment in which they grew up are thus naturally selected for certain traits, both genetic and cultural. These hypomanic people are naturally more entrepreneurial.

I have wondered about the validity of Gartner's theory in light of the fact that all countries of the world, and especially all countries outside Africa, were the result of immigration at some point in human history. But those ancient migrations were more like emigrations of whole populations, rather than of isolated individuals—and even to the extent they were of isolated individuals, the migrations may have been random, rather than the result of an adventure-some quest to set out for a better life alone or as a small nuclear family. Modern society makes it possible to emigrate much more freely as an individual, and thus heightens the selection effect.

I think of my own family history. All four of my grandparents came to America over a hundred years ago from Lithuania as single individuals. My paternal grandfather George Shiller emigrated alone, as he told me, to avoid conscription into the Russian army, by those he regarded as occupiers of his country. My paternal grandmother Amelia Miller emigrated alone to America at age eighteen, hardly speaking English, to avoid an arranged marriage to a man she loathed. Doing that no doubt took some spirit. My maternal grand-father Vincas Radziwil came to pursue an education at the Cleveland Institute of Art. My maternal grandmother Rosalia Šerys never told me her reasons for emigrating alone, but I know she suffered some difficulties on the trip, includ-ing being stranded alone in London for two years. All of them might be regarded as at least a shade hypomanic for launching on such independent adventures, and I wonder what such selection tells me about my own makeup.

The stories I have heard about illegal emigration from China to Hong Kong in the time of Mao Zedong—including swimming for miles down the Pearl River at night, only to be apprehended and punished by guards and then, weeks later, try it again—top even my grandparents' stories.

And I wonder how much the liveliness of urban areas around the world may have to do with hypomanic selection, for leaving the quieter countryside for a remote yet exciting big city suggests a similar self-selection process.

Limited Liability

Some forms of business also involve the selection of people. Financial institu-tions in economically successful countries have been designed to be conducive to the constructive expression of a speculative personality trait. The institu-tions themselves can select for hypomania, even within a single country, by bringing together hypomanic people into a single organization, where they form a larger hypomanic whole.

It is commonplace around the world today that investors in shares in pub-licly traded stocks are assured limited liability, which means that the investors cannot be sued for any transgressions of the firm. The investor can rest easy: the most that can be lost is the amount initially paid for the shares. For many it makes investment in shares almost a pleasurable experience, like buying a lottery ticket: having already paid for the experience, one can just sit back and savor the possibility that the investment will make a lot of money. In fact the inventors of general limited liability, centuries ago, understood this psychol-ogy, and it was part of their motivation for enacting limited-liability laws.[12]

Limited liability is an example of a financial institution designed to get people to express their animal spirits. The financial markets, with their limited liability, encourage a sort of gambling spirit that, while often unsuccessful, may on some rare occasions result in major entrepreneurial achievements. The idea that one can participate in a speculative venture with no other consequences than the loss of the money originally put up to purchase shares inspires a sense of playful excitement. Indeed the game one plays may likewise be acceptable to one's spouse, because the risk is plainly and unequivocally limited.[13]

That is why, ultimately, countries all over the world have seen fit to put in place limited liability laws that make it as clear as possible that there are no unexpected negative consequences to participating in the stock market. That is why we need such laws. True, firms could individually give their shareholders limited liability, even in the absence of a limited-liability law, merely by purchasing insurance for the shareholders against any losses beyond their initial investment, just as they currently buy insurance for directors against lawsuits brought against them individually. But such a move would never provide 100% coverage for shareholders, as they would have to check whether the insurance policy was sound, whether it had deductibles or exclusions, and whether the firm was keeping the policy in force as time went on. When we have shareholder limited liability as a fundamental, universal, and time-honored principle, then shareholders can bask in their fantasies of unlimited upside potential and sleep relatively easily at night since they have limited their losses.

A Shift Away from Partnerships toward Public Corporations with Limited Liability

The partnership is a natural structure in which a small number of people together go into a business in which reputation and integrity are of particular importance. Traditionally professional firms—whether in investment banking, law, consulting, or accounting—have taken the form of partnerships. The partners themselves are the owners, and they lack limited liability. But, particularly in investment banking, the partnership form has been dying out in recent decades, raising concerns that some of the factors contributing to the integrity of our financial markets are being lost, that careless speculation is being encouraged, and that this change may have contributed to the severe financial crisis that started in 2007.

Until 1970 the New York Stock Exchange required member firms to be partnerships because of the members' belief in the superiority of this form of organization (and probably for anticompetitive reasons as well).[14] Eventually, however, changes in the technology of business that encouraged large-scale enterprises led the exchange to relax this rule, and after the rule change there was a wholesale move away from the partnership structure in finance.

Donaldson, Lufkin & Jenrette changed its partnership structure and went public in 1970. It was followed by Merrill Lynch in 1971, Lehman Brothers in 1984 when it was acquired by Shearson/American Express and then spun off, Bear Stearns in 1985, Morgan Stanley in 1986, and Goldman Sachs in 1999. Among major Wall Street firms in the United States, only Brown Brothers Harriman retains the partnership structure, with its partners still suffering the burdens and risks of that structure.

In a traditional partnership, the partners' investment in their business is highly illiquid: they cannot easily get out, and its value is opaque, as shares are not traded minute by minute. They *are* their business, and tax law routinely accepts them as individual taxpayers, with no profits tax on the organization. They do not have limited liability; they are liable individually if the partnership is sued. They could lose everything if the partnership fails.

The partners are stuck with this investment, and this risk, for much of their lives, and therefore the partnership structure may be conducive to hard, cooperative, and effective work. Since they cannot exit easily by selling shares, when they discover problems in the firm they must endeavor to fix them. Thus the partnership form is widely thought to select for a different kind of person, to encourage partners to be very selective in finding new partners, and to create a strong sense of commitment among partners.

The most often cited problem with the partnership structure is that it is difficult for a firm to grow while adhering to that structure. Economies of scale for investment banks and broker-dealers are important. It is hard for partnerships to bring in new partners because partners, fearing the consequences of unlimited liability, feel they need to know everything about their peers. They need to know their character—which may take years to ascertain. Beyond that, they must have some sense of their wealth, for if one comes into a partnership with more wealth than the other partners, one is more vulnerable than they to the effects of unlimited liability.[15] The price of a share in the partnership is thus in effect different for each new partner, and the information-collection problem is significant. In contrast, with a corporation, all shares have the same value to everyone, and one need look only at the cash flow of the corporation in deciding whether to invest.

The decline in the partnership structure on Wall Street may have contributed to the severe financial crisis that began in 2007, as it would appear to have reduced the incentives to manage long-term reputation and long-term risks in favor of a structure that encourages rapid growth of the firm. Certainly speculative appetites are whetted by the spectacle of the rapid fluctuations of the stock market prices of firms that were once partnerships, and the ultimate collapse of firms such as Bear Stearns, Lehman Brothers, and Merrill Lynch—

and of the economy as a whole—may be related to the changes wrought by the end of the partnership structure.

Encouraging the Good in Financial Speculation

Charles Conant, quoted at the beginning of this chapter, was certainly right: speculative activity is central to the functioning of the modern economy. It is central because of conventional economic factors: the information that speculative markets reveal and the spurs to action that those prices generate. It is also central in the stimulus such markets give to animal spirits, in helping people of suitable risk-taking mien to come together and work together.

Some behavioral economists have embarked on efforts to channel the speculative impulse constructively, to help people make better financial decisions. For example, Peter Tufano and Daniel Schneider have proposed "lottery-linked savings," an alteration of government-sponsored lotteries so that they transform the gambling impulse into an impulse to save.[16]

But that is not to say that channeling every activity to speculative markets is necessarily a good thing. In retrospect, viewed from the vantage point of our severe financial crisis, it seems that investment banks might better have remained with the partnership structure, rather than having their shares traded on a daily basis in public markets, even if that structure diminished the flow of information and the rate of the firms' growth.

Every change in financial institutions is an experiment, and only after many years of experience with any institution do we know how well it will work. There is no simple answer as to what form our economic institutions should take. Designing financial institutions is difficult, for the designs have to accommodate a wide array of human foibles, and we have to consider such issues as the kinds of people who are selected into alternative forms of financial institutions and how the institutions would interact with each other in a financial crisis.

The next chapter considers the most salient of these foibles—the troubling tendency for markets to run into bubbles, the likes of which have caused numerous financial crises in history, including the most recent one. But, as we shall see, there can be comparable, or even bigger, analogues to speculative bubbles associated with economic activity even where we do not have speculative markets. We shall see that the problem with bubbles is a problem in dealing with the universal behavior of *people*, not the behavior of the abstract entities called markets.

Chapter 26

Speculative Bubbles and
Their Costs to Society

Economic history is peppered with stories of speculative bubbles, their bursting, and the resultant economic dislocation. There are more such stories than any of us can remember. Even before we had stock markets, there were economically important fluctuations in speculative asset prices. There are vague stories of housing booms in ancient Rome, in the time of Julius Caesar and in the time of Hadrian. Large swings in land prices wrought great distress even before we had stock markets of any size. After the invention of the newspaper in the early 1600s, stories of bubbles began to take on their modern form, and the intensity and frequency of reports of bubbles jumped significantly. The intermittent occurrence of these bubble stories seems an integral part of living in a system of financial capitalism.

Just What Is a Speculative Bubble?

When I wrote the second edition of my book *Irrational Exuberance* in 2005, I was struck by the fact that there didn't seem to be a good definition of a "speculative bubble." Dictionaries gave only vague general definitions for the word *bubble* in this context, as something insubstantial or filled with air. Finance textbooks in the efficient markets era generally did not even mention the term. It has, at least until recently, seemed a term used by writers for the popular news media rather than scholars. So I wrote my own definition, which seemed to capture what people typically mean when they refer to bubbles:

I define a speculative bubble as a situation in which news of price increases spurs investor enthusiasm, which spreads by psychological contagion from person to person, in the process amplifying stories that might justify the price increases and bringing in a larger and larger class of investors, who, despite doubts about the real value of an investment, are drawn to it partly through envy of others' successes and partly through a gambler's excitement.[1]

Looking back on this definition years later, I am struck by the fact that it contains many psychological, or emotional, terms: *enthusiasm, psychological contagion, doubts, envy, gambler's excitement*. Most economists would not put such words in the definition of any economic term, for they suggest the primacy of raw emotions in an economic decision. But it seemed to me then that the presence in large numbers of people of these emotions is what identifies a bubble.

Perhaps it would be better to define a list of symptoms of a bubble. Bubbles are a phenomenon that may be compared to a social mental illness, and not all bubbles are identical. We need something like the diagnostic criteria that the American Psychiatric Association has provided in its *Diagnostic and Statistical Manual of Mental Disorders*, now in its fourth edition (*DSM-IV*). Psychiatrists seeking to diagnose a patient's mental condition usually cannot rely on concrete factors like the bacterial cultures or x-ray images that other physicians use in diagnosis. *DSM-IV* provides a numbered list of the possible symptoms for all known mental disorders, and a required number of these symptoms from the list for a diagnosis to be valid, thereby allowing a diagnosis that should be replicable across different psychiatrists, and also allowing for useful statistical measures of the illness.

Social Epidemics

Yet a speculative bubble is different from a mental illness in that it is a social phenomenon, the result of an interaction among large numbers of mostly normal people. A positive bubble occurs when people observe price increases in some speculative market and the observation generates a feedback loop. Price increases attract attention, both in the news media and in popular talk, to theories—often so-called new era theories, inspirational stories of why the future is going to be dramatically better than the past—that justify the price increases, and more people decide to buy, thereby bidding up the price even further. At each stage of the loop prices have to be bid up enough that some existing holders of the asset will start to think that the price is too high and thus sell, preserving for the moment the equality of supply and demand. At each stage of the loop the contagion of the new era theories brings new demand and is in turn enhanced by the public attention generated by the price increases. As the loops repeat, the stories become ever more prominent and the price deviation ever larger.

In a negative bubble, it is the same, except that falling prices generate negative stories—catastrophe stories—that encourage selling. The feedback loop
means that falling prices encourage the catastrophe stories, the greater public
attention to them in turn leads to further price declines, and on and on. At
each iteration of the loop prices have to fall far enough that some investors
will buy the assets others are selling, despite the increased prominence of the
negative stories.

Bubbles generate profit opportunities for those who see and understand
what is happening, and the activity of such people tends to be stabilizing. Still,
such activity tends to be limited, as it is never known just when the bubble,
whether positive or negative, will end. Frequent short-run market reversals
seem to mark ends to the bubble—spurious though these are—which only
confuse people. Betting against a bubble is a risky business. And it all remains
a matter of opinion; there is no way to prove that there is indeed a bubble, for
bubbles cannot be well quantified. Changes in ratios, such as price-earnings
ratios, are never proof of a bubble. There are not enough major bubbles in one
market or country relative to a person's active professional lifespan to allow
one to establish a secure reputation as an exploiter of bubbles. Nor are there
enough to allow institutions or government organizations to gain the reputation
that would allow them to convince investors or taxpayers to provide massive
capital to lean against nascent bubbles and so prevent them from developing.

Sociologists have told us in the past about social epidemics, though most
of these are not related to finance and hence technically are not speculative
bubbles. Yet we have to rely on the understanding that modern sociology
gives us of these epidemics if we are to comprehend speculative bubbles.

We have to rely on modern neuroscience as well in understanding bubbles.
The coordination of all the different agents that make up the brain is imperfect,
for the evolutionary processes that shaped the human brain have not made
it into a perfect machine. In our evolution the mammalian brain was built
"on top of" the reptilian brain, and there is a degree of duplication and contradiction within our brains. Like a house to which new wings have been
added over the years, the structure is not a truly unified whole, and there are
cold spots and drafty areas. There still are "brain bugs"—similar to bugs in
computer programs—as neuroscientist Dean Buonomano has characterized
them in a book with that title: "Simply put, our brain is inherently well suited
for some tasks, but ill suited for others. Unfortunately, the brain's weaknesses
include recognizing which tasks are which, so for the most part we remain
blissfully ignorant of the extent to which our lives are governed by the *brain
bugs*."[2]

Speculative bubbles are the effect on the entire financial system of a number
of these brain bugs. I listed a number of them in *Irrational Exuberance*. The bugs
include

- *Anchoring,* a tendency to be influenced by extraneous cues when in ambiguous circumstances,
- A tendency to be overly influenced by *storytelling,* particularly human-interest stories,
- *Overconfidence,* particularly in ego-involving judgments,
- *Nonconsequentialist reasoning,* a difficulty in thinking through the array of hypothetical events that could potentially occur in the future, and
- *Social influence,* a tendency to adopt the attitudes of others around us without realizing we are doing so.

All of these factors create a vulnerability to thought viruses, or memes—ideas that spread across the population the same way disease viruses do.

There is also cognitive dissonance, which we discussed earlier. During a bubble, it operates on both an individual and a cultural level. At the cultural level, it contributes to the proliferation of a conventional wisdom that justifies the bubble-enhancing activities in which we are already involved. There are people who actively feed this conventional wisdom, as anything that disrupts the conventional wisdom will evoke cognitive dissonance in those who have internalized it—and who, moreover, may have made business arrangements or placed bets that are predicated on this wisdom.

Nonfinancial Investment Bubbles

It is important to recognize, when we think about how to regulate or prevent them, that speculative bubbles are just one particularly frequent and salient example of social epidemics. The above description of a social epidemic that creates speculative bubbles presumes the existence of financial markets that reveal the prices of speculative assets and news media that disseminate information about those prices, so that the price movements can accelerate the contagion of bubble thinking. But the process of a social epidemic involving the economy can proceed even in the total absence of financial markets—though the process would then necessarily be different.

To find clear examples, we have to look at economies that have no financial markets at all. Consider the centrally planned economies during the age of communism in the twentieth century. These examples are not normally referred to as "bubbles," since the central command of the economy did not involve a large segment of the population. The bubble thinking underlying these economies was less visible and less remarked on—but no less intense and disastrous.

In the Soviet Union, the collectivization plan of 1929 has aspects of a speculative bubble. The plan called for a massive reorganization of agriculture from small individual farms to giant collectives, which would be given modern farm equipment to increase productivity. The Soviet government promoted the plan to the general public to encourage its enthusiastic implementation. The initial forecasts for its success were as outlandish and wildly inflated as those in any financial bubble. The public participated in the enthusiasm, and it even became the fashion to name babies "Traktor," "Electrifikatsiya," and the like.

There was no way to buy shares in the collectivization schemes, though one could indirectly invest in a collective farm by throwing oneself into its workforce with hopes of promotion and rewards. More significantly, there was no price for such an investment recorded in any market, and no tempering forces for the bubble through comparing prices with alternative investments or making short sales. There was no broad publication of balance sheets and profit statements, and there were no independent analysts who could openly criticize the new enterprises. The bubble was ultimately proven to be a disaster. Eleven million people died in the famine of 1932–33, which was directly related to the disruption in agriculture that collectivization had produced.

The Great Leap Forward in communist China from 1958 to 1961 was another such investment bubble that took place in the absence of financial markets. The plan involved both agricultural collectivization and the aggressive promotion of industry, notably of the iron and steel industry. Once again there were no market prices, no published profit and loss statements, no independent analysts. Steel production was to be carried out in backyard furnaces that would be considered laughable by knowledgeable steel industry analysts, but those who understood that had no influence in China at the time. Of course there was no way to short the Great Leap Forward. As a result of this bubble, agricultural labor and resources were rapidly diverted to industry. The result was massive famine, with tens of millions of deaths.[3]

The Great Leap Forward also has aspects of a Ponzi scheme. There are reports that Mao Zedong, on visiting a modern steel plant in Manchuria in 1959, became doubtful that the backyard furnaces were a good idea. According to his personal physician and later biographer Li Zhisui, "he gave no order to halt the backyard steel furnaces. The horrible waste of manpower and materials, the useless output from the homemade furnaces, was not his main concern. Mao still did not want to do anything to dampen the enthusiasm of the masses."[4] The Great Leap Forward, as well as the Cultural Revolution that followed it, was essentially a calculated scheme to create a social contagion of ideas.

Accounting fraud played a major role in the disaster created by the Great Leap Forward, for the event created an incentive for collectives to overstate their harvest, and there were no regulators to ensure that the reports were honest. When the central government demanded its share of the reported produce, there was little left to feed the producers.

Some may object that these events were not really speculative bubbles because the activities were imposed on the population by totalitarian governments, and the deaths reflect government error more than investment error. But they nevertheless have aspects of bubbles. The simple fact that in each case the government was able to have its plans carried out for so long and on such a massive scale must mean that there was enthusiastic public support for the underlying ideas.

Fortunately no speculative bubble in any advanced financial country has ever had the disastrous consequences of Soviet collectivization or the Chinese Great Leap Forward. The presence of free markets, analysts, and balance sheets and income statements at least limits the magnitude of such disasters.

Wars and Bubbles

World War I was in a sense a bubble. As with many conflicts, the precipitating event, the assassination of Archduke Franz Ferdinand, became less significant as events progressed through a sequence of reactions and counterreactions—a feedback loop that no participant could seem to stop.

Emil Lederer, a sociologist, remarked in 1915 that he was struck by the transformation of society wrought by the war. The practice of universal conscription, he wrote, made the prospect of war an immensely personal matter, touching almost every family, which then invaded everyone's thinking and led to a change in interpersonal relationships. As he put it, *Gesellschaft* (society) was replaced by *Gemeinschaft* (community), which made it impossible to be detached from the feedback.[5]

World War I was so obviously a destructive feedback loop that it led to international mechanisms to curtail such feedback in the future. These included the League of Nations, which, after it failed to stop World War II, was replaced by the United Nations. An essential function of the United Nations is the mediation of disputes and the placement of peacekeeping forces to interrupt such feedback loops as close to their origins as possible. We could have analogous advances in curtailing speculative bubbles—though they will never be curtailed completely.

The Good Society

As with the founding of the United Nations in the twentieth century, the twenty-first century is seeing progress toward the achievement of the "good society." One example has been the development of the association of nations known as the Group of Twenty (G20), formed in 1999, as an effective economic policy institution. This development builds on centuries of progress in developing agencies of international cooperation among the great powers, starting with the Congress of Vienna in 1814–15. The League of Nations and the United Nations were important milestones, as were the Group of Seven and its successor the Group of Eight. The Economic and Social Council of the United

Nations, and the Second Committee of its General Assembly, did have some impact on economic policy formulation. But before the G20 no body of international agreement was effective in coordinating economic policy.

In the group's first summit statement, dated November 15, 2008, the leaders of the G20 nations committed themselves to ensuring "that all systemically-important institutions are appropriately regulated."[6] In their September 15, 2009, statement they announced their commitment to "policies designed to avoid both the re-creation of asset bubbles and the re-emergence of unsustainable global financial flows."[7]

Steps are being taken in the nations of the developed world to comply with these policies. In the United States, for example, the Dodd-Frank Act has set up, along with the Financial Stability Oversight Council, an Office of Financial Research, which is charged with collecting data that will allow informed decisions about systemic risks. In the European Union, the European Systemic Risk Board has an Advisory Technical Committee charged with helping it figure out how to deal with bubble-like problems.

But preventing speculative bubbles and overleverage in an economy is inherently difficult for any government agency. One wonders how well these agencies will succeed. Past examples are not uniformly encouraging. In 1987, right after the biggest one-day stock market crash in U.S. history, President Ronald Reagan created such an agency, the President's Working Group on Financial Markets, which consisted of the secretary of the Treasury, the chairman of the Federal Reserve Board, the chairman of the SEC, and the chairman of the Commodity Futures Trading Commission. It was similar to today's Financial Stability Oversight Council but had fewer members. That body apparently took no measures as a group to forestall the present financial crisis. On October 8, 2008, near the peak of the crisis, it issued only a weak statement that consisted of descriptions of the various actions that each of the four agencies constituting the working group had already undertaken, without offering any evidence that the existence of the group itself had been of any benefit.[8]

Descriptions of the activities of these agencies tend to be technical in nature, couched in terms of data on capital ratios, crossborder capital flows, and the like. They do not usually include the word *bubble*. The problem seems to be that accountants can often conceal the real meaning of the numbers. Recognizing a bubble is essential to preventing a financial crisis, but recognizing bubbles is as much a question of judging, from their actions, people's intentions and motives as it is of looking at the numbers themselves.

That is why formulating plans for new agencies to prevent bubbles is so difficult. And that is why the dislocations that we have seen during the present financial crisis will tend to recur.

Regulators play an important role, but they are human. Designing financial institutions around the imperfections of regulators—as much as that can be done—is just as important as designing financial institutions around the imperfections of market participants.

The Significance of Bubbles

Assuming all this is true, what good are prices in financial markets? What else can they do *besides* create bubbles and crashes? There is widespread talk among apologists for speculative markets that the markets provide price discovery, implying that they create important information. But what is the nature of the information the markets are revealing? What are the markets "discovering" in their prices?

The answer has to be that even though the fluctuating level of aggregate stock market prices over the past century has generally discovered little more than changing market psychology, stock prices still mean something. Notably, at the very least, *individual* stocks' prices clearly carry useful information.

The economist Paul A. Samuelson opined that stock prices are "micro efficient" and "macro inefficient." He meant that there is more truth to the efficient markets hypothesis for individual stocks (micro in the sense that we are talking about tiny parts of the aggregate market) than for the stock market as a whole (the macro side of the market). We call this Samuelson's Dictum.

In a paper I wrote with my former student Jeeman Jung, we found evidence that gives some support for Samuelson's Dictum.[9] We noted that excess volatility is most apparent for the aggregate stock market. For the aggregate market, there has never been much fluctuation in earnings or dividends; they have always followed a trend—with only short-run interruptions that tend to reverse themselves in a matter of a few years—and so should not have a significant impact on stock prices. There has thus never been much genuine information predicting substantial future movements in economywide earnings or dividends away from the trend. So, for the stock market for an entire country, the bubbles have dominated.[10]

But when one looks at individual stocks, and not just at the aggregate stock market, one finds that the percentage movements in dividends are much larger. Even if these stocks are just as vulnerable to booms and crashes, the large movements in the fundamentals, to some extent forecastable, provide a justification for fluctuations in the price-earnings ratio.

For example, Jung and I looked at those stocks that have never yet paid a dividend, typically young stocks, issued by relatively new companies that hope to reward their investors later with dividends. Efficient markets theory predicts that, while they are not paying dividends, these stocks will show higher price increases over time than other stocks, to compensate investors for the lack of dividend income. For stocks that pay no dividend, we find that in fact there *is* a higher capital gain on average. The market must know something; it somehow puts a value on these stocks, knowing that they will appreciate at a higher rate, and they in fact *do* tend to appreciate at a higher rate. So that valuation is meaningful.

In a research study titled "What Drives Firm-Level Stock Returns?" financial analyst Tuomo Vuolteenaho looked at the valuations of a large sample of U.S. stocks using over 36,000 firm-year observations over the years 1954–96. His conclusions imply that about two-thirds of the variability of individual company stock prices stems from responses to genuine information about the expected future cash flows of the firms, and only about a third of the variability can be attributed to changes in investor attitudes toward risk and time. He did not enumerate what might change these attitudes, but influences probably would include speculative bubbles, or possibly other factors that change investor willingness to pay, such as fashions or fads in investing, changing liquidity, publicity for individual stocks, market manipulation, or changing availability of shortable shares. But since these account for only about a third of the variability of individual stock prices, Vuolteenaho confirms that individual stock price movements mostly do make basic sense in terms of information about the future.[11]

Fischer Black, the co-author of the Black-Scholes option pricing theory, wrote in his presidential address to the American Finance Association that the efficient markets theory of the stock market "seems reasonable" if we adopt the right definition of "efficient." He defined "efficient" to mean that individual company stock prices are between half true value and twice true value almost all of the time. And he defined "almost all" to mean "at least 90%."[12] That judgment seems roughly to correspond to Vuolteenaho's assessment.

As I interpret the evidence, financial markets are not perfect, and a substantial fraction of the variation in individual stock prices is not explainable in terms of anything that makes good economic sense—at least not sense that we can discern today. Bubbles are frequent and, when they occur, salient. But enough of the variability of individual stock prices, or other individual asset prices, *does* make sense that the market remains an extremely important source of information for directing resources.

Chapter 27

Inequality and Injustice

We have ample reason to believe that financial markets are quite useful. And yet our wonderful financial infrastructure has not yet brought us the harmonious society that we might envision. There remains the ugliness of extreme economic inequality, of some who endure hardship while others are pampered. While some inequality is actually in many ways a good thing, for the motivation and stimulation it provides, arbitrary and extreme inequality poses problems.

The public aversion to inequality is deep seated and ancient. It has been shown that even our distant relatives, nonhuman primates, share with us an aversion to inequity.[1] It is an imperative that people feel society is basically fair to them.

We see this aversion most clearly today in the worldwide protests associated with Occupy Wall Street and its variants. The unfairness of the allocation of resources under financial capitalism is a major theme. Rising inequality is certainly a valid concern, and one that must be addressed. But financial capitalism does not *necessarily* produce unjust wealth distribution. Public policy can allow us to enjoy the benefits of modern finance without producing such inequality. We must examine the relationship between finance and our problems with inequality before we jump to unwarranted conclusions.

Finance and Injustice

We seem able to live with, even admire, wealthy people. There is no sense of injustice if we believe that the wealthy in some sense earned or deserve their wealth. Public awareness of inequality itself does not seem to be strongly associated with overt signs of anger, such as terrorism or antisocial acts.[2]

A college student with a good business idea who drops out, founds a company, raises the financing for it despite being an outsider to the system, and quickly becomes a billionaire does not seem to inspire resentment. To most people, that is just an interesting story. The greatest resentment is reserved for the social classes who focus their attention exclusively on amassing fortunes and keeping them from the eyes of the tax collector, year upon year and generation upon generation.

There is widespread skepticism that those who become extremely wealthy through financial dealings, or very high executive compensation packages, are sufficiently deserving of their wealth.

How the Rich Are Connected to Finance

If we define finance as broadly as in the introduction to this book, then most of the richest people in the world may be classified as connected to the field of finance. Looking at the Forbes 400 list of the richest Americans, all of them billionaires, one sees that the great majority of them have some real connection to finance, in the sense that they are in charge of large enterprises that participate frequently in markets and deal making.[3] Finance is usually not listed as their specialty: for only a quarter of them is the source of wealth given as investments, hedge funds, leveraged buyouts, insurance, or other distinctly financial businesses. But, though they may run a business with a specialized nonfinancial product, they do so on such a scale that they are surely involved in finance.

Forbes also maintains the Celebrity 100 list, the members of which are selected based not on their wealth but on other factors indicating their public presence, as well as their income.[4] Only three of those on this list—Oprah Winfrey, Donald Trump, and Steven Spielberg—are also on the Forbes 400 list. They are on both lists only because they are leading double lives as managers and entertainers—and big-time, as each manages a massive entertainment empire. Being famous is not at all the same as being rich, and finance is not by itself a route to celebrity.

The Forbes 400 billionaires have usually made use of some kind of specialized knowledge to achieve their wealth, but they rarely stand out for important contributions in any intellectual or creative fields. There are virtually no distinguished scientists on the list. There does not appear to be a single Nobel Prize winner on the list—though of course the Nobel Foundation might see little purpose in bestowing a mere $1.5 million on one of these billionaires.

There are only a few best-selling authors on the list, and even they are on the list because of their business ventures. If one searches Amazon.com for Oprah Winfrey, Donald Trump, or Steven Spielberg, many books come up, with numerous co-authors, but these books appear to be part and parcel of their media and entertainment enterprises.

Their wealth appears to be related to large-scale financial activities, not just artistic creativity. For example, Oprah Winfrey now has her own cable network, the Oprah Winfrey Network or OWN, and her own magazine, *O, The Oprah Magazine*. Donald Trump is more squarely situated in finance, with his Trump Organization and Trump Entertainment Resorts. Steven Spielberg has not been just a producer and director of films; he was a co-founder in 1994 of DreamWorks Studios, which has financed and distributed films, video games, and television shows. DreamWorks was sold to Paramount Pictures in 2005 for $1.6 billion.

As we have discussed, finance is a powerful tool because it has the ability to amass capital, pool information, and coordinate and incentivize people. It is no wonder that it is so central to the lives of the wealthiest. Their wealth comes not solely from their own efforts and talent, but often from their ability to form and lead huge and effective organizations composed of many other talented people.

Possible Bubbles in Financial Compensation

Still it remains a puzzle that those connected to finance can become so fabulously rich to the seeming exclusion of everyone else. Wouldn't you think that at least one scientist could come up with a patentable idea that would top all their successes? But that never seems to happen—not even close. Why is that?

Part of the answer might be that finance in recent decades has been going through an anomalous period. Perhaps the compensation that those in finance earn is going through a speculative bubble or an adjustment to new technology and will be corrected in the future. Indeed finance salaries have increased dramatically in recent decades, as a 2008 study by Thomas Philippon and Ariell Reshef has shown.[5] These authors found that the compensation of those in finance was also unusually high around 1930, just around the time of the 1929 peak in the stock market, and then fell dramatically for the next half century. In that interim period there were many low-paying jobs in finance. Philippon and Reshef also pointed out that the average education level of people in the finance professions was likewise high around 1930, after which it decreased; it has recently returned to a high level. These findings suggest that the path of financial salaries was not just a bubble—that it reflects an actual change in the composition of the financial labor force. In any event, their results encourage caution in making the assumption that because the compensation of people in finance is high now, it will always be high in the future.

But Philippon and Reshef were talking about the rank-and-file members of the finance professions, not the richest ones. It seems likely that finance will continue to produce a small number of super-rich people unless public policy changes the landscape.

And in considering the super-rich we have to come back to the fundamental nature of financial dealmaking, which enables the power of the dealmaker to be multiplied via his or her command over vast numbers of people. Scientists are, in their capacity as scientists, not dealmakers, and they depend largely on collegiality and professional courtesy to make the research progress they so value.

Although there does often seem to be injustice in this situation, in and of itself it is not extreme. The scientists are mostly living comfortably doing what they really want to do, and their everyday life is enriched with products that are provided by others doing less essentially gratifying work. The situation can still be improved, but it would not be without cost to eliminate inequality entirely from our society.

Family Dynasties

Part of the reason for a sense of injustice at the unequal distribution of wealth is that some of the inequality seems to be the result of family dynasties, through which the children of successful businesspeople become rich, whether or not they are deserving. Some of these children, for example Donald Trump, keep working in the family business. But in fact only about a third of family businesses are continued by the children of the founders, and only a tenth of them by the grandchildren.[6] Still, the later generations remain rich.

Having one's children and grandchildren become wealthy and perhaps continue the family business is a source of great meaning to many of those who have founded businesses. This sentiment endures despite the fact that studies have indicated that children who inherit large fortunes tend to feel a degree of meaninglessness in their later lives. According to one authoritative study, children of the very rich show "elevated disturbance in several areas— such as substance use, anxiety, and depression."[7]

And yet the dream of the family dynasty persists. Even though Karl Marx and Friedrich Engels cried "Abolition of the family!" in their *Communist Manifesto*,[8] today's hard-line communist countries pursue this dream. For example, in North Korea it drove Kim Il Sung to anoint his son Kim Jong Il and he in turn to anoint his son Kim Jong Un as leader of North Korea. It has even motivated Fidel Castro, who is a true communist, to bequeath his role as ruler of Cuba to his brother Raúl.

Positional Consumption

The tendency for wealthy families to annoy others by "showing off"—by spending extravagantly and wastefully on themselves—is often a cause for resentment. Consuming conspicuously feeds their ego. It may also help them convey social status to the next generation, by securing for their children a head start in the pecking order.

This tendency toward consumption for show has been dealt with for centuries, going back to ancient Greece and Rome, by means of sumptuary laws, that is, laws that directly forbid specified forms of wasteful consumption. For example, in seventh-century BCE Greece, women were forbidden by the Locrian code to wear extravagant clothing or jewelry unless they were prostitutes. Similarly, sumptuary taxes are special excise taxes on items of conspicuous consumption.

Sumptuary laws and taxes, however, have difficulty in actually preventing spending that invites the resentment of others. As one eighteenth-century observer sized up these laws, "they are null, because luxury employs itself upon objects which the laws have not foreseen, and could not foresee."[9] The laws' details were commonly ridiculed, and in modern times they are thought to be inconsistent with individual freedoms. They did, nevertheless, reappear again and again for thousands of years, reflecting the persistence of public disgust with the extravagance of the rich.

There is an economic theory that would seem to justify something akin to sumptuary laws or taxes. The theory was described by Thorstein Veblen in his 1899 book *The Theory of the Leisure Class* and the economic part of the theory was expanded by George Akerlof and other economic theorists.[10] Many people spend lavishly on consumption that they do not really even enjoy merely to signal to others their status—a practice called positional consumption because its value to the consumer depends on how it establishes his or her position relative to others. As argued convincingly by social psychologist Leon Festinger, with his 1954 "theory of social comparison processes," people are instinctively constantly comparing themselves with other people, and they delight when they are doing better.[11] They tend to compare themselves with others close to them in the social ranking and who are attempting to achieve similar things, and disregard those who are doing very much better or very much worse or who are very different in their measures of success.

The comparisons are substantially subconscious, and since such comparisons are generally frowned upon, many people deny to themselves as well as others that they are making them. From Festinger's other theory, of cognitive dissonance, we see that people often manage to convince themselves that they enjoy the positional consumption goods because the items consumed are intrinsically good; they experience a sense of enjoyment as if the enjoyment were intrinsic rather than positional. This is not to say that people cannot make value judgments independent of status considerations, just that such considerations impose a bias that affects their judgments, often subconsciously.

This theory has always been controversial, and even repugnant to those who dislike being accused of such low motives, even if the accusers recognize their good side as well. We should not overstress the theory of social comparisons, for people have sympathetic and communal aspects as well, but the theory is by now well established. A 2007 study even identified a region of the brain (the ventral striatum) that is stimulated especially strongly after a reward if others nearby are seen as not receiving the same reward.[12] There is thus a physical basis for the social comparison theory.

A modern version of sumptuary laws calls for progressive consumption taxes: taxes based on the amount one consumes rather than the amount one earns, and with higher tax rates on higher levels of consumption. Such a tax was proposed in the United States Senate by Democrat Sam Nunn and Republican Pete Domenici in 1995. Adding a progressive consumption tax is like adding a sumptuary tax, but one that is broadly applied to overall levels of consumption, not just consumption of particular items. Recently economist Robert H. Frank has advocated replacing the income tax with such taxes, to help reduce the problem of positional consumption.[13]

Switching from a progressive income tax to a similarly progressive consumption tax might be a good idea, for such an approach does not penalize one from earning a large income; it simply discourages excessive spending from that income, and it might encourage saving, philanthropy, or both.

However, there are serious implementation problems that make progressive consumption taxes difficult. For example, in implementing such a new tax regime, it would be hard not to effectively reduce taxes on the highest-income people, and it would be hard to manage withholding on income, since responsible withholding would have to depend on unknown future consumption.[14] Neither a sumptuary tax nor a progressive consumption tax is an easy and obvious solution to the problem of wasteful and resentment-inducing positional consumption. We need to keep such ideas in mind, though, as fodder for public financial innovation, possibly in some altered form or through reliance on future advances in information technology.

Estate Taxes

Whether or not rich people actually feel any sense of connectedness to others in their country, their countrymen will feel that they ought to. Upon their death, distributing their estates to their own children seems selfish, especially as their children may not seem particularly deserving, at least in the eyes of others. Levying estate taxes is one of the most effective ways of restoring a sense of fairness in society. Many countries tax estates heavily at the time of death.

If estate taxes were pursued aggressively, they would do much to reduce economic inequality. But there remains an issue: often the most important reason people try to make money is to pass it to their children. Such desires to promote the welfare of one's children are in some ways instinctive. Leaving a financial estate for them may not be the most fundamental expression of such instincts, but it is a desire that crops up repeatedly in human societies.

Estate taxes can seem extremely onerous to some. In late 2010, when a law abolishing the federal estate tax in the United States was set to expire on January 1, 2011, bringing the maximum estate tax rate up from 0% to 55%, the media told unconfirmed stories of elderly people in poor health asking their doctors to cut off further treatment so they would die before the year was over.[15] Representative Cynthia Lummis of Wyoming said, "If you have spent your whole life building a ranch, and you wanted to pass your estate on to your children, and you were 88-years-old and on dialysis, and the only thing that was keeping you alive was that dialysis, you might make that same decision."[16]

She makes a good point: some people do spend their lives trying to promote their children's welfare—a goal that, one has to admit, is far from evil. But here we have an essential conflict, for their doing so very successfully can create a situation of social resentment.

There is no way to eliminate this essential conflict, and so the best solution would seem to be setting estate taxes at some intermediate level, neither confiscating wealth at death nor allowing its complete transition. In fact, most people think about the issue in this way. Most believe that society should give in somewhat to the natural desire to make one's children rich, but simply limit the exercise of that desire. A 1990 survey that Maxim Boycko, Vladimir Korobov, and I conducted found that people in both the United States and the Soviet Union—people from two very different economic traditions— thought that the estate tax should take about a third of an estate.[17]

We may consider tragic the stories of people losing the family farm—having to sell the farm and move to an apartment in the city just to pay the estate tax, thus upending a family's whole way of life, possibly for generations to come. But we also have to consider the resentment caused by wealthy children holding such wealth indefinitely, and the feelings of society as a whole.

In fact, the form of estate tax favored by most people actually allows wealthy people to leave their children a ranch or a family farm. In this case parents are perceived as transferring not just wealth but also a set of responsibilities, and meaningful work, to their children. But transferring responsibilities and work does not *require* a massive transfer of wealth. The people that Representative Lummis talked about could probably have paid any higher estate tax in 2011 by taking out a mortgage on the farm and paying it off through time. Finance offers many flexibilities, and if the ranching lifestyle is important to a family, they can probably find a financial strategy that will allow them to continue it.

Inequality Indexation or Inequality Insurance

Besides estate taxes, one of the most important weapons society already has against economic inequality is the progressive income tax system. Progressive income taxes have higher tax rates on higher levels of income, and so revenue is raised disproportionately from high-income people, and much of the benefit of the proceeds is directed to, or at least shared by, the poor. Moreover, government expenditures on many things (education, public goods) are shared among all people. Over the years, income tax systems have become more sophisticated in managing inequality. For example, the tax systems in the United States and other countries have forms of the "earned income tax credit" that in effect gives low-income workers a negative income tax on their wages.[18]

But, strangely, the income tax system has never been expressly designed with the objective of managing inequality. The word *inequality* does not seem to be in the tax code. So the system deals with economic inequality in a haphazard way purely as a by-product of its stated goals, and tax law is not written in a way that allows it to respond to economic inequality.

I have proposed that in the future nations should *index* their tax systems to inequality.[19] Under inequality indexation (which I have also called inequality insurance) the government would not legislate fixed income tax rates for each tax bracket, but would instead prescribe in advance a formula that would tie the tax rates to statistical measures of pretax inequality. If income inequality were to worsen, the tax system would become automatically more progressive. This is a "financial" solution to the problem of inequality in the sense that we impose the indexation scheme *before* we know that income inequality will worsen, and *before* people know who might effectively be highly taxed by it. So the indexation scheme is dealing with a *risk*, the risk of rising inequality, before it happens, much as insurance contracts do. In fact, inequality indexation could be considered a kind of insurance—inequality insurance.

The inequality indexation scheme could be designed either to gradually reverse the level of inequality, to bring it eventually to a more acceptable level, or to merely freeze it at the present level, so that it does not get worse. The latter course may be the most politically acceptable. A scheme could be designed that would allow substantial income inequality to persist forever, that would merely be aimed at preventing a serious *worsening* of income inequality. It would after all be easier to accustom people to inequality indexation of taxes if such a system had no immediate impact, and no chance of changing the current social order. People would still be able to get rich, as they can today, but we would plan in advance not to let income inequality get much worse. If inequality never worsened, then the inequality indexation scheme would have no effect.

The combined wealth of the Forbes 400 in 2011 was $1.5 trillion, or 2.6% of the national household net worth.[20] As the percentage of total societal wealth is small, and as most of these people are seen as contributing to society by running large businesses, this degree of inequality may be acceptable, or at least there may not be the political will to address it. But the inequality could get worse. How much of a concentration of economic blessings do we really want to allow? The possibility that the 400 could come to have a much greater—perhaps an extraordinary—share of our national wealth, in return for a contribution to society that is not at all proportionate, seems odious. If such changes were to occur, it would not be because the distribution of talents or skills in their genes had suddenly changed. The change would no doubt be widely perceived as an injustice.

It would be easier to legislate contingency plans in advance against any future worsening in income inequality than to wait until the inequality became a reality. It is much easier to insure a house *before* it burns down. The same principle implies that it is easier to construct a tax system that deals with increasing inequality before it happens. If the day should come when we have a much larger class of wealthy people, then these people will tend to feel entitled to what after-tax income they already have and will have the economic clout to lobby forcefully to maintain that status. We need to put mechanisms in place now, not later, that will prevent that cycle from ever starting, and this is one route to limiting the power of the lobbyists who were discussed in Part One. It will seem unfair if we change the tax laws after the fact. So we should deal with the potential problem now.

An inequality indexation formula might be enacted as a political quid pro quo for some pro-growth policy that is controversial because of its possible consequences for income inequality. The formula would promote average economic well-being as well as deal with risks to that well-being.

Leonard Burman at Syracuse University and I did a historical analysis of the possible effects of inequality indexation, had it been imposed many years ago.[21] We found that if an inequality indexation scheme had been legislated in 1979 that would have frozen after-tax income inequality at the then-current level, the marginal tax rate on high-income individuals would have increased to an extraordinarily high level, over 75%. This finding provides stark evidence of how much economic inequality has worsened since 1979. We were concerned that full inequality indexation might be too much to be accepted, and so we also proposed partial inequality indexation, as part of a broader attack on random economic influences that create inequality, using other insurance and hedging schemes. An inequality indexation scheme also has to be designed, and constrained, to minimize effects that encourage welfare dependency or provide strong incentives to immigrate or emigrate.

The Need to Be Systematic and to Apply Financial Theory

Progressive income taxes and estate taxes—and possibly also progressive consumption taxes—are important tools for dealing with excessive economic inequality. Real public concerns about inequality have already made some of these taxes common around the world.

But societies have great trouble dealing with the issue of inequality in a systematic manner. The principle has never been articulated that some degree of inequality is a good thing, that there should be some who are richly rewarded for their business success (or their parents' success), but that society has to systematically put some limits on this inequality. Because that principle has never been established, the effects of various tax laws are never considered systematically and holistically. Thus the wealthy instinctively oppose any increase in their taxes, fearing that acquiescing even to a limited extent might leave them open to a haphazard series of tax increases that, in combination, could amount to confiscatory taxation.

Measures to deal with economic inequality should be implemented holistically and articulated clearly, in terms of achieving some appropriate level of inequality. The inequality indexation scheme described here is one trial balloon for such an idea. It may not ultimately prove to be the right course, but it is at the very least illustrative of the principle that we should be considering more complex systems of tax rates that are grounded in risk management theory and behavioral economics. Our tax system is still hampered by that old impulse for conventionality and familiarity. But given our rapidly advancing information technology—in an age when computers are increasingly calculating our taxes and we are increasingly filing our taxes electronically, and looking forward to the day when tax paying can be automated even further—we can introduce quite a bit more responsiveness and nuance into the tax system to help achieve a better society—a society in which people feel that basic economic justice is assured.

Chapter 28

Problems with Philanthropy

Why is it that gifts to causes (charitable, religious, artistic, scientific, environmental, educational, and so forth) are not more common? In the United States in 2010 only 2.2% of national income was given away by individuals and organizations.[1] It would seem that people would give more. With just a little thought one naturally concludes that we suffer what economists would call diminishing marginal utility of consumption; that is, one cannot really consume a large amount of wealth. Certainly there are always others who are in greater need. So why don't people see this and do something about it?

Giving as we observe it today seems often to be a distinctly unrewarding experience. People often give merely in response to immediate social pressure.[2] They seem to respond better to charities that offer them some kind of prestige in return for the giving, as if that were all that mattered.[3] It is hard to imagine that such giving, apparently motivated by the wish to avoid opprobrium or to impress others, can be as rewarding to the giver as giving intended to fulfill his or her own moral purpose.

One challenge to motivating donations without external pressure or rewards may be that there is a lack of fulfillment when those who give to philanthropic organizations do not feel any real gratitude from the recipients, for they never meet the people who benefit from their contributions. Psychologists have shown that people are not well motivated in their charitable giving by mere statistics about human suffering: they have to see a suffering individual and put a human face on the need.[4]

Many of the hopes that are expressed for philanthropy seem to take the form of a national sense of community. One feels a responsibility toward others in one's own country, as if the *country* were one's family. Political scientist Benedict Anderson has asserted that the modern nation-state is an "imagined community," standing in place of family.[5] But it is only an *imagined* community, since the people in it have never met most of the other people in it and have no relationship whatsoever with them.

Those who advocate sharing with others face a problem: generosity seems to require a sense of community. Friedrich Hayek, in his 1944 book *The Road to Serfdom*, discerned a "universal tendency of collectivist policy to become nationalistic."[6] The imagined community has to be elevated to people's constant attention to encourage their sympathy with or acquiescence in the collectivist policy. Of course, when Hayek wrote in 1944 his prime example was the German National Socialists, the Nazis. But he argued that promotion of the idea of a national community was a universal tendency. Socialists may pay lip service to the notion that theirs is an international movement, but underneath it all the appeal they make to their constituents is distinctly nationalist.

In many ways modern political leaders have created a sense of family for a whole nation, and people are up to a point willing to sacrifice for the nation as if it were their family. But there are definite limits to the satisfaction one may obtain by considering the nation as one's family. One is repeatedly reminded of the stark reality that all those millions of other people in one's country do not know or care about you.

Philanthropy in today's world is made doubly unrewarding by the typical giving process. A paid caller for some philanthropic organization telephones at dinner time, beginning to read from a script that has been carefully worded by professional marketers. The paid consultants who write these scripts have years of experience with telemarketing. The scripts are such a powerful force that local governments in the United States require that charities register their scripts with the attorney general or the charitable trust division.

The script is designed to elicit a cash contribution, by one tactic or another. Readers are likely very familiar with the typical response when one hesitates to promise a particular dollar amount: "I need to enter a minimum amount that you are prepared to give," perhaps with the additional explanation that the organization needs to set its budget. Obviously the real reason for this line in the script is that organizations have found that asking the potential donor to come up with a number that will be put down in black and white on a pledge card is motivational. Even when one supports the organization's cause, the tactics used to collect donations typically leave one feeling manipulated.

The sense that, in contributing to a philanthropic organization, one is giving in to manipulation puts a chill on the whole process, detracting from the sense of fulfillment and purpose in earning an income and giving a portion of it to good causes. One would rather feel that one has been creative in supporting causes that are personally meaningful, that are congruent with one's sense of identity. It is not just a question of personal satisfaction. It is also a matter of principle. People, whether of modest or high income, who justifiably want to see their lives as building or creating something of value might best focus on making substantial (relative to their own incomes) gifts to no more than a few causes. For it is only in this way that one can have the time and energy to think carefully about and truly identify with these causes, and fulfill the moral imperative of actually directing one's own resources, on one's own terms, to a cause one considers meaningful.

The *Gospel of Wealth* by Andrew Carnegie, discussed earlier in this book, has become an inspiration for many, notable among them Bill Gates and Warren Buffett, who modeled their "giving pledge" on it.[7] Recall that Carnegie considered it the moral duty of those who achieved great financial success to retire from their business careers early enough to begin managing the purposeful disposal of their wealth for the public good. But what if anything has been the lasting effect of Carnegie's theory?

Carnegie's theory, now over a century old, has still not succeeded in convincing most wealthy persons to take personal charge of giving their wealth away. A 1995 study concluded that there are 35,000 active family foundations in the United States with combined assets of $190 billion. That may sound like a lot. However, it is but a fraction of 1% of U.S. household net worth. Another study estimated that the annual giving of the top one hundred family foundations in 2008 was $7.049 billion in the United States, £1.174 billion (US$2.198 billion) in the United Kingdom, and €725 million (US$920 million) in Germany—each amount representing a tiny fraction of 1% of the countries' respective national incomes.[8]

Improving Incentives for Philanthropy

The emptiness that is often felt in making philanthropic contributions—and that may underlie the low national charitable-giving figures just cited—could perhaps be remedied by improving the process whereby it is managed. For example, it is well known, and controlled experiments have confirmed, that giving is enhanced if the solicitation involves a promise that the donor will be identified to his or her peers, along with a broad indication of the amount given.[9] The desire for publicity for one's gifts is an understandable human impulse; not only do people enjoy recognition for having made substantial gifts, but they may also want the publicity for their gifts to influence their friends to give to the same or similar causes, which they consider important. Further research may reveal that there are yet better ways, not in the current repertory of charity solicitors, to fulfill this desire for recognition—perhaps recognition that is longer term or more personalized.

Research has shown that giving can also be increased if the giver is made to feel that the charity is not all one-way. One study demonstrated that a seemingly generous promise to refund the contribution if the goal of the drive was not met substantially improved the level of giving.[10] Also, a reward for giving also appears to heighten the incentive to give. A field experiment showed that people give more to a charity if they are primed by first receiving a gift from the organization.[11] Human relationships are normally reciprocal—even if the exchanges are not equal in monetary value—and designs for charitable campaigns might better reflect that fact.

The advent of social media should offer new means for promoting giving by creating a sense of community and providing for more personal recognition. Child sponsorship is a significant example. Save the Children, established in the United Kingdom in 1919, led the way by assigning a single child in poverty to each contributor, who would correspond by mail, giving the contributor a sense of personal relationship. Save the Children is now an international organization, and a number of other such organizations have followed. Some now employ more advanced communications tools, such as Skype calls between donors and recipients, to allow a closer bond to develop. One can look the child in the eyes and feel empathy as never before.[12]

It seems that we are gradually learning more about how to make the giving experience more meaningful, and that current strategies are not the final word in encouraging such giving. Perhaps new kinds of social organizations—relying on innovations in social media—could lend a better sense of a shared experience, and of true community between the giver and the receiver.

Tax Laws Favoring Giving

To help humanize finance, and reduce inequality of incomes without destroying incentives, it may also be helpful to change the nature of our tax laws regarding charitable contributions, so that people will find it more rewarding to give their wealth away themselves, to disperse it widely and on their own terms. Even though consideration of tax implications seems to appeal to our self-interest, appropriate redefinitions of the tax laws might still have the effect of encouraging altruistic behavior. The tax deduction itself stands, psychologically, as a kind of affirmation and recognition that helps make one's generosity personally meaningful.

There is a precedent for increasing the deduction for contributions as a sweetener for the wealthy when tax rates on them are sharply increased. It was in fact such a quid pro quo that was responsible for the contribution deduction in the United States in the first place. There was no contribution deduction in the first year of the U.S. income tax, 1913. It was not until 1917 that such a deduction was introduced. That was the same year that, because of the need to finance World War I, the top federal income tax rate was raised to 67% (from 15% in 1916 and 7% in each of the years 1913, 1914, and 1915). At that time Senator Henry F. Hollis of New Hampshire argued successfully for adding the deduction. He quoted a letter from one of his constituents, Felix Warburg, who represented a Jewish philanthropic organization: "I fear that with heavy taxes rightly placed upon the people during this war, if no allowance be made as suggested above, many institutions will be forced to close their doors and the State will have to carry the burdens in their stead, which will be most deplorable."[13]

Before the increase in tax rates went into effect, philanthropic contributions had been rising sharply.[14] It was a time when the suffering associated with the war was prominent in people's thinking, and U.S. soldiers were dying abroad. It was also a time when U.S. allies in the war were suffering horrendous losses, indirectly on behalf of the United States. It thus seemed only appropriate that the nation acknowledge and encourage generosity closer to home.

The same thing happened during World War II, when the war pushed the maximum federal income tax rate up to 94% in 1944 (after the highest marginal tax bracket had been lowered to 25% between the wars). Because of continuing war anxieties caused by the cold war, including the revolution in China in 1949 and the Korean War from 1950 to 1953, the top tax bracket remained very high: it was still 91% in 1963, when tax cuts were enacted under President John F. Kennedy. The reaction to these high tax rates—which must have been expected to continue for the foreseeable future—began around 1948, when a number of U.S. national leaders began to ask for an increase in the 15%-of-income limit on charitable deductions that had been in place since the beginning in 1917.

J. K. Lasser, best known as the author of a series of popular tax guides, asked that the limit be raised drastically or abolished altogether; he saw it as "penalizing the public-spirited individual who has a social conscience."[15] The limit on contribution deductions was raised, to 20% in 1953 and to 30% in 1954, and in 1956 an unlimited deduction was given to those whose donations plus income tax payments exceeded 90% of their income for eight of the past ten years.

All of these changes in the law, intended to encourage philanthropic contributions, were made in response to high tax rates. When tax rates were cut—after the Kennedy tax cuts in 1963 started a downtrend in the top marginal tax rate, to 77% in 1964 and then all the way down to 35% by 2003—the limit on contributions was also cut. In 1969 the unlimited contribution deduction was abolished, though the limit on contribution deductions was raised to 50% for some kinds of contributions.

Thus it is entirely plausible that if we raise the top tax bracket again there would be public support for some extension of the tax system's mechanism for encouraging charitable contributions. That must be part of our plan to deal with even worse economic inequality, should it arise.

At this point some more ambitious changes to our tax system might help reduce income inequality and also serve as a sweetener for any proposed increase in income tax rates. Here I propose a number of ideas that may be controversial; they would certainly need to be considered carefully. I do feel we need to be more creative in thinking about how to achieve a more just and equal society, and our tax laws potentially provide us with useful tools to achieve that goal.

There Is Less Need Today for Tax Simplification

Incentives for giving in the United States took a big hit in 1944 when Congress passed, and President Franklin D. Roosevelt signed, a new law that aimed to simplify tax preparation. That law introduced a "standard deduction," which anyone could claim even if he or she made no contributions. The standard deduction was put in place so that most people would not have to go through all the effort of assembling the paperwork to prove their various deductions. Today, about two-thirds of U.S. taxpayers avail themselves of the standard deduction, and so for them there is effectively no tax benefit from donating.[16]

The standard deduction was enacted in 1944, when paperwork really was paperwork. Certainly we do still need to keep tax preparation simple. But today, when computers are at hand to calculate taxes on our behalf, we should not have to resort to tax simplification methods that eliminate important charitable incentives.

Today a system could be set up so that philanthropic organizations would themselves be responsible for reporting to the tax authorities individual contributions they receive. The system would automatically make the necessary adjustment to the individual's tax form, even if the individual chose the standard deduction. There would be no need for a standard deduction to simplify taxes, and the taxpayer would need to do nothing to obtain the benefit of the deduction. Moreover, a truly comprehensive automated system could immediately adjust withholding for income tax purposes, and thus the donor's paycheck would immediately rise in response to the charitable contribution.

We must always bear in mind that our existing tax system was created taking into account computation limits that are no longer relevant. All its various "simplifying" measures should be reexamined with the goal of building real incentives into the system.

More Finely Focused Contribution Deductions and Tax Credits

The contribution deduction as an active tool in achieving a better society has not been much considered in public discourse. Usually contributions either do or do not qualify as deductible—it is all or nothing. In the United States, there are no gradations in the rate of deductibility, no responsiveness to changing public needs for charitable activities, nor is there active use of tax credits instead of deductions. There are different deductibility limits for different kinds of philanthropies (for example, a private foundation may have only a 30% limit, while a private operating foundation may have a 50% limit), but these differences do not appear to have been motivated by any sense of public purpose. A better-thought-out system of contribution deductions and credits could lead to an improved society, one in which people feel more purpose in their economic lives and in which government policies are fulfilled in more creative ways.

The government could give special tax incentives for contributions to organizations designated as filling particular national needs, instead of just raising taxes to pay for government expenditures for those needs. This would be an alternative form of public financing of important activities. For example, in a time of recession, directed contribution tax incentives could be implemented that would encourage donations to organizations helping to create jobs for the unemployed. Or, at a time of rising inequality, there could be a special tax incentive for donations to organizations that embrace the concerns of the poor or that help to foster a sense of community between rich and poor. The tax breaks would be much bigger than the usual contribution deduction. They could take the form of a partial tax credit, rather than just a deduction, so that the gift-giving would be just as meaningful for people in lower tax brackets.

The government could afford such high tax incentives if the specifications for the qualifying organizations were written so as to encourage them to carry out work that the government itself would otherwise have to do. And the resulting complexity in the tax code could be dealt with by suitable improvements to the information technology infrastructure.

Such tax breaks would allow people to put their own mark on these causes, giving their own personal direction to the expenditures while at the same time promoting the public-goods programs of the government. They would give the wealthy a sense of personal satisfaction and at the same time allow them to feel the gratitude of others for their contributions. Such a plan might receive far greater public acceptance than one to merely "tax the rich and give to the poor."

Tax Incentives for Interpersonal Gift Giving

We ought to consider giving people at least a partial tax deduction when they disperse some of their income irrevocably to others, even if the recipients are individuals and include friends or relatives.

Such giving is in fact already commonplace, even without a tax break. According to one study, 40.8% of U.S. households made substantial gifts to relatives not living in their own homes, and 26.2% made direct gifts to friends, neighbors, or strangers.[17] But even though such interpersonal gifts should tend to reduce income inequality, there is generally no encouragement in the tax law to support this form of giving.

I have seen firsthand some examples of such charitable giving. A close friend and colleague of mine and his wife often give away or loan substantial sums of money to students. The institution where he teaches assigns all entering students from outside the United States a "host family." Over the years he and his wife have hosted more than two dozen such students; many of them experience financial difficulties at some stage in their lives. My friend has provided personal emergency assistance to them. He has thus far financed seven automobile loans, three graduate school tuitions, countless trips home, and at least three dental procedures. In one case, a student needed several crowns and root canals totaling about $12,000 which were not covered by her dental insurance. The dentist agreed to do what was needed for half the price, and my friend picked up the rest.

If the tax law's progressivity is intended to reduce inequality, governments might consider giving some kind of encouragement to such generosity, including tax breaks. If gifts to other individuals (excluding one's own children) were made fully tax deductible for the giver, but taxable for the receiver, then in any given case there would be no effect on total government tax revenue unless the two persons' tax brackets were different. With progressive taxes, a total government revenue effect would occur only when an individual in a higher tax bracket gave to someone in a lower tax bracket, thus promoting income equality. If so much giving from higher to lower tax brackets went on that total government tax revenue was too low, the government might have to raise tax rates overall to achieve the same level of revenue—but we would have achieved a degree of social equality with the same overall amount of taxes collected.

The principal concern about such a scheme for tax encouragement of interpersonal gifts would be tax fraud, if an individual made a gift and got the money back under the table. The gifts might also be disguised payments for services. But in our informationally advanced society, it should be possible to create surveillance mechanisms to verify large such gifts and to limit tax fraud. All tax systems are subject to fraud, and governments learn to limit it.

There are some who doubt that there should be any such interpersonal gift giving, for doing so may create an expectation of such gifts and therefore some uncomfortable situations. Indeed this may be an unavoidable consequence of the proposal. But offsetting that would be the atmosphere of social connectedness and caring that would be engendered.

Instead in the United States today we have a gift tax. The gift tax was created by the U.S. Congress in 1932 to prevent evasion of the estate tax by those who gave their wealth away to their heirs before their deaths. Gift tax rates mirror those of the income tax, currently up to a maximum of 35%. Currently one can give up to $13,000 annually as a gift to any one individual before that person is requited to pay the gift tax. It should be just the opposite: instead of a gift tax we should have a gift *deduction* from current income, designed to encourage small- to moderate-size gifts to many people, without making it possible for the clever to completely frustrate the estate tax.

To some extent the current tax treatment of contributions already supports a form of such interpersonal giving. Taxpayers are allowed to deduct contributions to religious organizations, and it is no surprise that the biggest single component (35%) of contributions in the United States today is to churches.[18] People typically give to their *own* church. It is not just because they are religious; it is also because they know some of the people who will thus benefit and have a sense of family and connection with them. Such giving allows them to be appreciated by those whom they know. The second biggest category of contributions in the United States is to schools and colleges. Again most people give to their *own* schools, not to others'. And again there is a sense of connection to these people.

The Participation Nonprofit

There could be instituted a new kind of organization that I will call a participation nonprofit corporation. It would be a nonprofit, aimed at a public purpose such as running a hospital, but in a different sense. The participation nonprofit would raise money by issuing shares, but buying shares in it would be a charitable contribution for tax purposes. Selling shares in it would have no tax consequences as long as the proceeds were donated to other charitable causes, such as by buying shares in other participation nonprofits. The shareholder could sell the shares and consume the money from the sale, but such actions would be subject to a substantial tax penalty. The organization would distribute profits to shareholders with the stipulation that they could use their share of the profits only for charitable purposes, including possibly investing in other participation nonprofits. By distributing its profits, the organization would solve the "trapped capital" problem to which I alluded in Chapter 17: the profits would come back to the participation nonprofit itself only if the shareholders saw value in that.

If one donates to a cause, such as a new nonprofit hospital or a new college, by buying shares in a participation nonprofit corporation, the story is not over after one makes the donation, as it is with conventional charitable contributions. One now has a psychological stake, akin to ownership, in the nonprofit. One can look forward to receiving dividends and watching one's stake in the organization grow. One can watch the market price of the nonprofit rise and fall; those price changes are (admittedly imperfect) indicators of the underlying success of the nonprofit. With their dividends, shareholders can even set up their own private foundations (with their names on them), though they cannot consume the dividends without incurring a serious penalty.

If the investment proves highly successful they can use their dividends to underwrite new buildings with their names on them, or they can make other charitable donations with their names attached. They might also be allowed to spend the money on themselves, without incurring a tax penalty, in the case of a certified family emergency. Allowing investing in such a participation nonprofit might be a way to generate more widespread interest in public causes, since it would give people a sense of participation and accumulation, allow for memories of one's past largesse, provide what would in a sense be a "playable game" to occupy time, and allow for more ego involvement in a chosen cause. We saw earlier that the invention of tradable common stock shares in for-profit corporations was an important innovation because, by making investing in companies fun, it increased the amount of capital available to them. The establishment of participation nonprofits may well offer the same advantage.

And yet the participation nonprofit will probably still be viewed by most people, such as patients in a hospital or students at a new school, as a nonprofit, and so they will be likely to have the same goodwill toward it. They may even have greater goodwill, if they are connected to institutional or other shareholders in the participation nonprofit.

Other Ways to Improve the Effectiveness of Philanthropy

Many wealthy people may see a problem with the contribution deduction in its present form, in that donations have to be made every year during the period that one is earning the income to accumulate a fortune. If one does not make contributions regularly each year, one misses the deduction almost completely. If one defers giving, one has paid heavy taxes on the income and does not recoup the past taxes upon finally making a gift. U.S. tax law allows up to a five-year carryforward of deductible contributions, which means that amounts contributed in any year that exceed the percentage-of-income limit can be deducted in subsequent years—but there is no carryback.

Most wealthy people would like to accumulate a huge fortune first and then give it away later when they have had time to think about what they will do with the fortune—time to think carefully about the mark they are making on the world. If marginal tax rates were much higher, we might rule out altogether the possibility of the wealthy accumulating a fortune at the same time they are busy making a living and then undertaking a major philanthropic project like funding a school or research foundation with the accumulated money after they retire. This problem is purely one of timing—and if not addressed, it may make higher-than-current income tax rates seem far more onerous than they would really be.

In fact, current U.S. law allows people to substantially solve this problem, by giving away a significant share of their income while they are young to a private foundation or donor-advised fund, which will accumulate their fortune for them tax-free and then allow them, years later, to choose (within certain limits) how to give it away. (Donor-advised funds are like private foundations without the hassle: they are designed for the general public and even allow people to put their names on their charitable contributions.)

So one may think that donor-advised funds eliminate the timing problem. Even if income tax rates for high-income individuals were raised substantially, wealthy people could still have the satisfaction of accumulating large fortunes (within their private foundations or donor-advised funds, to which we might also add participation nonprofits) and still see their names in the Forbes 400 (if Forbes decides to include such funds in their calculations, which would be a logical step)—even though in effect they would have already given the bulk of their wealth away. Problem solved? Not quite.

Tax provisions on private foundations and donor-advised funds are still not well designed from a behavioral economics perspective. People plainly enjoy accumulating wealth, even if it is only symbolic. Yet at the present time under U.S. law these funds are required to distribute 5% of their assets to qualifying contributions each year (with some exceptions for special projects, but then too only a five-year exception). This means that in most cases increases in the assets of the foundation or fund will be small or nonexistent. And there is a limit—currently 30% of income—for deductions made for contributions to donor-advised funds that delay spending contributions for more than a year.

Something isn't working well with these funds. The five largest donor-advised funds in the United States together have total assets of less than $10 billion, and so they represent about two-hundredths of 1% of the national wealth. Private foundations and donor-advised funds should be allowed to accumulate.

Presumably something could also be done to make these funds more convenient, such as offering a check-off on the tax form that would automatically create a donor-advised fund account to enable a last-minute deduction for the tax filer, thereby dramatically lowering his or her tax liability.

We can imagine other advantages to amassing a large fortune that is dedicated to helping others. For example, there could be a new provision in the law that the founder of a private foundation could withdraw any amount of the money, before it is spent on philanthropy, to pay medical expenses for anyone of the founder's choosing. Paying a family member's (or anyone's) medical expenses directly is not currently considered a deductible contribution. If this were changed, then a wealthy person who had contributed his or her fortune to a private foundation would still be perceived as wealthy and as a pillar of strength on whom others could rely. This change would further encourage giving.

There should be no limitation on the share of income that could be given away—unlike the provisions of current U.S. law, under which contribution deductions are limited to 50% of income (in some situations to 30% or even 20%) and the deduction appears to be in danger of being reduced even further.[19] Moreover, deductions for gifts abroad should also be allowed, as philanthropy knows no borders. Gifts made directly abroad are now deductible in the United States only when the gift is to certain organizations in Canada.

The law could also be changed to permit new kinds of organizations devoted to the public good that may be better able to reward their donors. The benefit corporation, described previously, is an example of such innovation. We need to experiment with such new organizations, and to continually improve their structure in light of our knowledge of human nature and our experience with existing organizations.

Goals and Our Lives

We all need to think more about the ultimate purpose of our wealth. The basic theme of this book is finance as a means for achieving goals. But we have seen that most of us have trouble with the final step of actually realizing a basic goal. We become involved in the steps along the way, and some of us may accumulate large fortunes, only to see our grip weakening as the goal comes into sight, so that the fortunes are never spent constructively.

Psychological research has shown that when people act altruistically, they are happier, less likely to be depressed.[20] Altruistic acts in a social context are an effective antidepressant. Showy houses and luxury cars do not bring happiness. Individual fulfillment depends on a sense of meaning and purpose, and society should act so as to encourage individual actions that reinforce such meaning, including encouraging the giving away of accumulated wealth.

There is a positive externality for all of us in seeing a society in which altruistic acts are common, and so governments should encourage such acts, even if the encouragement might be interpreted by some as appealing to selfish motives. There is often a fine line between selfishness and altruism, but a tax law that encourages people to accumulate wealth in order to gain recognition for giving it away should have the effect of promoting the general sense of a good society.

The real risk, if we do not set up policies that encourage philanthropy, is that many may be left with meaninglessness, individually and collectively. Finance concerns itself with risk management—but not with the risk of meaninglessness. Dealing with that risk is left to our conscience and to our human spirit.

Chapter 29

The Dispersal of Ownership of Capital

The history of financial capitalism is to a substantial extent a history of deliberate government policies to disperse financial interests, to disperse ownership across a wider segment of the population. Such policies have helped democratize finance.

People seldom realize to what extent we live in a society that is structured by financial design to become better and better over time. The history that brought us to certain financial arrangements is often forgotten, and it is useful to remind ourselves of some of that history. Here I offer some examples of past progress that is unseen and unappreciated today.

A modern market economy seems to many observers increasingly to be run by a relatively small number of business leaders who are, by virtue of their financial and general business savvy, excessively influential. To these same observers it may seem at times that the more free-spirited among us will not want to participate in top management at all, for such a role seems to entail a mindset that they find repugnant. The wealthiest and most influential people in our society may come to seem like ensconced feudal lords, lacking in essential humanity, who set the pace for society as a whole. Then the majority of us may feel as if we are mere serfs in a society that puts the ambitious and inhumane at the top.

William O. Douglas, the second head of the SEC and later a U.S. Supreme Court justice, wrote as follows in 1940:

In big business, management tends to become impersonal. The huge aggregations of capital of big business mean that the number of public security holders is large. These investors are largely scattered. Management acquires a sort of feudal tenure as a result of the utter dependence of the public security holders on them. . . . There can be no question that the laxity in business morals has a direct relationship to the size of business. Empires so vast as to defy the intimate understanding of any one man tend to become playthings for manipulation.[1]

Douglas was part of President Franklin D. Roosevelt's New Deal: Roosevelt nominated him to the Supreme Court in 1939. The New Deal was a relatively humanizing social force, even as it retained the real strength and integrity that characterize the best financial solutions.

This loss of a sense of individual participation in society was the concern that occupied Friedrich Hayek in his 1944 book *The Road to Serfdom*. He tended to focus on excessive *government* intervention as the source of the problem, rather than the practices of big business, but he also spoke of government being captured by big business.[2] Excessive reliance on such large controlling entities, Hayek believed, leads to a defeated attitude, the attitude of serfs.

It may seem odd that his major treatise on capitalism was published near the end of World War II, a time when one might think society would have been occupied by much more pressing concerns. But the timing is not as surprising as it might seem, for World War II was also a time of struggle between economic systems, and a time when people wondered how the Nazi leaders could command such outrageous crimes from some of those they governed— even going so far as to carry out the orders that resulted in the Holocaust. Hayek wondered at the deeper underpinnings of support for such a party, or for any organization. The serf mentality of which he spoke was a social phenomenon of the utmost interest.

The modern capitalist system with all of its regulatory machinery may, if power within it does not become too centralized and institutionalized, be *liberating* from just such a serf mentality. If the right rules are in place, they may pave the way for the development of a multitude of creative organizations that can achieve far more than any individual, however free, ever could. The set of rules and assumptions that allow orderly businesses to be initiated and then to proceed represents a kind of social capital that is enabling for creativity.

The dispersal of *information* about the economy and its opportunities across millions of people—with their different situations, different locations, different eyes and ears—is a given. Hayek emphasized this.[3] We need also to facilitate, on top of that arrangement, a dispersal of *control*. This can be done by encouraging broader public participation in shareholding in corporations, or by giving tax preferences to small firms, or by other means to encourage the dispersal of property holding throughout the population.

Collectively we can make a deliberate decision to plan a more broadly based financial capitalism. Such a plan can be compared with traditional communism, which similarly sought to equalize ownership. But that system had control over property, if not its actual ownership, centralized in the government, in the hands of a bureaucracy. This centralized model has been falling out of favor around the world, since such centralization of control does not allow truly broad participation and does not allow people to use their diverse information actively to direct the use of capital.

The term *ownership society*, referring to a society in which citizenship and responsibility are encouraged by the widespread ownership of and control over individual properties, is attributed to President George W. Bush; he popularized the term in his 2004 reelection campaign. It is an expression of the desirability of the democratization of finance. But the idea goes back much further in history than that.

Land Reform

In centuries past, when agriculture constituted the bulk of national product, policies to disperse ownership of capital were concentrated on land. Land reforms that encouraged (or forced) landlords to give up their holdings and that distributed farmland took their impetus from the French Revolution at the end of the eighteenth century, which transferred ownership of land from the ancien régime to individual family farms.[4] Following this example, there were numerous land reforms in the nineteenth and twentieth centuries, in Albania, Bolivia, Brazil, Bulgaria, Canada, Chile, China, Colombia, Croatia, Cuba, Czechoslovakia, Denmark, Egypt, El Salvador, Estonia, Ethiopia, Finland, Germany, Greece, Guatemala, Hungary, India, Iran, Ireland, Japan, Kenya, Lithuania, Mexico, Namibia, Nicaragua, Peru, the Philippines, Poland, Romania, Russia, Slovenia, South Africa, South Korea, Syria, Taiwan, Venezuela, Vietnam, and Zimbabwe.

These land reforms, while sometimes imposed harshly, did usually represent real social progress, and they helped economic growth. For example, the South Korean postwar economic growth miracle has been attributed to that country's land reform and the resulting lessening of income inequality after the Japanese occupiers were expelled with the end of World War II. The South Korean Agricultural Land Reform Amendment Act (ALRAA) of 1950 specified that anyone could own agricultural land but only if he or she actually farmed it, set at three hectares the maximum amount of agricultural land that any one individual could own, and prohibited tenancy arrangements and land-renting. Landlords were forced to sell their lands in exchange for government debt, the land to be redistributed to smallholders.

Even before the ALRAA took effect, after World War II the rich landlords were already selling much of their land to small owners at relatively low prices. The landlords' position in Korean society was growing untenable because they were generally viewed as having been complicit with the Japanese occupiers, and many even began to fear for their personal safety. The end result was that wealth was extracted from the South Korean landlords (in a more peaceful way than in China or North Korea after the communist revolutions there) to lower inequality, effect a modernization of Korean society, and launch that country's economic miracle.[5]

The United States has a long and unusual history of land reform since it had available vast undeveloped public lands. Andrew Johnson, Horace Greeley, and others argued that ownership of one's own farm was healthy for democracy. Their efforts led to the passage of the Homestead Act of 1862, which divided up public lands and sold small farms to individual families. The act was passed during the U.S. Civil War, after southern votes representing the plantation system had been removed from Congress. The rationale underlying northern support for individual small farms was succinctly explained, just before the war, by the *Chicago Press and Tribune:*

> It should be the policy of our government to encourage the multiplication of landed proprietorships. The history of the world proves that the larger the proportion of land-owners in any given country, the greater is the degree of personal liberty, the greater the progress in civilization, and the greater the security of the nation from external attack. Slavery is impossible, as a permanent institution, except where the ownership of the soil is confined almost exclusively to the slave-holding class. . . . A prosperous non-slaveholding class, identified with the country by the ownership of a portion of it, would soon become powerful and dangerous opponents of slavery.[6]

A good part of the sense of equality and common good feeling that exists in America today probably owes its origin at least in part to this democratic nineteenth-century land reform.

Homeownership

Government policies to encourage urban individual home ownership, instead of just farm ownership, tended to come later, as the world became urbanized. These policies have discouraged the development of huge corporations that might have operated rental properties for the general public. Instead we have a large home-owning population in the United States and other more developed countries. This did not happen by accident.

The concept of a "property-owning democracy" was developed by Conservative British member of Parliament Noel Skelton in the 1920s and 1930s. His cause was taken up by Prime Minister Harold Macmillan in the 1950s, with a home building program, and Prime Minister Margaret Thatcher in the 1970s, with a program to sell council houses (public housing managed by local councils) to their renter inhabitants.

In the United States major policies to promote homeownership came in the 1930s with President Franklin D. Roosevelt's New Deal. The Federal Housing

Administration was created in 1934 to provide for government insurance of new mortgages, and the Federal National Mortgage Association (later called Fannie Mae) was created in 1938 to buy mortgages from their originators to support the housing market.

China, with its communist ideology, came late to the ownership society concept. But the Chinese government eventually made homeownership a priority. In 1998 China created a Housing Provident Fund for all its citizens, a compulsory saving plan with employer matching. The government also created an affordable housing program that subsidized construction of low- to moderate-income housing. Associated with these initiatives has been a rapid expansion of the Chinese home mortgage market (although it is still relatively small). As of 2004 total mortgages in China amounted to US$1.6 trillion, or a little over $1,000 per capita. Total mortgage value then was only 5% of total urban residential property value, but it was growing fast.

The idea of encouraging homeownership pops up everywhere. Noel Pearson, an Australian aborigine who has campaigned for the rights of indigenous peoples, in 2004 founded an advocacy organization for them, the Cape York Institute. On their web site we find a plea for public policy to encourage homeownership:

> There is now an inter-generational expectation within Indigenous communities, that governments will provide, maintain, and in the end replace their housing. Like other forms of passive welfare over the past three decades, public housing in Indigenous communities has promoted dependency and passivity. The Institute believes that we must break this dependency and reintroduce personal responsibility. This must entail moving towards home ownership solutions where families make sacrifices to acquire or build a home of their choice and take ongoing responsibility for its maintenance.[7]

Homeownership, in contrast to land ownership or stock ownership, does not usually directly involve people in any specific business. But it has been widely thought of as helping to create a market-oriented psychology that encourages other kinds of property ownership as well, and as encouraging a feeling of participation and equality in society.

In some other countries—notably Switzerland, which recently has had a low homeownership rate (only 35% of households, per its 2000 census, compared with 65% in the United States)—it is apparently the ownership of stocks and bonds that contributes to a feeling of participation. In Switzerland—where the mountainous land is considered a common heritage of all Swiss, and where the banking system and financial sophistication are elements of national pride—it is rather natural that the ownership society would take this form. Swiss laws regarding rentals make the rental market work to a high level of satisfaction among the renters. Because of a high level of confidence in their financial system, the Swiss have not supported government subsidies of their owner-occupied housing.

In other countries—such as Spain, in which over 90% of households owned their own homes before the recent severe financial crisis—the high ownership rate is substantially the result of government policy. Spanish rental policy, instituted after the Spanish Civil War of 1936–39, had made it very difficult to evict renters, and hence few properties in that country are offered for rent. Starting in the 1950s, Spanish laws facilitated the conversion of apartment buildings into condominiums suitable for purchase.[8]

Government policy should not overemphasize homeownership, for the overreaching of the ownership society concept has in the past led to government policies that tried—particularly in certain countries, notably the United States and Spain—to get too high a fraction of the population into homeownership. This in turn helped feed a housing bubble that eventually burst and served as a prime cause of the severe financial crisis that began in 2007. But in general a degree of government support for individual homeownership, particularly targeted at lower-income and marginal households, will contribute to a better society.

Ownership of Investment Portfolios

A real sense of participation in society and the economy may be promoted more broadly by policies that encourage more business-oriented ownership, notably ownership of broad portfolios representing the real productive assets of the country.

Singapore, under Lee Kuan Yew, led the way to an ownership society with its Central Provident Fund, a mandatory saving plan for its citizens, with both employer and employee contributions, that allowed them to purchase both international investments in stocks and bonds and also housing for themselves in Singapore. He reflected: "The CPF has made for a different society. People who have substantial savings and assets have a different attitude toward life. They are more conscious of their strength and take responsibility for themselves and their families."[9]

Defined contribution pension plans, which began in the early 1980s in the United States, also encourage people to become owners of investment portfolios, ostensibly to provide a pension for them, an income in retirement. They do not serve pensioners optimally in their present form, for they leave them open to making mistakes in planning for their retirement. But they do get people involved in financial decision making and allow them to feel more a part of a society that takes so much of its structure from finance.[10]

All of these policies, in many different countries around the world, were efforts to democratize and humanize finance, to make finance serve people and to encourage people to consider themselves participants in a society built on the principles of finance.

Policies That Promote Employee Ownership of Business

Louis O. Kelso (the founder of the private equity firm Kelso & Co.) and Mortimer J. Adler (who created the Syntopicon series of great books), in a pair of best-selling books, *The Capitalist Manifesto* in 1958 and *The New Capitalists* in 1961, presented a plan aimed at achieving more dispersed ownership of business. These books are probably almost totally forgotten today. And yet they have left a legacy of better employee morale.

The books were published at a time when people were troubled about the state of relations between labor and management. In the 1950s, when the labor movement in the United States was gaining strength, there was much concern about the unfortunate "dual loyalty" of workers.[11] It was claimed that no one could be loyal to both labor union and firm. To achieve good morale and high effectiveness in the workplace, it is helpful if the worker feels loyalty to the employer. On the other hand, when there is a contentious labor-management situation, the worker may feel greater loyalty to his or her union. The conflict creates stress for workers and may lead to perplexing ethical quandaries.

There is a basic tribal instinct to be loyal to a group with which one associates on a daily basis. Membership in the group becomes a source of identity. George Akerlof and Rachel Kranton, in their book *Identity Economics*, stress that this identity is fundamental to economic behavior.[12] A psychological experiment they describe randomly divided boys into two groups. The experiment showed that even though everyone knew the groupings were random, there was a dramatic change in the boys' behavior as group identities began to develop: the groups became rivals and the boys became intensely motivated by the rivalry. We form these identity-defining relationships casually, almost randomly, based on who we encounter, and our beliefs then tend to conform gradually to those of the group. Akerlof and Kranton stress that this all makes for a rather absurd element of the human experience.

The development of modern communications technology and means of transportation, and the rise of multinational corporations, have tended to change tendencies toward loyalty in unpredictable ways. The general tendency may be to reduce national loyalties. The automobile allows the formation of separate enclaves of rich and poor. The Internet allows people to define for themselves the subgroup from which they will learn and with which they will communicate every day.

Both of the Kelso and Adler books envisioned changes to our financial institutions that would improve our sense of loyalty to our business colleagues. And while they didn't completely "solve" the problem of dual loyalty, they have helped lead us to a better form of financial capitalism.

The first of the two books was a plea for what are now called employee stock ownership plans (ESOPs), whereby companies encourage their employees to participate in the ownership of the firm by obtaining stock in the firm.

The authors argued that such a plan would motivate employees to work more effectively and help create a capitalist culture.

The ideas in the book may at first have seemed rather unlikely to be implemented, but sixteen years later the U.S. Congress enacted tax incentives for such plans with the Employee Retirement Income Security Act of 1974, which institutionalized the ESOP.

It took many years before serious research was done to see whether the Kelso-Adler proposal for ESOPs had really had any of the intended effects. It has been learned that indeed, as Kelso and Adler predicted, on-the-job shirking is common in businesses everywhere, and that when such plans are introduced they reduce the tendency of workers to shirk. This happens even though rational-person economics implies that ESOPs would have virtually no such effect, except in the tiniest of firms. Under that calculation, each worker would rationally conclude that he or she might as well shirk, even with an ESOP in place, because the positive effects of an individual worker's efforts are divided up over all stakeholders in the enterprise, while the negative feeling of effort is experienced by just the worker, and thus effort has a negative effect on just that worker. Yet apparently, in a firm with an ownership plan, an anti-shirking culture develops.[13] It has also been found that employees of firms with ESOPs have higher wealth overall, perhaps because the ownership plan encourages a more capitalist culture.[14] The intuitive foundations on which Kelso and Adler built their theory were shown to have some validity, based on latter-day behavioral economics research, even though they could not articulate their vision in terms that would have been taken seriously by the mainstream economists of their time.

In their 1961 book *The New Capitalists*, Kelso and Adler proposed a Capital Diffusion Insurance Corporation that would guarantee loans to encourage the founding of small businesses, thereby increasing the diversity of such businesses and allowing for new startups that might someday grow into bigger businesses. This is another proposal that would serve to bring more and more people into the process of financing business, while creating positive externalities in terms of a better business culture.

At the time, this proposal was greeted by some as just another strange idea. But once again Kelso and Adler were simply ahead of their time. Their argument actually convinced some congressional leaders to effect change. The U.S. Small Business Administration (SBA) had been created in 1953 to replace the Depression-era Reconstruction Finance Corporation, and it was then a maker rather than a guarantor of loans. The SBA, in its original form, might well have been shut down because of its excessive quantity of bad loans, which ultimately defaulted, at cost to taxpayers. To follow Kelso and Adler's proposal and involve the public in the selection of loans to be made, it became evident that the SBA should leave the actual lending to the public. Thus the SBA was transformed from a lender into a partial guarantor of small business loans.

Today the public has an incentive to participate in the risk-taking, relieving the taxpayer of the full burden.[15] The activities of the SBA as they are today are useful, but they could be further improved by placing more emphasis on subsidizing the most innovative small business ideas.[16]

Concentration Limits

Competition law, which dates back to ancient times, has long attempted to reduce the power of large monopolies. The development of modern capitalist institutions brought with it newfound opportunities for very large organizations, and in response competition law has become more aggressive in antitrust policies, in breaking up (or preventing the formation of) companies that are so large that they seriously inhibit competition. Lobbyists for these companies will try to derail such efforts and argue that much is lost by such breakups. But there can be many advantages as well.

The current financial crisis has generated calls for preventing the increased concentration of economic power, but so far the response has not been very effective. In the United States the Dodd-Frank Act of 2010 introduced a concentration limit for financial firms: subject to some discretion and with a few exceptions, no financial company may merge with, consolidate with, or acquire another company if the resulting company's consolidated liabilities would "exceed 10 percent of the aggregate consolidated liabilities of all financial companies."[17]

The motivation for creating this concentration limit was ostensibly to reduce the "too big to fail" problem, the concern that some financial companies had become so central to the economy that they would have to be bailed out by the government in the event of pending failure. But this limit plausibly had something to do as well with some of the issues emphasized in this chapter— those of making our financial markets more democratic amidst widespread resentment of the concentration of wealth and power.

This is a significant, though rather weak, limit on the size of financial companies. According to a 2011 study by the U.S. Financial Stability Oversight Council, based on currently available data sources and definitions it is difficult to ascertain just how many financial firms are already near or over this 10% limit; however, there may well be some to which the Dodd-Frank provision would apply.[18]

It may be that the framers of Dodd-Frank settled on a limit of 10% because it seemed just beyond a situation that would require action today. And indeed no actions have been taken, or appear to be in immediate prospect, to reduce the concentration of power in U.S. financial firms.

As an alternative to concentration limits, the government could merely impose an incentive system to discourage large concentrations of power in financial firms. The corporate profits tax in the United States today is progressive; that is, it taxes large corporations at a higher rate. But the tax brackets are set so that only the smallest of firms have lower tax rates. The tax laws could be arranged differently, so as to discourage the formation of really massive financial firms in favor of less-dominant ones. Moreover, as suggested by the Squam Lake Group, capital requirements on large and systemically important financial institutions could be systematically raised.[19]

The Combined Effects of Policies to Disperse Capital

The policies of the past to disperse ownership of farms, homes, and companies are part of the reason we have a sense of equality and participation in our society today. The policies themselves are largely unknown to most people, but they see their effects. We often seem inclined to think that the current ownership structure happened naturally. In fact the widespread ownership of farms, homes, and companies and the various forms of employee participation plans that we see today are all part of a public policy that has as a tangible benefit a significant improvement in public morale. These are not best described as "government plans," for, though they were in fact implemented through government action, the ideas come from the people themselves and in response to popular concerns.

In the future we will need to be vigilant to prevent the concentration of economic power, and we should work to disperse the ownership of capital even further. Doing so effectively and efficiently, so that the net results are beneficial and not destructive of productivity, and in ways that take account of new developments in finance and information technology, will require continuing attention and innovation.

Chapter 30

The Great Illusion,
Then and Now

In 1910 Norman Angell, a British member of Parliament, documented a widespread and dangerous misconception through his best-selling book *The Great Illusion: A Study of the Relation of Military Power to National Advantage*. The great illusion was, in Angell's words, an "optical illusion" that stood as "an all but universal idea": the belief that

> a nation's financial and industrial stability, its security in commercial activity —in short, its prosperity and well-being, depend upon its being able to defend itself against the aggression of other nations, who will, if they are able, be tempted to commit such aggression because in so doing they will increase *their* power and consequently *their* prosperity and well-being, at the cost of the weaker and vanquished.[1]

In short the illusion was that military conquest brings economic advantage. This misconception persisted despite Angell's book and, quite arguably, led to uncompromising and provocative actions by governments, and ultimately to World War I. Despite the fact that the book did not bring about peace, in 1934 Angell won the Nobel Peace Prize for it.

Angell argued that this "universal idea" was without merit, and yet he saw evidence that people deeply believed in it, in numerous speeches, newspaper articles, and books. It was a politically destabilizing meme that had spread throughout society. The idea became widely and uncritically accepted that human nature is inherently warlike—that we should not lament that reality but understand that we who are alive today are descended from the victors

219

in previous wars, and accept that military victory is an expression of human excellence. The idea, and the assumption that other nations thought similarly, led to expectations of future attack and a justification for preemptive strikes—strikes that might start a war.

Today we no longer widely share this once-commonplace illusion. Few people in the twenty-first century think that it would be economically advantageous for Europe to attempt to conquer the United States or the reverse, or for Japan to conquer Korea or the reverse.

But we still suffer from an analogous illusion: an illusion that those in the business world will stand to benefit from business conquest, from aggressive and inhuman business tactics. Thus people *think* that the wealthy in our society —among them the financiers—have a real and genuine incentive to use devious means to attack and subjugate, economically, the majority of the population.

To take a concrete example, people widely assume that it was in Goldman Sachs's interest to deliberately double-deal its clients, as it allegedly did in 2007, urging securities on them that Goldman thought would eventually fail, because the securities were designed to benefit a different client, Paulson & Co.—a fact not disclosed to the clients. At the same time Goldman Sachs was effectively taking short positions in these same securities.[2]

As another example, people widely assume that Countrywide Financial Corporation deliberately issued and securitized mortgages that they believed would ultimately default. It has been claimed that the subprime mortgage collapse that brought on the current financial crisis was a deliberate plot by Countrywide and other mortgage lenders.[3]

There may well have been some moral lapses behind these events, but it is not correct to claim that these institutions acted deliberately in full knowledge of the actual outcome. To the extent that they misbehaved, it was not really in their ex ante interest to do so.

The assumption today, analogous to Angell's great illusion, often seems to be that businesses have a real incentive to behave in an aggressive and evil manner. This assumption, if left unchallenged, will create resentment toward business that will inhibit its proper functioning, thus threatening to slow the advance of the world's prosperity in coming years.

The Great Illusion, 1910

Concerns about the possibility of war were widespread at the time Angell wrote, just before World War I: the arms race among the countries of Europe was taking on alarming proportions. The race created an unsettled psychology throughout the continent. It appeared that every country was arming itself because of a fear of attack by another. But that situation was absurd on its face, since no government was in fact threatening to attack. They were all only talking about defense. The fear of attack came not from their words but from the great illusion.

The great illusion, the belief in the primacy of human aggression, must have seemed plausible to many in the years before World War I and World War II because of a careless and loose extrapolation of Darwin's theory of evolution to the affairs of modern states. Yet the extrapolators of Darwin's theory typically paid little direct attention to his works, and one of the most influential of them, Friedrich Nietzsche, actually labeled himself as "anti-Darwin." But even Nietzsche adopted something akin to a survival-of-the-fittest frame of reference.[4]

Humankind has been in a perpetual state of warfare, it was argued by many at the time, as with all living things. We who are alive today, it was thought, are the survivors of a bitter struggle, and our very intelligence and talents are the result of that struggle.

Angell argued that it would be absurd for any country to attempt to conquer another, for in the modern economy no conceivable economic advantage could accrue from such an attack. Armed warfare may have made sense in ancient times, but no longer. According to the synopsis at the beginning of the 1910 book,

> wealth in the economically civilized world is founded upon credit and commercial contract (these being the outgrowth of an economic interdependence due to the increasing division of labour and greatly developed communication). If credit and commercial contract are tampered with in an attempt at confiscation, the credit-dependent wealth is undermined, and its collapse involves that of the conqueror; so that if conquest is not to be self-injurious it must respect the enemy's property, in which case it becomes economically futile. Thus the wealth of conquered territory remains in the hands of the population of such territory.[5]

Angell emphasized that there is nothing really to be gained by conquering another country because the victor could find little of value that could actually be taken from the conquered. He provided an analysis of the reparations payments imposed by the victor, Germany, on the vanquished, France, after the 1870–71 Franco-Prussian War, and he concluded that, paradoxically, the French who were making the reparations payments fared better than the Germans who were receiving those payments. The problem, as Angell emphasized in a chapter entitled "The Indemnity Futility," was that countries by and large do not have large amounts of gold or other transferable things of value—far too little to pay the huge reparations demanded by the victors in modern warfare. So the reparations must take the form of exports of new goods and services. The paying country must somehow develop a huge export industry, of unnatural proportions, to pay the reparations. Making the payments must entail something like the "dumping" or "unfair competition" that free traders deplore. And receiving the payments drives out the businesses in the same sector in the receiving country, thereby depressing that country's economy. So there can in fact be no benefit to the conqueror:

> For a modern nation to add to its territory no more adds to the wealth of the people of such nation than it would add to the wealth of Londoners if the City of London were to annex the county of Hertford. It is a change of administration which may be good or bad, but as tribute has become under modern economic conditions impossible (which means that taxes collected from a given territory must directly or indirectly be spent on that territory), the fiscal situation of the people concerned is unchanged by the conquest.[6]

Another element of this great illusion is taken up by Angell in a chapter entitled "The Psychological Case for War." Advocates of military aggressiveness argued that military victory, by demonstrating heroism, hardiness, and tenacity, reinforces national morale, and that it has a psychological benefit to the victorious country in stimulating its economy. It is hard to quantify such an effect, but, Angell argued, we do know that against these presumed advantages of a warlike philosophy there is the perpetual burden of maintaining a military force, and of occupying a sullen and angry vanquished country. The resentment of the oppressed ultimately proves so costly, in terms of emotional ambience and risk of future war, as to wipe out the psychological advantages gained from victory. This is the burden of empire, noted many times throughout human history.

Angell's book was for the most part misinterpreted in its time. People thought he was asserting that because the economies of the modern world were so interconnected, war was no longer possible. So the sudden outbreak of World War I in 1914 discredited the book in the eyes of many. It was widely derided and was cited by some commentators as evidence of great naïveté among intellectuals about the real prospect of war in the modern world.

But Angell's book did not actually assert that war was no longer possible. In a 1933 edition of the book, lamenting that the great illusion was still very much with us, Angell explained that he had, when he first wrote the book in 1908, actually suppressed his fears of something like World War I:

> To have given the very first emphasis to the fact that war was certainly coming unless we changed our ideas and our policy, would have had with the ordinary reader of 1908 just one effect—to make him shout for more Dreadnoughts. The author saw and expressed this difficulty. . . . But in clarifying the fact of avoidability he may have allowed an impression of improbability or "impossibility" to grow up in some reader's mind.[7]

As had happened many times before and has happened many times since, even the most thoughtful discussions are curtailed by considerations of their effects on public confidence and the possible results of talking openly about worries for the future.

The Great Illusion as the Ultimate Cause of World War I

The fears generated by the arms race before World War I created a state of mind that led to a startlingly swift descent into war in 1914. There were count-less proximate causes of this descent; we have to drill down to the ultimate causes. The war began with a seemingly minor event, the assassination of Archduke Franz Ferdinand of Austria in Sarajevo by a small fringe group, on June 28, 1914. The assassination would not at the time have seemed significant on a worldwide scale. The assassin, Gavrilo Princip, explained his motives after his capture: "I am a Yugoslav nationalist and I believe in unification of all South Slavs in whatever form of state and that it be free of Austria."[8] Most people around the world, occupied with their own concerns, wouldn't have cared one way or another about his cause, and so it may seem a puzzle that this event was the immediate trigger for World War I.

But a feedback loop took its first turn when Austria demanded that neigh-boring Serbia take action against an underground railroad that supported the terrorists. Serbia, whose relations with Austria were strained, acceded to only some of the demands. Austria in turn invaded Serbia on July 28, 1914. Both countries had military alliances with other countries, who were thus drawn into the conflict. The events drew public attention to long-standing animosities among these other countries as well, and a war fever erupted that proved unstoppable. Politicians, after mobilizing their armies in response to the pub-lic's appetite for war, could not realistically demobilize for fear of the internal political consequences. According to historian Gordon Martel's 2008 assess-ment of the public spirit at the very beginning of that war,

> It may now be difficult for us to imagine a time and a place in which war was not only acceptable but popular. . . . The kind of thinking that led people to re-joice at the prospect of war is now difficult to recapture—but rejoice they did: there was dancing in the streets and spontaneous demonstrations of support for governments throughout Europe; men flocking to recruitment offices, fear-ful that the war might end before they had the opportunity to fight; there was a spirit of festival and a sense of community in all European cities as old class divisions and political rivalries were replaced by patriotic fervor.[9]

That fever pitch was not purely psychological, for it was ultimately informed by an idea—the idea that Angell had called the great illusion, which inspired a genuine feeling of individual self-actualization through war.

The Great Illusion in Business Today

The great illusion lived on long enough in public discourse to pave the way for a second world war, just as Angell had suggested in the 1930s.[10] But by now we are much less afflicted by his illusion—as it applies to nation-states.

Yet we still must deal with the popular notion that corporations and wealthy individuals have an interest in "conquest," just as states were once thought to have. The idea is widely held that extremely wealthy people in our society have an interest as a group in aggressively preventing even the most modest redistribution, through taxes or regulation, that would tend to diminish their extreme wealth.

Amassing a large fortune may seem to many to be a real way to boost one's self-esteem; many of the honors that are routinely awarded for achievement are considered suspect, as they may have been awarded carelessly or for ulterior motives. But we tend to feel that when someone amasses a significant fortune it is proof of some real talent associated with genuine business acumen. There appears to be no "nonsense" about such an undeniable achievement. The winner was not announced by an effete intellectual society or obscure government bureaucrat. But people are admired for such an accomplishment only if they stay within certain limits in their business dealings. Being too zealous in acquiring and defending wealth does not inspire admiration, and so we should not expect most wealthy people to engage in such behavior.

Something similar to the indemnity futility that Angell described between nations also applies between social classes in business. If the wealthy do somehow manage to economically subjugate the majority of the population, thus angering them, what then can the majority still transfer to the wealthy that is of real value to them? Once again, it cannot be gold or other tangible goods, for the subjugated majority will no longer have much of such things. It must take the form of services provided to the wealthy. Yet in providing these services, they would be taking away those industries from the wealthy themselves. The wealthy and the members of their families would lose a sense of involvement and purpose.

The "psychological case for war" that Angell described is another part of the great illusion that is used to argue that people and social classes derive an inherent advantage from having, and maintaining a tight grip on, great wealth. It is true that acquiring great wealth does appear to provide an ego boost to the members of a wealthy family. And, within some limits, it permits them to achieve more by granting them better education and time to devote to pursuits beyond earning a living. But it does not give them a boost in terms of their overall psychological well-being, and it does not appear to motivate them, or their children, to achieve on a higher level.

Such an illusion threatens to halt the very kind of financial development that the world desperately needs. Just as the news media perpetuated Angell's great illusion before the world wars, doing so because it made for an attention-grabbing story, so too are they perpetuating the great illusion today.

The great illusion that Angell discerned was an *idea*—and there can be great danger in ideas, such as this one, that sow mistrust. This particular idea may have, for all practical purposes, caused two world wars. There is similar danger in the idea that people will relentlessly pursue wealth in business, for it too sows mistrust, which in turn diminishes the possibilities for constructive business.

Life Satisfaction

Most of the real satisfaction one gets from business is not really closely related to the level of profit. One derives pleasure from making a fine product or from helping customers, from providing jobs to employees. And one simply enjoys being involved with others in a shared activity and shared business interests.

There is absolutely nothing in financial theory that says that people should value making money to the exclusion of all other rewards. On the contrary, the theory holds that people can have preferences regarding anything and everything, and it is perfectly consistent with people's natural willingness to sacrifice some income for quality of life. It is true that those in fiduciary positions, such as managers of investment funds or businesses, outside of nonprofits or benefit corporations, may be under some obligation to focus exclusively on making money for their clients or shareholders. But even then they are under such an obligation only to the extent that their principals have so informed them.

It may seem hard to believe that one might go into finance for reasons other than making money. It seems that the scorecard for this game is the money earned, and one naturally falls in with the idea that amassing the biggest possible fortune is everything.

But if one looks at the lives of *real* people in finance, the impression one gets is quite different. For example, in his autobiography, John L. Moody, the founder of Moody's Investors Service, spoke of his mission in founding the company. He admitted that he had the dream of making millions, but he also recounted that he was following a "literary or writing bent," even though it may seem implausible that there is anything literary about publishing investment manuals.[11] His motivation wasn't quite profit maximization: it was indulgence of himself in a certain pursuit that gave him personal satisfaction—and this led him ultimately to success in finance.

Many people interested in finance go into regulation. Here there is no sport in making money. Some may be surprised to learn that there are those who actually *prefer* a job in regulation, dealing with finance without the possibility of making a fortune. They find finance inherently interesting and understand that it offers satisfactions other than profit.

The futility of conquest in business mirrors the futility of conquest in war about which Angell wrote. Angell noted that it is impossible to extract much wealth from conquered countries. It is likewise impossible to extract much happiness from wealth that has been earned by antisocial financial means. There is little that one can do personally with a large fortune that is really satisfying, except to give it away. Owning a mansion or mansions is not intrinsically satisfying, as the law of diminishing returns soon sets in. One also suffers a degree of emotional distance from most people, as well as a sense of selfishness and social isolation when one is conspicuously wealthy and not sharing with others, to say nothing of fears about kidnapping or extortion.

And yet there is a common presumption, replicated constantly in the news media, that business is relentlessly selfish—and ready to attack us all, if we ever let our defenses down. This presumption leads to an atmosphere of excessive suspicion, and that atmosphere has some of the same social costs that Angell envisioned.

Just as that great illusion led in substantial measure to the world wars, so too does that same illusion in business lead to economic inefficiency and disappointment. There is a significant role for people of influence, including educators, in working to correct this illusion, and making that correction will be a fundamental step toward building the good society.

Aggression in Life and in Business

A financially sophisticated economy provides an outlet for aggression that is substantially constructive and does not result in loss of human life. That is what Montesquieu wrote about in his *Spirit of the Laws* in 1773: "The spirit of commerce is naturally attended with that of frugality, oeconomy, moderation, labour, prudence, tranquility, order, and rule. As long as this spirit subsists, the riches it produces have no bad effect. The mischief is, when excessive wealth destroys the spirit of commerce; then it is that the inconveniences of inequality begin to be felt."[12] Montesquieu did not have the benefit of knowing Darwin's theory. Nor is it clear how we should understand the word *spirit* in this context. But perhaps we are not far amiss in inferring that he is talking here about a social environment, a unique construction of the human species, that can induce changes in our aggressive tendencies.

Ethologist Konrad Lorenz, in his 1966 book *On Aggression*, concluded that most animals have evolved inhibitions against attacking their own species—inhibitions that prevent unnecessary destruction of the species. The effect of the inhibitions depends on the environment, and throughout the development of species evolution has made these inhibitions work in the environment as it is usually encountered. But alter the environment and these inhibitions may fail to function normally. Lorenz points out, as an example, that even though doves are to us the symbol of peace, if one cages two of them close together, putting them in an artificial environment where they cannot separate from each other, the stronger of the two will torture the other to death, without the arousal of any inhibition.[13]

Another ethologist, Frans de Waal, in his 1990 book *Peacemaking among Primates*, detailed how four different species of primates—chimpanzees, rhesus monkeys, stump-tailed macaques, and bonobos—all separated from humans by millions of years of evolution, have methods of reducing conflict among themselves after an argument—methods that sometimes resemble and sometimes differ significantly from analogous behavior patterns among modern humans. The exact forms of controlled aggression and reconciliation behavior are specific to the species. Chimpanzees tend to uses kisses, putting fingers in one another's mouth, and love bites, while stump-tailed monkeys tend to present their rear ends, followed by genital inspection. But all these behaviors serve a common purpose as "buffering mechanisms" to reconcile conflicting interests.[14] De Waal wonders why patterns of limited aggression, in the context of the patterns of reconciliation that follow aggression, are not seen by more people today as a good thing, worthy of appreciation as promoting a stable and effective society. Unfortunately, these patterns of aggression and reconciliation evolved in small groups, and they do not always function well on a national or international scale: human institutions must be built that exploit these behavior patterns in a constructive manner.

Steven Pinker, in his 2011 book *The Better Angels of Our Nature: Why Violence Has Declined*, reviews a number of studies showing that in the past few thousand years human society has evolved into one that makes better use of these built-in behavior patterns to reduce aggression, and that violence has dramatically subsided since the hunter-gatherer days of our species. He notes that the brain has built-in patterns of aggressiveness. For example, a sudden fit of anger can be artificially stimulated by current to an electrode implanted near the "rage circuit" of the brain, and it can be stopped by merely cutting off the current. The brain even appears to have a program that can launch a rampage, or "forward panic." The program facilitates joining a group to commit carnage against another, vulnerable, group, if a particular circuit is triggered. But Pinker argues that such violence "is not a perennial urge like hunger, sex, or the need to sleep," and that people can go through their entire lives without seeing a forward panic triggered. These "inner demons" can be controlled in a society that encourages "gentle commerce," an "expanding circle" of connections, and other socially constructive institutions.[15]

Modern society is the result of centuries of thinking about how to manage human aggressive tendencies and avoid situations in which people are confronted with others' selfish behavior, resentments become intolerable, and aggression turns into open violence. This progress has done much to sustain financial capitalism, and among its products are restraints on the inconveniences of inequality of which Montesquieu spoke. We have a tax system and a system of public goods provision that work against human aggression leading to vexing inequality—albeit, as we have noted, somewhat unsystematically and haphazardly.

Finance and Conflict Management

Albert O. Hirschman, in his 1977 book *The Passions and the Interests*, traces a history of thought about human evils and of the origin of the concept of capitalism.[16] Hirschman traces the idea that man "as he really is" is driven by passions that often create conflict. There is no escaping these passions. They are part of the natural human condition. Indeed one of the results of these passions is that the history of the world has in large measure been a succession of wars and rebellions. But, Hirschman argues, starting around the 1600s the idea gradually emerged that the best hope for reducing the damage from the unconstrained expression of these passions was to create a situation in which people have interests that countervail these passions. A modern economy, in which complex business interests develop, is just such a means of restraining passions.

Hirschman traces this train of thought from Francis Bacon to Thomas Hobbes to Niccolò Machiavelli to Charles de Montesquieu and to James Steuart. He sees the development of capitalism in terms of a gradual decline in the concept of military glory as an end that might justify the expression of angry passions, and a recognition of the imperfectability of humankind, an understanding that human passions need to be controlled to prevent war. Given this imperfectability, the concept arose of setting up a structure that would provide "countervailing passions," that is, one within which people have "material interests" that work against these passions. Material interests usually means financial interests: ownership of property, of shares, and of bonds, and long-term employment contracts.

Some academic articles have attempted to test the hypothesis that economic interconnectedness helps prevent wars. The political scientists Bruce Russett and John Oneal, in their book *Triangulating Peace*, have presented a statistical analysis of data on wars around the world from 1886 to 1992.[17] They conclude that three variables, measured for any given pair of countries, help explain the likelihood that those countries will be at war: economic interconnectedness, democratic traditions, and membership in international organizations. All three factors help prevent wars, and when all three are at their most favorable, the probability of war is reduced by 71%.

Among these factors, Russett and Oneal found economic interconnectedness to be the most important. Of course, there are difficulties in interpreting just why interconnectedness fosters peace. International economic activity may foster international communications and hence a "transnational identity," to use a term due to political scientist Bruce Cronin, or an "imagined community," to use a term from political scientist Benedict Anderson.[18] The relation could also be spurious: perhaps friendlier countries are more likely to trade with each other in the first place.

But Russett and Oneal have interpreted the effect of economic inter-connectedness, measured by volume of trade flows relative to GDP, as sup-porting the line of thought described by Hirschman. Economic trade creates an interest in maintaining peace. While other interpretations are possible, it appears that trade raises the cost of conflict and thus raises the benefits of maintaining peace.[19]

Montesquieu argued centuries ago that "movable wealth" prevents wars by creating a sudden and intense consequence for any military action. If coun-tries are financially free to invest in each other, and have done so but have the freedom to withdraw their investments, then this situation creates an incentive for the owners of that capital to use their influence to prevent war.

Most studies of the incidence of war have, like Russett and Oneal, used trade flows to measure economic interconnectedness. But another study by Erik Gartzke, Quan Li, and Charles Boehmer found that *financial* inter-connectedness, namely capital flow, is a better predictor of war than any of the factors studied by Russett and Oneal.[20] They showed, using world data for the interval 1951–85, that foreign direct investment as a percentage of GDP helps explain militarized interstate disputes between pairs of countries: the higher the percentage, the lower the probability of a dispute, even after con-trolling for the variables used by Russett and Oneal.

Financial interconnectedness may help prevent war for deeper reasons than those associated with the perceived risk to capital movements. Financial interconnectedness provides another outlet for aggressions, a civilized stage for the playing out of aggressive impulses and an environment in which exposure to risk is carefully chosen by each player, not determined arbitrarily by a military commander. Creating a large and varied playing field for busi-ness may be like giving Lorenz's two doves, closely caged together and fighting as a result, a larger environment, one in which their conflictual tendencies have space to roam. Thus financial development may lead to a kinder and gentler—if not altogether kind and gentle—society.

With the development of modern weapons of mass destruction, the cor-responding development of means for limiting aggression becomes an impera-tive. It is not unrealistic to suppose that we can achieve such a mechanism, and that we will achieve it by improving financial capitalism, democratizing and humanizing it, and putting a final end to the "great illusion" and its consequences.

Epilogue:
Finance, Power, and Human Values

There is one more aspect of financial capitalism, not fully dealt with in this book so far, that bothers many people deeply. And that is the economic power that some in the financial community attain. Their power in itself rankles. It offends our sense of participation in a society that aspires to respect, appreciate, and support everyone. The pursuit of power that so often seems to drive financial capitalism seems contrary to the concept, promoted in this book, that finance is all about the stewardship of society's assets.

If one searches the bookseller Amazon.com today for the phrase "wealth and power," one finds that almost eighty-five thousand books come up.[1] People may be reading these books to learn how to *achieve* wealth and power, but a good fraction of the books seem to regard the existence of the wealthy and powerful as a scandal that deserves our contempt.

Yet part of the reason successful societies develop power elites is that they need a leadership that has the power to get things done. We have to make it possible for a relatively small number of people—a management—to use their personal judgment to decide on the direction of our major activities. One of the themes of this book has been that despite rapid advances in information technology, we are still just as dependent as ever on the judgment of individual human beings. The faculties of "complex communication" and "expert thinking" that Levy and Murnane found to have survived the information technology revolution are needed as much as ever for coordination of the economy, and a system of financial capitalism will eventually imbue those in possession of such faculties with wealth and power.

But there is still a reason that the level of resentment of the wealthy and powerful is so high: a free capitalist system can support an equilibrium in which some kinds of social *conspiracy* pay off. George Akerlof, in his 1976 article "The Economics of Caste and of the Rat Race and Other Woeful Tales," has provided an economic theory of the human tendency for certain social groups to form a sort of business conspiracy against outsiders.[2] He takes the caste system—most notorious in traditional India, but in fact to some degree a part of human society everywhere—as a long-standing example of this. People who belong to a higher caste realize the immense economic advantage provided by their membership in that caste. Fearful of compromising that status, they adhere to the caste's social norms—which include ostracizing fellow caste members who fail to adhere to the norms. They favor their own caste in business and reject those who do not belong to the caste or who *do* belong but flaunt its norms by offering jobs and business to outsiders. Akerlof's point was that an economic equilibrium with castes can be stable, and that no business that flaunts caste norms can outcompete the caste businesses, so there is nothing to upset the equilibrium.

Business communities can be caste-like if there is a suitable culture and there are leaders who encourage exclusionary behavior. Those who have gained admittance to such a community value their connections and favor others in the caste in their business activities and financial dealmaking. In modern society a "caste" may be defined in terms of connections to a specific business culture, or in racial or sexual terms, or it may take form among graduates of elite colleges. If one is in a position of power and uses this opportunity to make an important deal with someone who is not connected with the business group, a member of a minority group, a woman, or merely a nondescript outsider, this behavior may cause one to lose power or even become an outcast. So, instinctively, one shuns outsiders and reconfirms the existing concentration of wealth and power.

But these are problems that we associate with finance only because advanced finance is used as a tool by some who wish to preserve their special status. It is not the financial tools themselves that create the caste structure, though their mechanisms are part of the equilibrium. The same financial tools can also, if suitably designed and democratized, become a means to break free from the grip of any caste equilibrium. Truly democratic finance can enable one to escape outcast status.

Financial capitalism is a work in progress. It is not yet perfected, but it is gradually improving. As we have seen, it is defined by a long list of financial practices and specific roles and responsibilities for people within those practices. Watching most of these people in operation from day to day, one comes to feel that in our modern society caste-like behavior has been much attenuated.

Even the caste system itself has never been accepted by the Buddhist, Christian, and Muslim religions, though caste-like behavior nonetheless continues among many of their adherents. It has survived in the Hindu religion, at least in some of its schools of thought, which have incorporated the notion of caste into their fundamental concepts, so caste loyalty is still very much alive. But even there the system—which was deplored by Mahatma Gandhi and other spiritual leaders—is now declining.

The same distaste for castes or their analogues was promoted by Vladimir Lenin in Russia, Kemal Atatürk in Turkey, Yukichi Fukuzawa in Japan, Sun Yat-sen and Mao Zedong in China, Eva Perón in Argentina, and Nelson Mandela in South Africa. These thought leaders couldn't be more different from each other, but together they provide evidence of a worldwide trend that finds castes or their analogues repugnant. Just as these beliefs represent a trend toward greater social enlightenment, there is a parallel trend toward enlightenment about caste-analogues in the business world.

I have been teaching at Yale University for some thirty years. Even my own university has seen a gradual transformation over the centuries from a training center for elite American families to an educational institution serving the people of the world. It has also become a financially sophisticated institution, given its success in investing its endowment. It is private and internationally focused, not connected with the U.S. government—a nonprofit, with its own goals. Those goals are substantially social and benevolent, and reflective of the views of a unique intellectual community.

The concept of an aristocracy or "high society," so strong in the nineteenth century, is fading around the world. The *Social Register* is a publication listing the wealthy and socially prominent families in the United States. Inclusion in it was once a coveted symbol of membership in the elite. Today it is largely a list of the descendants of the same families who were wealthy and prominent a century ago, and it has largely been forgotten by mainstream society.[3] Much the same has happened to *Burke's Peerage* in the United Kingdom and its European counterpart, the *Almanach de Gotha*, which ceased publication in 1944.[4] In China the national records of degree-holding literati and the local gazetteers died out before the end of the Qing dynasty in 1912. There is a more egalitarian spirit abroad in the world, and this spirit is supported by democratized finance.

Partly it is the presumption, the arrogance, that accompanies economic power that rankles. And the fact that so many people seem to admire the wealthy and powerful bothers us. Why do people think the wealthy are so special? Even presidents wonder about that. Franklin D. Roosevelt once said,

> I am simply unable to make myself take the attitude of respect toward the very wealthy men which such an enormous multitude of people evidently feel. I am delighted to show any courtesy to Pierpont Morgan or Andrew Carnegie or James Hill, but as for regarding any of them as, for instance, I regard . . . Peary, the Arctic explorer or Rhodes the historian—why I could not force myself to do it even if I wanted to, which I don't.[5]

Most of us might think that Roosevelt himself was rich. After all, in the 1940s his family was the most prominent of all in the *Social Register*, with no less than a page and a half of entries.[6] But he was not among the extremely rich, and apparently he did not *feel* that he was one of them either.[7] He seems to have considered himself at the same distance from these people that most of us do, and this mindset must have been a factor in his New Deal policies, which helped democratize U.S. financial markets.

At times we seem to be stuck in an economy that arbitrarily elevates a small number of the undeserving and forces the rest of us to pamper and flatter them. Resentment of such circumstances can suddenly build up to an intense level. For example, in 2011 the board of the Miami Art Museum announced that the museum would be renamed the Jorge M. Pérez Art Museum of Miami-Dade County in recognition of a donor, a real estate developer, who had given $35 million to the museum in the form of his personal collection of Latin American art, valued at $15 million, and a pledge of another $20 million.[8] A storm of protest followed. The museum had been funded mostly by tax-payers, and a $220 million capital campaign relying on numerous small donors was under way. It appears that the acknowledgment to Mr. Pérez was mis-applied. Perhaps the board should have offered only to name a wing of the museum or an auditorium within the museum after him, and then refused his gift if that was not enough for him. The granting of recognition in exchange for gifts has to be handled sensitively.

But we are usually not so sure that we bear any resentment toward such wealthy donors, for sometimes they *do* seem deserving. Often we set aside our social comparison processes because these donors do not seem in any way comparable to ourselves, and sometimes we imagine that we or our children could actually be as successful as they are

It has always been a source of satisfaction to me that Yale University, where I teach, has not followed a policy of selling naming rights to the high-est bidder. For example, the names of all twelve of its residential colleges are those of distinguished alumni, not merely wealthy donors who "bought" their way onto the colleges' walls. The Yale Law School and the Yale School of Management are not named after anyone—yet. If one or the other is someday named after a philanthropist donor, there will have to be general agreement within the university community on the worthiness of that person.

Part of this acceptance of wealthy donors is just the natural human willing-ness to live and let live. Each of us has other ways of maintaining self-esteem besides achieving wealth. So we want an economic system that allows for the attainment of human potential in various forms; we want it to be basically fair. Most of us will choose not to try to get rich, and we will pursue meaning in our lives in our own ways. We realize that we can't build an economic system that allows most of us to be prosperous and healthy and able to pursue our own individuality without producing some unusually successful, and possibly arrogant, people

The democratization of finance entails relying more on effective institutions of risk management that have the effect of preventing random redistributions of power and wealth—a system of financial contracts. Finance is supposed to *reduce* randomness in our lives, not increase it. To make the financial system work well, we have to further develop its inherent logic, its own ways of making deals among independent and free people—deals that leave them all better off.

The democratization of finance as spelled out in this book calls for an improvement in the nature and extent of participation in the financial system, including awareness of fundamental information about the workings of the system. The public needs to have reliable information, and that can only be provided by advisers, legal representatives, and educators who see their role as one of promoting enlightened stewardship. When people can benefit from such help, they will come to feel less strongly that our economy is run by a power elite. At present most people have little or no such information. Instead they are routinely confronted by salespeople for financial products, who have inadequate incentive to tell them what they really need to know. But it could be different, under a truly enlightened system of financial capitalism.

We have seen that some government interventions are needed, including redistributions through a progressive income tax, and this could be done more deliberately and judiciously than at present, without raising alarms that wealth might be unfairly confiscated. There needs to be a social safety net, and this safety net has to be continually improved and reworked. But under financial capitalism many of our best protections, and inspirations, come not directly from the government but from our own private financial arrangements. The government can merely be a facilitator.

The democratization of finance works hand in hand with the humanization of finance. To that extent it is important that finance be humane, and that it incorporate our increasingly sophisticated understanding of the human mind into its systems, models, and predictions. The rise of behavioral economics and neuroeconomics in recent decades provides a foundation for such an approach, for understanding how people really think and act. People are not inherently and uniformly loving to their neighbors, but our institutions can be changed to reward the better side of human nature.

One of these better sides is the philanthropic impulse, and the tendency, at least in the right social environment, for wealthy people to give much of their wealth away constructively. As we have seen, such a tendency ought to be considered central to financial capitalism. The gifts of the wealthy might in some respects be self-serving or motivated by ego, and they may in some cases generate resentment rather than gratitude, but financial capitalism makes full sense only when we recognize the importance of their gifts.

A problem with philanthropy is that, in the words of Craig Calhoun, president of the Social Science Research Council, there is a "loss of dignity for workers and citizens to feel they are dependent on charitable gifts—rather than on protections rightly available to them."[9] Yes indeed, the financial power that some achieve is resented, even if they eventually give away much of the wealth from which that power derives. But wealth accumulation followed by charity will still play a fundamental role in the good society, for, as we have seen, allowing or even actively encouraging people to amass wealth and give much of it away creates a system that motivates them to do good things. The loss of dignity that Calhoun notes can be minimized, and it may be more than offset by the overall beneficial results of such a system.

This conclusion is perhaps more sobering than inspiring. From what we know of human nature, we must continue to perfect a system that provides outlets for people's aggressive nature, that allows them to be egotistical. The system must also give them the opportunity to express their better natures at some point in their lives, for the good of society as a whole.

In my Financial Markets class, I ask students to read the philosopher Peter Unger's 1996 book *Living High and Letting Die*.[10] The book remarks at the widespread indifference—not just among the rich, but among the majority of the population—to the true suffering of poverty-stricken people we do not see every day. Unger tells us that it is not so easy for those of us in developed countries—or in the advanced parts of less-developed countries—to justify this neglect. He takes apart the moral arguments we use to justify this indifference, concluding that they are self-serving and specious. However, there is something futile about his exhortations, for relatively few people read Unger's book or change their behavior after having heard his message.

Other philosophers have taken the view not only that it is futile to ask people to be charitable, but also that human nature is essentially focused on a quest for power. Friedrich Nietzsche was very influential in promoting this view, and he was an inspiration for aggressors in both World War I and World War II. He wrote in *The Will to Power* (1901) of his theory

> that the will to power is the primitive form of affect, that all other affects are only developments from it; that it is notably enlightening to posit *power* in place of individual "happiness" (after which every living thing is supposed to be striving): there is a striving for power, for an increase of power;—pleasure is only a symptom of the feeling of power attained . . . that all driving force is will to power, that there is no other physical, dynamic or psychic force except this.[11]

Nietzsche seems to a modern ear almost to be saying that the brain is hardwired for a lust for power.[12] However, he overstates his case: neuroscience shows many patterns of behavior in the brain, including altruistic impulses, which cannot all be derived from any unitary "psychic force."[13]

One singularly important human impulse, which Nietzsche did not seem to appreciate but that is emphasized by Adam Smith in his book *Theory of Moral Sentiments*, is not a desire for power per se but a desire for *praise*.[14] We see this desire plainly in the behavior of the youngest children and the oldest and weakest people, those with no hope of attaining "power" over others.

There is an enormous literature in modern psychology confirming the importance of self-esteem. But Smith gave his discussion of the desire for praise a different slant, one perhaps more closely aligned with the contemporary psychological literature on essentialism,[15] and one still not as appreciated today as it ought to be. Smith wrote that in mature people the desire for praise is transformed into a desire for *praiseworthiness*:

> The desire of the approbation and esteem of those we live with, which is of such importance to our happiness, cannot be fully and intirely contented but by rendering ourselves the just and proper objects of those sentiments, and by adjusting our own character and conduct according to those measures and rules by which esteem and approbation are naturally bestowed. . . . We are pleased not only with praise, but with having done what is praise-worthy.[16]

He seems almost to be saying that this craving is inherent in the human psyche and that our brain wants to categorize the praise we receive by its essential truth, by the real category of people into which it places us. Smith notes that most people would find it unsatisfying to be praised by mistake, for something they did not do. No one is satisfied merely to *look* praiseworthy. One wants to *be* praiseworthy. This is an aspect of human nature that is essential to the success of our economic system.

It is human to view a forged painting in entirely different terms than a genuine one, even though in many cases no one but an expert could tell the two apart. One might think that we would be just as happy to have a nice forgery hanging on the wall—after all, it gives us the same visual gratification. But we most certainly are not. In the same way, one does not want to be a forged *person*. Even criminals who commit frauds and violent crimes probably do not either. They merely imagine that they are praiseworthy within the confines of a moral philosophy that they perceive as sharing with their social group.

Economic development is in substantial measure the development of a social milieu in which it is harder and harder to find others who will truly feel that corrupt behavior is actually praiseworthy.

Pablo Escobar, the notorious Colombian drug lord, had hundreds of public figures, including a presidential candidate, assassinated, and he even had a commercial passenger airliner bombed, killing 110 people. When he was finally hunted down and killed by Colombian security forces in 1993, his mother, Hermilda Gaviria, demonstrated a strong conviction that her son, however brutal, was a good man because of what he had done for his family and the poor people in his community. At his funeral, amidst adoring throngs of his supporters, she said, "Pablo, you're in heaven, and the people acclaim you. The people love you. You have triumphed, Pablo."[17] Escobar probably did have a generous side. Had his business been legal and run within a system of financial capitalism, his aggressive instincts might have been channeled into mostly productive directions.

When a society is fragmented into fiefdoms run by primitive warlords, it is easier to feel praiseworthy for one's antisocial activities. The same society may in time evolve to a higher level at which the warlords are gone, but the government and business sectors remain filled with corruption, bribery, and caste-like behavior. Once again, those involved may still feel praiseworthy because there is a viewpoint—which they view as well entrenched in their society—that the laws they are breaking are meant to be broken and that one must do so to support one's friends and family.

As we mature we come to have the inner sense that we are praiseworthy, and not just superficially so. That, as Adam Smith observed, is a fundamental aspect of human nature that makes human society, and the economy, work as well as they do.

Ultimately, a well-constituted financial capitalism creates a safe venue for power struggles without violence. Achieving such a system requires appropriate innovations that humanize finance, taking account of our increasing knowledge from behavioral economics and neuroeconomics. There is no known economic system that can perfect aggressive human impulses—but they can be softened.

Financial institutions and associated regulations are like the rules of war. They lessen the unnecessary damage from human aggression, and they work to encourage the expression of other, more charitable, human impulses. We have seen that alternative economic systems work less well than a developed financial capitalism in their handling of the more difficult aspects of human nature.

Before modern financial capitalism, power was wielded in much more stark ways. For example, throughout most of human history, hostage exchange was used to guarantee agreements between governments.[18] A king might be forced to give up his son to spend years in the land of a rival leader, with the understanding that the son would be killed if the king did not live up to a treaty or other bargain. Because of the outrageous inhumanity of such a practice, it is now eschewed by respectable governments the world over.

Many of us will remember Brendan Behan's 1957 play *The Hostage*, which tells the story of an eighteen-year-old British soldier who is taken hostage by the Irish Republican Army. He strikes up a romance with an Irish woman of the same age who has been given the job of taking care of him in captivity—

and then he has to be killed. The play vividly reveals the inhumanity of war and its tactics.

But modern finance has not done away with all forms of hostage exchange to seal deals. The term for modern-day hostage exchange is *collateral*, and the hostages are financial assets instead of people. The practice was elevated to a high level before the severe financial crisis that began in 2007, with the widespread use of repurchase agreements, or repos, to carry financing farther forward. Even the home mortgage is in essence a hostage exchange, one in which the home (and the sense of equilibrium and well-being it provides to its inhabitants) is the hostage. The foreclosure on a house for failure to make the mortgage payments has its human consequences too, and it may lead to tragedies not entirely unlike that described in Behan's play. But the home mortgage could not have been made in the first place without such a collateral arrangement.

Many of our hopes for the future should be pinned on further development of the institutions representing financial capitalism. We are easily dazzled today by advances in information technology, and these advances can certainly interact positively with financial innovations. But the advances in our economic institutions may ultimately be more important than those in our hardware and software. The financial system is itself an information-processing system—one built out of human, rather than electronic, units—and the field of artificial intelligence is nowhere close to replacing human intelligence.

The key to achieving our goals and enhancing human values is to maintain and continually improve a democratic financial system that takes account of the diversity of human motives and drives. We need a system that allows people to make complex and incentivizing deals to further their goals, and one that allows an outlet for our aggressions and lust for power. It must be a system that redirects the inevitable human conflicts into a manageable arena, an arena that is both peaceful and constructive.

Notes

Preface

1. Videos of the complete set of lectures for my course Economics 252, Financial Markets, can be found on http://oyc.yale.edu/economics and a number of other web sites that collect such lectures. The lectures for 2008 and 2011, two different versions of the same course, are both available free to the public. When they are fully up on the site, the 2011 lectures (which were given while I was writing this book) will include problem sets and their answers, final exams and their answers, and self-scoring questions and answers. However, there is no provision for obtaining credit at Yale for taking this course online.

2. National Commission on the Causes of the Financial and Economic Crisis in the United States (2011): 188.

3. This trend, visible in many individual countries, has been offset for the world as a whole by the rise of the emerging countries. See Sala-i-Martin (2006).

4. Smith (1776).

Introduction: Finance, Stewardship, and Our Goals

1. Edwards (1938).

2. Nicolas Sarkozy, from his speech at the symposium "New World, New Capitalism," Paris, January 8, 2009, http://www.gouvernement.fr/gouvernement/ouverture-du-colloque-nouveau-monde-nouveau-capitalisme.

3. Tony Blair, from his speech at the symposium "New World, New Capitalism," Paris, January 8, 2009, http://www.tonyblairoffice.org/speeches/entry/speech-by-tony-blair-at-the-new-world-new-capitalism-conference/.

4. Yavlinsky (2011): 48.

5. http://www.imf.org/external/pubs/ft/weo/2011/01/, Figure 1.6 data, "Global Outlook."

6. Marx (1906): Volume 1, Chapters 13 and 26, pp. 365, 785–86, 786.

7. Duflo (2011): 4.

8. Government subsidies for small businesses are used today to help solve the problem. Social programs to provide early education have been the subject of some experimentation, and effective methods of developing talent among the poor are starting to be implemented. See Heckman and Carneiro (2003).

9. A living history of this revolution can be seen on my behavioral finance web site (http://www.econ.yale.edu/~shiller/behfin/index.htm), which shows a list of the seminars that Richard Thaler and I have organized since 1991, and my behavioral macroeconomics web site (http://www.econ.yale.edu/~shiller/behmacro/index.htm), which shows a list of seminars that George Akerlof and I have organized since 1994. Books about behavioral economics include Shleifer (2000), Shefrin (2007), and Thaler and Sunstein (2008).

10. Laird (2009).

11. http://www.research.ibm.com/deepqa/deepqa.shtml.

12. Levy and Murnane (2005).

13. Gilpin and Wallace (1905).

14. U.S. National Income and Product Accounts, Table 1.14, "Gross Value Added of Domestic Corporate Business," http://www.bea.gov/national/nipaweb/SelectTable .asp?Selected=Y. This figure excludes many finance-related activities, which are not directly part of financial corporate business.

15. According to the U.S. Bureau of Labor Statistics, 20.3% of the total employed U.S. population in 2008 was engaged in finance and insurance (activities related to credit intermediation, plus other investment pools and funds, insurance agencies and brokerages, other insurance-related activities, and insurance and employee benefit funds). National Employment Matrix, http://www.bls.gov/data/#employment.

16. Food services: Purchased meals and beverages was $528 billion or 3.7% of GDP in 2009. National Income and Product Account Table 2.4.5, "Personal Consumption Expenditures by Type of Product," http://www.bea.gov/national/nipaweb/TableView .asp?SelectedTable=70&Freq=Year&FirstYear=2009&LastYear=2010.

17. Jayadev and Bowles (2006) also report international estimates excluding police and private security personnel (for which they were unable to find reliable data in many countries). By this definition, the United States ranks quite high in terms of guard labor as a fraction of the population, but even the countries with the lowest fraction of guard labor, notably the Scandinavian countries, still have about half the U.S. level of guard labor.

18. *The Federal Reporter: With Key-Number Annotations . . .*, Volume 160, p. 467, http:// books.google.com/.

19. Ibid., p. 472.

Chapter 1. Chief Executive Officers

1. Long (1983).

2. "Romneys Reported $3 Million Income from 1955 to 1966," *New York Times*, November 26, 1967, p. 46.

3. Iacocca (1984).

4. Iacocca said afterwards that he had only "kidded with" reporters when he expressed interest in running. Ibid., p. 291.

5. French et al. (2009).

6. Dodd-Frank Act, H.R. 4173-579, Section 954.

7. Bebchuk and Fried (2006): 4.

8. Hellman and Puri (2002).

9. Khurana (2004).

10. Djilas (1983 [1957]).

11. "In fact, the Party committees are extremely active in their 'protection of the stock-holding interest,' far more than is the case of their counterparts in American business. With the duty and obligation of 'supervision' over industrial management, they have in fact injected themselves deep into the management function." Granick (1960): 203.

12. "Both in Russia and in the United States, managerial incentives are very strong. Since top-management posts are not restricted to candidates qualifying through family or friendship connections, junior executives have opportunities for major advancement. Income differences are sharp, and promotion up the managerial ladder can lead to sharp rises in income." Ibid., p. 130.

Chapter 2. Investment Managers

1. Gruber (1996).

2. Bodnaruk and Simonov (2011).

3. Redleaf and Vigilante (2010): 8.

4. Milgrom and Stokey (1982).

5. Grossman and Stiglitz (1980).

6. This 14.2% is based on a geometric average of gross returns, as it should be.

7. Chevalier and Ellison (1999).

8. Li et al. (2008).

9. That is, among the individuals inducted into the army between 1982 and 2001, those who had higher IQ scores had higher Sharpe ratios for their 2000 portfolios, controlling for other factors, reflecting greater exposure to small-cap and value stocks and better diversification. Grinblatt et al. (2011).

10. Kat and Menexe (2003).

11. Kaplan and Schoar (2005).

12. Berk and Green (2004).

13. Bogle (2009): 47.

14. Levine (1997).

15. French (2008).

16. Goetzmann et al. (2002).

17. Dugan et al. (2002).

18. Dugan (2005).

19. Acharya et al. (2010).

20. Kaufman (2005): 313.

21. Bernasek (2010): 48.

Chapter 3. Bankers

1. Diamond and Dybvig (1983) lay out the issue of bank runs as a problem of multiple equilibria in a model of banks as creators of liquidity, thereby providing both a clear rationale for the existence of banks and an understanding of their vulnerabilities.

2. http://fraser.stlouisfed.org/publications/bms/issue/61/download/130/section10 .pdf, Table 130.

3. There were some forms of capital requirements before 1982, but no national systematic and regular enforcement of them for banks until then. See Gorton and Winton (1995).

4. Akerlof and Romer (1994).

5. Mayer (1990) and Mishkin (1996).

6. Gorton (2010): Chapter 5.

7. Gorton (2010) argues that the Federal Reserve was mistaken to have stopped calculating and publishing the M3 measure of the money supply, which included some repurchase agreements, in 2006, just before the severe financial crisis that began in 2007. They should instead have expanded the coverage of repurchase agreements in M3, which might have helped them see the origins of the speculative bubbles and the risks of a crisis.

8. This trend was seen long before the beginnings of the financial crisis in 2007. See Marcus (1984).

9. Yunus (2003).

10. Karlan and Zinman (2011). Banerjee and Duflo (2010) report that microcredit has numerous effects, including promoting self-control and saving on the part of the borrowers.

11. Bucks et al. (2009): Table 6B, p. A18.

12. Barr (2004).

13. Blank and Barr (2009).

Chapter 4. Investment Bankers

1. Malmendier (2005: 38) quotes Cicero referring to "partes illo tempore carissimae" (shares that had a very high price at that time).

2. "Modern Banking in Europe," *Bankers' Magazine and Statistical Register* 14(3): 183–214 (1864), p. 188.

3. Seavoy (1972): 89.

4. Moss (2004).

5. Myers (1984).

6. Fama and French (2005).

Chapter 5. Mortgage Lenders and Securitizers

1. Park (2011). Of course, the market value of these securities took a greater hit because of the possibility of more losses in the future. The U.S. Financial Crisis Inquiry Commission, in its final report, emphasized that 83% of Moody's Aaa-rated mortgage-backed securities tranches were eventually downgraded to lower ratings—downgrades that affected their market price. But downgrades do not necessarily represent much in the way of losses because of actual defaults. National Commission on the Causes of the Financial and Economic Crisis in the United States (2011): xxv.

2. A lucid account of the nature of the disparity between actual default losses and market turmoil can be found in a review by Gary Gorton (2011) of books by Michael Lewis (2010) and Gregory Zuckerman (2009). See also Gorton and Ordoñez (2012).

3. Some mortgage securities had also been issued by the Government National Mortgage Association (Ginnie Mae) as early as 1968. See Fabozzi and Modigliani (1992).

4. Acharya et al. (2011).

5. Ibid.

6. Canada has an entity similar to Fannie Mae and Freddie Mac, the Canada Housing and Mortgage Corporation (CHMC), which insures mortgages and buys pooled mortgages and resells them to the public as its bonds. It is not bankrupt, as there was no comparable collapse in Canadian home prices, but the possibility that there could be problems with CHMC in the future, like the problems experienced by Fannie Mae and Freddie Mac, has been the subject of some concern in Canada. The Japan Housing Finance Agency also pursues mortgage securitization, but on a relatively small scale. In much of the rest of the world, although there has been some limited attempt at mortgage securitization, investors have mostly held mortgages indirectly by owning shares in the mortgage originators.

7. Franco Modigliani and Merton Miller (1963) assumed that investors did not have to expend any resources to acquire information about the assets they invest in. George Akerlof shared the 2001 Nobel Prize in economics for a 1970 article that detailed how information asymmetry sometimes prevents markets from existing.

8. Akerlof (1970).

9. Hill (1997).

10. National Commission on the Causes of the Financial and Economic Crisis in the United States (2011): 196.

11. Shiller (2008).

12. Davis (2006) and Caplin et al. (1997).

Chapter 6. Traders and Market Makers

1. Montesquieu (1773 [1748]): Volume II, Book XX, Chapter II, p. 2.

2. Montague (2007): 119.

3. O'Reilly et al. (2002).

4. It has been discovered that some dopamine neurons, which are part of an anatomically distinct second dopamine system, are stimulated by aversive, rather than rewarding, events. See Brischoux et al. (2009).

5. Vickery et al. (2011): 166.

6. Schultz et al. (1997).

7. Schultz (1998). See also Glimcher (2011).

8. Compare Brickley (1983) and Schultz (1998).

9. "Commercial Summary," *The Sun* (Baltimore), February 13, 1847, p. 4.

10. U.S. Commodities Futures Trading Commission and Securities and Exchange Commission (2010). For broader perspectives, see Melamed (2009).

11. Berg et al. (2008).

12. Wolfers and Zitzewitz (2004).

13. The Eurozone HICP futures settle on the harmonized Index of Consumer Prices, http://www.cmegroup.com/trading/interest-rates/interest-rate-index/eurozone-hicp-futures_contract_specifications.html. The CME Group nonfarm payroll futures were delisted on December 5, 2011. See also Labuszewski et al. (2010).

14. Thomsen and Andersen (2007).

15. The real estate futures settle on the S&P/Case-Shiller Home Price Indices, http://www.cmegroup.com/trading/real-estate/. See John Dolan's homepricefutures.com.

16. See Fabozzi et al. (2010) for a discussion of options on real estate prices.

Chapter 7. Insurers

1. Chen and Ravallion (2007).

2. Townsend (1994).

3. Barnett and Mahul (2007).

4. Shiller (2003).

5. Scharlach and Lehning (2012).

6. O'Leary (2012).

7. Jaffee et al. (2008) and Kunreuther and Useem (2010).

8. Shiller (1994, 2003, 2008).

Chapter 8. Market Designers and Financial Engineers

1. Shapley and Scarf (1974) and Roth et al. (2005).

2. Kremer and Glennerster (2004).

3. Horesh (2008).

4. "A New Matrimonial Plan," *New England Galaxy and United States Literary Advertiser*, May 13, 1825, pp. 8, 396.

5. "New Matrimonial Plan," *The Port-Folio*, November 7, 1801, pp. 1, 45.

6. Gale and Shapley (1962).

Chapter 9. Derivatives Providers

1. Dixit and Pindyck (1994).

2. Aristotle (1977): 16.

3. Milgrom and Stokey (1982).

4. Arrow (1964).

5. Ross (1976): 75.

6. MFAO in Spain first began trading olive oil futures in 2006.

7. Gross (1982): 166, as quoted in Shefrin and Statman (1993).

8. Schwed (1940): 140.

9. Bachelier (1900).

10. Boness (1964) and Sprenkle (1964).

11. Boness (1964): 163.

Chapter 10. Lawyers and Financial Advisers

1. The sources for the figures, all for 2010, are as follows: Israel—Israel Bar Association, http://www.israelbar.org.il/english_inner.asp?pgId=103336&catId=372. Brazil—Ordem dos Advogados do Brasil (Brazilian Law Board), http://www.oab.org.br/relatorioAdvOAB.asp. United States—American Bar Association, http://www.americanbar.org/content/dam/aba/migrated/marketresearch/PublicDocuments/2011_national_lawyer_by_state.authcheckdam.pdf. Japan—Japan Bar Association, http://www.nichibenren.or.jp/ja/jfba_info/membership/index.html. Korea—Korean Bar Association, http://www.koreaherald.com/opinion/Detail. jsp?newsMLId=

20101209000705. China—inferred from information supplied by the Chinese Ministry of Justice, http://www.moj.gov.cn/index/content/2010-05/27/content_2157168.htm.

2. Castor (2002): 189.

3. http://data.bls.gov:8080/oep/servlet/oep.nioem.servlet.ActionServlet.

4. http://www.napfa.org/membership/OurStandards.asp.

Chapter 11. Lobbyists

1. Levitt (2003): 251.

2. http://ourfinancialsecurity.org.

3. "National Realtors Call for Reforms," *Washington Post*, January 29, 1933, p. SP19.

4. Harriss (1951).

5. U.S. Congressional Budget Office (2011): 1.

6. Hacker and Pierson (2010): Kindle edition, location 5089.

7. Stratmann (1991).

8. http://www.thedailymaverick.co.za/article/2011-05-26-how-really-powerful-are-the-people-with-brains-and-money.

9. Lessig (2011).

10. http://www.opensecrets.org/lobby/top.php?indexType=c.

11. "Good Lobbyists, Good Government," *Los Angeles Times*, January 13, 2006, http://articles.latimes.com/2006/jan13/opinion/oe-odonnell13.

12. Miller (2008): 158, 157, and 163.

13. Committee on Disclosure of Corporate Political Spending, Petition for Rule-making, August 3, 2011, http://www.sec.gov/rules/petitions/2011/petn4-637.pdf.

14. Bartels (2005).

15. Visser (2003).

Chapter 12. Regulators

1. Friedman and Kuznets (1945) and Friedman (1962).

2. Stigler (1971): 3.

3. Kleiner and Krueger (2009).

4. Bhagwati and Srinivasan (1994).

5. Rajan and Zingales (2004).

6. Markopolos (2011): Kindle edition, locations 270, 2589–96.

7. Mongelli and Mangan (2009).

8. Laura Cha, lecture to Shiller Financial Markets class, March 23, 2011, video and transcript available online as part of Shiller's 2011 course, http://oyc.yale.edu/economics.

Chapter 13. Accountants and Auditors

1. Allen (1993): 58.

2. Levitt (2003): 266.

Chapter 14. Educators

1. Franklin (1787): 212–14.

2. "Education in Finance," *Friends' Intelligencer*, April 16, 1881, p. 140.

3. "A College Education," *Washington Post*, June 15, 1890, p. 9.

4. Miller (1991): 207.

Chapter 15. Public Goods Financiers

1. Hill (1837): 6.

2. Bush (1945): Chapter 6.

Chapter 16. Policy Makers in Charge of Stabilizing the Economy

1. Our study compared the out-of-sample performance of large-scale structural econometric models, single-equation autoregressive models, vector-autoregressive models, and a form of autoregressive model that we called the "autoregressive components" model. See Fair and Shiller (1990).

2. Efforts to confirm that expert political judgment can result in useful forecasts have yielded results that are hard to interpret, reflecting the essential ambiguity of their forecasting problem. See Tetlock (2006).

3. In the United States, the Federal Reserve was also in part modeled on another U.S. institution. For more than half a century before the founding of the Federal Reserve System, temporary interruptions of liquidity in bank accounts were made more bearable by a private institution, owned by its member banks, that issued clearing house loan certificates to member banks. The Clearing House Loan Committee of the New York Clearing House decided on the loan policy, and in doing so it was performing a task analogous to that carried out today by the Federal Open Market Committee of the Federal Reserve Board, although it was an entirely private, not a government-associated, committee. See Gilpin and Wallace (1904). This was a private-sector financial invention, of some utility, that is by now virtually forgotten. Although it served its purpose in its time, its principal flaw was that the system did not protect against bank suspensions of payments to the public, which were associated with sharp recessions.

4. Bagehot (1896): 131, 189.

5. Woodward (2001).

6. U.S. Federal Open Market Committee, Press Release, May 10, 2006, p. 1, http://www.federalreserve.gov/newsevents/press/monetary/20060510a.htm.

7. Jean-Claude Trichet and Lucas Papademos, "Introductory Statement," July 6, 2006, p. 1, http://www.ecb.int/press/pressconf/2006/html/is060706.en.html.

8. International Monetary Fund, *World Economic Outlook*, April 2006, p. 1.

9. The IMF *World Economic Outlook* for April 2006 did mention concerns about the U.S. housing market, calling it a "key uncertainty" (p. 17).

10. Bank for International Settlements, *Quarterly Review*, June 2006, p. 6.

11. Čihák (2006): 19.

12. Rajan (2010).

13. Higgins (1943): 188.

14. Shubik (2009).

15. Shiller (2008).

16. Shiller (1994, 2003, 2008, 2011) and Athanasoulis and Shiller (2001).

17. Kamstra and Shiller (2010).

18. Shiller (2012a).

Chapter 17. Trustees and Nonprofit Managers

1. http://compforce.typepad.com/compensation_force/2008/02/bonusincentive
.html.

2. Berle and Means (1932).

3. Salacuse (2003).

4. The requirement to have labor representatives on the *Aufsichtsrat* is codified in German Corporate Law (*Aktiengesetz*) Section 96, http://www.gesetze-im-internet.de/aktg/BJNR010890965.html. This same German law, Section 88, forbids board members from competing with the company, but it has no explicit provision for a duty of loyalty, no stipulation that the board's exclusive responsibility is to the shareholders.

5. http://www.bcorporation.net/publicpolicy.

6. http://nccsdataweb.urban.org/NCCS/V1Pub/index.php.

7. Sometimes nonprofits do produce millionaires. See Buettner (2011).

8. Schumpeter (1950): 125–26.

9. Hansmann et al. (2003).

10. Hansmann (1990).

Chapter 18. Philanthropists

1. Smith (1761): 272–73.

2. Saint-Exupéry (1943): 38.

3. The concluding sentence in Carnegie's original 1889 article was "Such, in my opinion, is the true Gospel concerning Wealth, obedience to which is destined some day to solve the problem of the Rich and the Poor, and to bring 'Peace on earth, among men Good-Will'" (p. 664). The article was republished in London that same year as "The Gospel of Wealth," and it was later altered by Carnegie to include that title when it became a part of his book of collected essays (1901).

4. Carnegie (1889): 656.

5. "The price which society pays for the law of competition, like the price it pays for cheap comforts and luxuries, is also great; but the advantages of this law are also greater still, for it is to this law that we owe our wonderful material development, which brings improved conditions in its train. . . . It is best for the race, because it insures the survival of the fittest in every department." Carnegie (1889): 655.

6. Buffett (2010) and http://givingpledge.org/.

Part Two. Finance and Its Discontents

1. Freud (1952 [1930]): 776, 788.

Chapter 19. Finance, Mathematics, and Beauty

1. Weyl (1952).

2. There is an extensive psychological literature on how people judge facial beauty. See Rhodes (2006).

3. Lederman (2004).

4. Black and Scholes (1973).

5. Miller and Modigliani (1961) and Modigliani and Miller (1963).

6. Barro (1974).

7. Whitman (1892): Book XV, "A Song for Occupations!"

Chapter 20. Categorizing People: Financiers versus Artists and Other Idealists

1. Ross (1977).

2. Swafford (1996).

3. Swafford (1996): 403.

4. http://www.christies.com/LotFinder/lot_details.aspx?intObjectID=5101408.

5. Thoreau (2008 [1863]): 4. See also Shiller (1994): 79.

6. From a book review (of William Channing, *Henry Thoreau, The Poet-Naturalist*, Boston: Roberts Brothers, 1873) reprinted from the *British Quarterly Review* in *Littell's Living Age*, March 14, 1874, pp. 643–71; quote on p. 643.

7. Kasper (1980): B1.

Chapter 21. An Impulse for Risk Taking

1. Akerlof and Shiller (2009). See also Chapter 25.

2. Fiorillo et al. (2003).

3. Zuckerman et al. (1978) and Arnett (1994).

4. Patoine (2011).

5. Martin et al. (2007).

6. Joseph et al. (2008).

7. Smith (1761): 183.

8. For an elaboration on this point, see Krueger (2003).

9. Weber (2010 [1905]).

Chapter 22. An Impulse for Conventionality and Familiarity

1. The Federal Farm Loan Act of 1916 established amortizing mortgages for farms, amidst opposition from those who thought the government was overreaching in making farm mortgages a "compulsory savings fund." See "Finds Flaws in New Loan Plan," *New York Tribune*, January 30, 1916, p. B10. An example advocating amortizing mortgages is Davis (1917). Amortizing mortgages for homes did not become common in the United States until Congress established them with the Home Owners' Loan Corporation in 1933.

2. Shiller (2005a).

3. Shiller (1997).

4. Locke (1841 [1690]): 352.

5. Bloom (2004): 49.

6. Mac Cormac (1985) and Lakoff and Johnson (2003).

7. Pulvermüller (2002): 59.

8. It has been found, for example, that the brain stores words as "unique objects." Neuroscientist Laurie Glezer and her colleagues used functional magnetic resonance imaging to study the "visual word form area" in the visual cortex of the brain, and they found that words have nonoverlapping neural representations there. Glezer et al. (2009).

9. Wittgenstein (1953): Part I, Sections 164–65.

10. Newcomb (1879): 230.

11. There are other factors to consider in understanding the lack of interest in indexation. See Shiller (1997).

12. Ibid.

13. http://valoruf.cl/.

14. Shiller (2003, 2009).

15. Shiller (2008), Kroszner and Shiller (2011), and Shiller et al. (2011).

16. United Nations (1948).

17. Gollier (2008).

Chapter 23. Debt and Leverage

1. Adelino et al. (2011) confirmed that access to mortgage credit has significant effects on house prices in the United States by using changes in conforming loan limits as instruments to detect exogenous changes in credit supply.

2. Mian et al. (2011).

3. Mian and Sufi (2010).

4. Glick and Lansing (2010): Figures 3 and 4.

5. Fisher (1933). See also Shiller (2012b).

6. Geanakoplos (2009).

7. Geanakoplos (2010).

8. Jayachandran and Kremer (2006).

9. Berger and Ritschl (1995).

Chapter 24. Some Unfortunate Incentives to Sleaziness Inherent in Finance

1. Kahneman and Tversky (1979).

2. Simmons and Novemsky (2009).

3. "Mr. Prowler Discourses This Week on One Kind of Bucket Shop," *National Police Gazette*, June 14, 1879, p. 14.

4. Schwed (1940): 19.

5. Festinger (1957).

6. Van Veen et al. (2009).

7. Tarbell (1904).

8. Shiller et al. (1991).

Chapter 25. The Significance of Financial Speculation

1. The essay "The Functions of the Stock and Produce Exchanges" was reprinted in Conant (1904): 83–116; quote on p. 83.

2. Marx (1906): 440.

3. Keynes (1936): 159.

4. Fama (1965): 56.

5. Working (1934) and Kendall (1953).

6. Shiller (1981). My paper was followed by some others, with John Campbell, that made significant improvements in the analysis (Campbell and Shiller 1988a, 1988b). See also LeRoy and Porter (1981) and Summers (1986).

7. For a discussion of the controversy see for example Cochrane (1991).

8. Keynes (1965 [1936]): 161, 162.

9. Akerlof and Shiller (2009).

10. Proust (2002 [1913]): 46–47.

11. Gartner (2005).

12. Moss (2004).

13. Andrew Hertzberg (2011) has shown how households composed of partly altruistic and partly selfish individuals can behave very differently from a rational single individual.

14. Morrison and Wilhelm (2008). Professional organizations and professional norms are the dominant explanation for the prevalence of the partnership form in law, consulting, and accounting. See Nordenflycht (2008).

15. Esterbrook and Fischel (1985).

16. Tufano and Schneider (2009).

Chapter 26. Speculative Bubbles and Their Costs to Society

1. Shiller (2005b): 2.

2. Buonomano (2011).

3. Becker (1997).

4. Li (1994): 291.

5. Lederer (1915).

6. http://www.g20.utoronto.ca/summits.htm, http://www.g20.utoronto.ca/2008/2008declaration1115.html.

7. http://www.g20.utoronto.ca/2009/2009communique0925.html.

8. http://www.treas.gov/press/releases/hp1177.htm.

9. Jung and Shiller (2005).

10. Shiller (1981).

11. Vuolteenaho (2002). See also Cohen et al. (2003).

12. Black (1986): 533.

Chapter 27. Inequality and Injustice

1. Brosnan (2009).

2. Krueger (2007).

3. The analysis here refers to the thirtieth annual Forbes 400 list, the cover story of the October 10, 2011, issue of *Forbes*. The list can be found at http://www.forbes.com/forbes-400/list/.

4. http://www.forbes.com/wealth/celebrities/list.

5. Philippon and Reshef (2008).

6. Stanley (1991): 271.

7. Luthar and Latendresse (2005).

8. Marx and Engels (1906 [1848]): 39.

9. De Lazowski (1788): 689.

10. Veblen (1899) and Akerlof (1976).

11. Festinger (1954).

12. Fliessbach et al. (2007).

13. Frank (2011).

14. Graetz (1979) lists eight practical problems with a progressive consumption tax and concludes that until these problems are solved "a progressive personal tax on consumption should remain low on the list of political priorities" (p. 1661).

15. In fact, the U.S. Congress passed an act on December 16, 2010, that reinstated the estate tax but also gave a new stepped-up basis for capital gains, so that after the fact there was no unambiguous tax advantage to dying in 2010 rather than 2011.

16. Quoted in Tarlow (2010).

17. Shiller et al. (1991).

18. A wage subsidy could be used to augment and regularize the earned income tax credit. See Phelps (2007).

19. Shiller (2003).

20. *Forbes*, October 10, 2011, p. 218. Household net worth was $57.4 trillion in the fourth quarter of 2011, according to the Federal Reserve Flow of Funds Accounts, Table B-100, http://www.federalreserve.gov/releases/z1/Current/z1r-5.pdf.

21. Burman et al. (2007).

Chapter 28. Problems with Philanthropy

1. The Center on Philanthropy at Indiana University (2011) reports that $290.89 billion was given to charity in the United States, which is 2.2% of U.S. third-quarter national income, as seen from the National Income and Product Accounts, http://www.bea.gov/national/nipaweb/TableView.asp?SelectedTable=43&Freq=Qtr&FirstYear=2009&LastYear=2011.

2. Della Vigna et al. (2011) constructed an experiment in which potential donors in an experimental group were allowed to opt out of even having to confront a representative of a charity. The total giving by the experimental group was significantly lower than that of a control group not given the option.

3. Harbough (1998).

4. Small et al. (2007).

5. Anderson (1991).

6. Hayek (1944): 161.

7. Carnegie (1901), Buffett (2010), and http://givingpledge.org/.

8. Pharoah (2009): 9. Data are for the most recent year for which information was available in 2009 for each foundation.

9. Karlan and McConnell (2009) showed experimentally that such publicity increases the amount given. The desire for recognition may be evidence that gift-giving is at least in part a form of disguised exchange. See Stark and Falk (1998).

10. List and Lucking-Reiley (2002).

11. Falke (2004).

12. One such Skype call, complete with smiles and kisses, is shown at "Meeting Our Compassion International Sponsored Child OVER SKYPE!!!" at http://www.youtube.com/watch?v=tT3CY8Lwiak.

13. "Except Gifts from Income," *New York Times*, June 17, 1917, p. 3.

14. The *Chicago Tribune* estimated in 1920 that $4 billion had been given to war organizations, the Red Cross, religious and educational movements, and other causes since 1915. "$4,000,000,000 to Philanthropy," *Chicago Tribune*, April 25, 1920, p. 8.

15. "Tax Revision for Charity," *New York Times*, February 11, 1948, p. 26.

16. Prante (2007).

17. Toppe et al. (2001): Table 1.7, p. 35.

18. Ibid., p. 6.

19. The U.S. National Commission on Fiscal Responsibility and Reform (chaired by Alan Simpson and Erskine Bowles), in its 2010 report to President Obama and the U.S. Congress, recommended replacing the charitable deduction with a 12% tax credit. There were public concerns that Congress's Joint Select Committee on Deficit Reduction (the "Supercommittee") would in 2011 propose the weakening of the charitable deduction, but in fact the committee reached no agreement on the question.

20. Post (2005).

Chapter 29. *The Dispersal of Ownership of Capital*

1. Douglas (1940): 16.

2. "It should be noted, moreover, that monopoly is frequently the product of factors other than lower costs of greater size. It is attained through collusive agreements and promoted by public policies." Hayek (1944): 2.

3. "Today it is almost heresy to suggest that scientific knowledge is not the sum of all knowledge. But a little reflection will show that there is beyond question a body of very important but unorganized knowledge which cannot possibly be called scientific in the sense of knowledge of general rules: the knowledge of particular circumstances of time and place. It is with respect to this that practically every individual has some advantage over all others." Hayek (1945): 521.

4. Sargent (1961).

5. Jeon and Kim (2000).

6. "Land for the Landless," *Chicago Press and Tribune,* August 30, 1860, p. 2.

7. Cape York Institute, "Land and Housing," http://www.cyi.org.au/landhousing .aspx.

8. Cabré and Módenes (2004).

9. Lee Kuan Yew (2000): 105.

10. French et al. (2009).

11. See for example Dean (1954).

12. Akerlof and Kranton (2010).

13. Freeman (2000) and Freeman et al. (2008).

14. Buchele et al. (2009).

15. Subsidizing small businesses is analogous in a way to subsidizing early childhood education, in that it helps people approach the economy on an even footing. Careful evaluation of early childhood education programs has helped us see better which such programs work and which do not work. See Heckman and Carneiro (2003).

16. Phelps and Tilman (2010).

17. Dodd-Frank Act, H.R. 4173-37, 2010, Section 622. In its first annual report, the Financial Stability Oversight Council concluded that "the concentration limit will reduce moral hazard, increase financial stability, and improve efficiency and competition within the U.S. financial system." http://www.treasury.gov/initiatives/fsoc/ Pages/annual-report.aspx 127.

18. U.S. Financial Stability Oversight Council (2011): Figures 1–4, pp. 24–25.

19. French et al. (2009).

Chapter 30. *The Great Illusion, Then and Now*

1. Angell (1910): 29–30.

2. Goldman Sachs agreed in 2010 to a settlement with the SEC, which had Goldman pay a $550 million penalty.

3. Countrywide agreed to pay settlements according to agreements with numerous state attorneys general. http://countrywidesettlementinfo.com/.

4. Nietzsche (1968 [1901]) wrote: "Man as a species is not progressing. Higher types are indeed attained, but they do not last. The level of the species is *not* raised" (Section 684, p. 365). "The influence of 'external circumstances' is overestimated by Darwin to a ridiculous extent: the essential thing in the life process is precisely the tremendous shaping, form-creating force working from within which *utilizes* and *exploits* 'external circumstances'" (Section 647, p. 344).

5. Angell (1910): vii–viii.

6. Ibid., p. viii.

7. Angell (1933): 53.

8. Owings (1984): 56.

9. Martel (2008): 8.

10. Angell (1933) refers to "the Japanese adventure" and the "semi-mystic nationalism" of Hitlerism (p. 296). He justifies the new edition of his 1910 book as follows: "The problem is not merely to show that 'war does not pay' (is not, that is to say, either advantageous to our country, a satisfaction of our pride in it, or necessary to the assertion of its rights), but to show why the policies which we pursue and which we believe do pay, must lead to war" (p. 5). His idealized policies, "that organization [of nations] be based on clear political and diplomatic obligation" (p. 54), sound like a proposal to create what eventually became the European Union.

11. Moody (1933): 91.

12. Montesquieu (1773): Volume 1, pp. 54–55.

13. Lorenz (1966). The dove example appears on p. 232.

14. De Waal (1990): 234.

15. Pinker (2011): Kindle edition, locations 15155, 15295.

16. Hirschman (1977).

17. Russett and Oneal (2001).

18. Cronin (1999) and Anderson (1991).

19. Acemoglu and Yared (2010) present a case for reverse causality—that shifting political currents may raise the level of militarism in a country, and this then appears to have the effect of diminishing that country's foreign trade. Kupchan (2010: 400) argues from consideration of a number of case studies of stable peace breaking out that economic integration does not seem to promote the early phases of development of stable peace, when unilateral accommodation and reciprocal restraint are first attempted. But economic integration does advance it in later phases, when trust is gradually built.

20. Gartzke et al. (2001).

Epilogue: Finance, Power, and Human Values

1. If one searches on the parallel phrase "poverty and weakness" only some eight hundred titles come up.

2. Akerlof (1976). See also Mailath et al. (2000) and Scoville (2006). Much of this literature has focused on racial discrimination, though the theoretical principles apply more broadly to other forms as well; for a literature survey see Arrow (1998).

3. A ProQuest search for "Social Register" shows a massive downtrend since the 1930s in newspaper articles mentioning the phrase. Broad (1996) documented that the *Social Register* (http://www.socialregisteronline.com/) shows a strong continuity with prominent families from the long past.

4. http://www.burkespeerage.com. An attempt was made to start a new Almanach de Gotha in the twenty-first century, replacing the French language with English. See http://www.almanachdegotha.org/.

5. Quoted in Fraser (2009): 41.

6. "Social Register Drops Notables: Page and a Half Devoted to Roosevelts," *New York Times*, November 21, 1941, p. 19.

7. Members of the Roosevelt family were not mentioned on the short list of the very richest Americans in their time, but one of them, Betsey Cushing Roosevelt Whitney, the former wife of Franklin D. Roosevelt's son James (since remarried into more wealth and then widowed), made it onto the first Forbes 400 list in 1982. She was ranked 92.

8. Pogrebin (2011).

9. Calhoun (2012): 12.

10. Unger (1996).

11. Nietzsche (1968 [1901]): 366.

12. Nietzsche (1968 [1901]: 354) in places sounds like a modern neuroscientist. He wrote: "Affects are a construction of the intellect, an invention of causes that do not exist. . . . Frequent rushes of blood to the brain accompanied by a choking sensation are interpreted as 'anger': persons and things that rouse us to anger are means of relieving our physiological condition."

13. As summarized by Samuel Bowles and Herbert Gintis (2011: 20), "In experiments we commonly observe that people sacrifice their own payoffs in order to cooperate with others, to reward the cooperation of others, and to punish free-riding, even when they cannot expect to gain from acting this way." See also Gintis et al. (2005) and Fehr (2009).

14. Smith (1761).

15. Gelman and Bloom (2000).

16. Smith (1761): 191, 193.

17. "Death of a Drug Lord," CNN, December 5, 1993.

18. Griffiths (2003).

References

Acemoglu, Daron, and Pierre Yared. 2010. "Political Limits to Globalization." *American Economic Review* 100(2):83–88.

Acharya, Viral, Thomas Cooley, Matthew Richardson, and Ingo Walter. 2010. "Manufacturing Tail Risk: A Perspective on the Financial Crisis of 2007–9." *Foundations and Trends in Finance* 4:247–325.

Acharya, Viral, Matthew Richardson, Stijn van Nieuwerburgh, and Lawrene J. White. 2011. *Guaranteed to Fail: Fannie Mae, Freddie Mac, and the Debacle of Mortgage Finance*. Princeton, NJ: Princeton University Press.

Adelino, Manuel, Antoinette Schoar, and Felipe Severino. 2011. "Credit Supply and House Prices: Evidence from Mortgage Market Segmentation." Unpublished paper, Tuck School, Dartmouth College.

Akerlof, George A. 1970. "The Market for 'Lemons': Quality Uncertainty and the Market Mechanism." *Quarterly Journal of Economics* 84(3):488–500.

———. 1976. "The Economics of Caste and of the Rat Race and Other Woeful Tales." *Quarterly Journal of Economics* 90(4):599–617.

Akerlof, George A., and Rachel E. Kranton. 2010. *Identity Economics: How Our Identities Shape Our Work, Wages, and Well-Being*. Princeton, NJ: Princeton University Press.

Akerlof, George A., and Paul M. Romer. 1994. "Looting: The Economic Underworld of Bankruptcy for Profit." National Bureau of Economic Research Working Paper R1869.

Akerlof, George A., and Robert J. Shiller. 2009. *Animal Spirits: How Human Psychology Drives the Economy and Why It Matters for Global Capitalism*. Princeton, NJ: Princeton University Press.

Allen, Noelle. 1993. *Confessions of a Tax Accountant*. Cupertino, CA: Canyon View Institute.

Anderson, Benedict. 1991. *Imagined Communities: Reflections on the Origin and Spread of Nationalism*. London: Verso.

Angell, Norman. 1910. *The Great Illusion: A Study of the Relation of Military Power in Nations to Their Economic and Social Advantage*. New York: G. P. Putnam's Sons.

———. 1933. *The Great Illusion 1933*. New York: G. P. Putnam's Sons.

Aristotle. 1977. *Politics*, trans. Benjamin Jowett. New York: Forgotten Books.

Arnett, Jeffrey. 1994. "Sensation Seeking: A New Conceptualization and a New Scale." *Personality and Individual Differences* 16(2):289–96.

Arrow, Kenneth. 1964. "The Role of Securities in the Optimal Allocation of Risk Bearing." *Review of Economic Studies* 31:91–96.

———. 1998. "What Has Economics to Say about Racial Discrimination?" *Journal of Economic Perspectives* 12(2):91–100.

Athanasoulis, Stefano G., and Robert J. Shiller. 2001. "World Income Components: Measuring and Exploiting Risk-Sharing Opportunities." *American Economic Review* 91(4):1031–54.

Bachelier, Louis. 1900. "Théorie de la Spéculation." *Annales Scientifiques de l'École Normale Supérieure, 3e Série* 17:21–86.

Bagehot, Walter. 1896. *Lombard Street: A Description of the Money Market*, Tenth Edition, London: Kegan Paul, Trench, Trubner & Co. Ltd.

Banerjee, Abhijit V., and Esther Duflo. 2010. "Giving Credit Where It Is Due." Unpublished paper, Department of Economics, Massachusetts Institute of Technology.

Barnett, Barry J., and Oliver Mahul. 2007. "Weather Index Insurance for Agriculture and Rural Areas in Lower-Income Countries." *American Journal of Agricultural Economics* 5:1241–47.

Barr, Michael S. 2004. "Banking the Poor." *Yale Journal of Regulation* 21:121–237.

Barro, Robert J. 1974. "Are Government Bonds Net Wealth?" *Journal of Political Economy* 82(6):1095–117.

Bartels, Larry M. 2005. *Economic Inequality and Political Representation*. Princeton, NJ: Princeton University Press.

Bebchuk, Lucian, and Jesse Fried. 2006. *Pay without Performance: The Unfilled Promise of Executive Compensation*. Cambridge, MA: Harvard University Press.

Becker, Jasper. 1997. *Hungry Ghosts: Mao's Secret Famine*. New York: Free Press.

Berg, Joyce, Robert Forsythe, Forrest Nelson, and Thomas Rietz. 2008. "Results from a Dozen Years of Election Futures Markets Research." In Vernon Smith, ed., *Handbook of Experimental Economic Results*, Volume 1, 742–52. Amsterdam: North-Holland.

Berger, Helge, and Albrecht Ritschl. 1995. "Germany and the Political Economy of the Marshall Plan 1947–52: A Re-Revisionist View." In Barry J. Eichengreen, ed., *Europe's Post-War Recovery*, 199–245. Cambridge: Press Syndicate of the University of Cambridge.

Berk, Jonathan B., and Richard C. Green. 2004. "Mutual Fund Flows and Performance in Rational Markets." *Journal of Political Economy* 112(6):1269–95.

Berle, Adolf A., and Gardiner C. Means. 1932. *The Modern Corporation and Private Property*. New York: Commerce Clearing House.

Bernasek, Anna. 2010. *The Economics of Integrity*. New York: HarperCollins.

Bhagwati, Jagdish, and T. N. Srinivasan. 1994. *India's Economic Reforms*. Delhi: Ministry of Finance.

Black, Fischer. 1986. "Noise." *Journal of Finance* 41(3):529–43.

Black, Fischer, and Myron Scholes. 1973. "The Pricing of Options and Corporate Liabilities." *Journal of Political Economy* 81(3):637–54.

Blank, Rebecca M., and Michael S. Barr, eds. 2009. *Insufficient Funds: Savings, Assets, Credit and Banking among Low-Income Households*. New York: Russell Sage Foundation.

Bloom, Paul. 2004. *Descartes' Baby: How the Science of Child Development Explains What Makes Us Human*. New York: Basic Books.

Bodnaruk, Andriy, and Andrei Simonov. 2011. "Do Financial Experts Make Better Investment Decisions?" Unpublished paper, Department of Economics, University of Notre Dame.

Bogle, John C. 2009. *Enough: True Measures of Money, Business, and Life*. New York: Wiley.

Boness, A. J. 1964. "Elements of a Theory of Stock Option Value." *Journal of Political Economy* 72:163–75.

Bowles, Samuel, and Herbert Gintis. 2011. *A Cooperative Species: Human Reciprocity and Its Evolution*. Princeton, NJ: Princeton University Press.

Brickley, James A. 1983. "Shareholder Wealth, Information Signalling and the Specially Designated Dividend." *Journal of Financial Economics* 12:187–209.

Brischoux, F., S. Chakraborty, D. Brierley, and M. Ungless. 2009. "Phasic Excitation of Dopamine Neurons in Ventral VTA by Noxious Stimuli." *Proceedings of the National Academy of Sciences of the USA* 106(12):4894–99.

Broad, David B. 1996. "The Social Register: Directory of America's Upper Class." *Sociological Spectrum* 16(2):173–81.

Brosnan, Sarah. 2009. "Responses to Inequity in Non-Human Primates." In Paul Glimcher, Colin Camerer, Ernst Fehr, and Russell Poldrack, eds., *Neuroeconomics: Decision Making and the Brain*, 285–302. Amsterdam: Elsevier.

Buchele, Robert, Douglas Kruse, Loren Rodgers, and Adria Scharf. 2009. "Show Me the Money: Does Shared Capitalism Share the Wealth?" National Bureau of Economic Research Working Paper 14830.

Bucks, Brian K., Arthur B. Kennickell, Traci L. Mach, and Kevin B. Moore. 2009. "Changes in U.S. Family Finances from 2004 to 2007: Evidence from the Survey of Consumer Finances." *Federal Reserve Bulletin* February: A1–A56.

Buettner, Russ. 2011. "Reaping Millions in Nonprofit Care for Disabled." *New York Times*, August 2, http://www.nytimes.com/2011/08/02/nyregion/for-executives-at-group-homes-generous-pay-and-little-oversight.html?pagewanted=all.

Buffett, Warren. 2010. "My Philanthropic Pledge." *Fortune*, July 5, 86–87.

Buonomano, Dean. 2011. *Brain Bugs: How the Brain's Flaws Shape Our Lives*. New York: W. W. Norton.

Burman, Leonard, Robert Shiller, Gregory Leiserson, and Jeffrey Rohaly. 2007. "The Rising Tide Tax System: Indexing the Tax System for Changes in Inequality." Unpublished paper, Department of Economics, Syracuse University, http://www.newfinancialorder.com/burman-nyu-030807.pdf.

Bush, Vannevar. 1945. *Science: The Endless Frontier*. Washington, DC: U.S. Government Printing Office.

Cabré, Anna, and Juan Antonio Módenes. 2004. "Homeownership and Social Inequality in Spain." In *Home Ownership and Social Inequality in a Comparative Perspective*, 233–54. Stanford, CA: Stanford University Press.

Calhoun, Craig. 2012. "Shared Responsibility." In Jacob Hacker and Ann O'Leary, eds., *Shared Responsibilities, Shared Values*, 8–16. New York: Oxford University Press.

Campbell, John Y., and Robert J. Shiller. 1988a. "The Dividend-Price Ratio and Expectations of Future Dividends and Discount Factors." *Review of Financial Studies* 1(3):195–228.

———. 1988b. "Stock Prices, Earnings and Expected Dividends." *Journal of Finance* 43(3):661–76.

Caplin, Andrew, Sewin Chan, Charles Freeman, and Joseph Tracy. 1997. *Housing Market Partnerships: A New Approach to a Market at Crossroads*. Cambridge, MA: MIT Press.

Carnegie, Andrew. 1889. "Wealth." *North American Review* 148(391):653–64.

———. 1901. *The Gospel of Wealth and Other Timely Essays*. New York: Century.

Castor, Belmiro V. J. 2002. *Brazil Is Not for Amateurs: Patterns of Governance in the Land of "Jeitinho,"* trans. A. W. McEachern. Bloomington, IN: Xlibris.

Center on Philanthropy at Indiana University. 2011. *Giving USA 2011: The Annual Report on Philanthropy for the Year 2010—Executive Summary*. Giving USA Foundation, http://big.assets.huffingtonpost.com/GivingUSA_2011_ExecSummary_Print-1.pdf.

Chen, Shaohua, and Martin Ravallion. 2007. *Absolute Poverty Measures for the Developing World, 1981–2004*. Washington, DC: World Bank, Development Research Group.

Chevalier, Judith, and Glenn Ellison. 1999. "Are Some Mutual Fund Managers Better Than Others? Cross-Sectional Patterns in Behavior and Performance." *Journal of Political Economy* 54(3):875–99.

Čihák, Martin. 2006. *How Do Central Banks Write on Financial Stability?* Working Paper WP/06/163. Washington, DC: International Monetary Fund.

Cochrane, John. 1991. "Volatility Tests and Efficient Markets: A Review Essay." *Journal of Monetary Economics* 27:463–85.

Cohen, Randolph, Christopher Polk, and Tuomo Vuolteenaho. 2003. "The Value Spread." *Journal of Finance* 58:609–42.

Conant, Charles A. 1904. *Wall Street and the Country: A Study of Recent Financial Tendencies*. New York: G. P. Putnam's Sons.

Cronin, Bruce. 1999. *Community under Anarchy: Transnational Identity and the Evolution of Cooperation*. New York: Columbia University Press.

Davis, Ed L. 1917. "The Refunding Mortgage: A [*sic*] Amortizing Method for Small Mortgage Loans." *Bankers' Magazine* 95(3):323–26.

Davis, John E. 2006. *Shared Equity Ownership: The Changing Landscape of Resale-Restricted, Owner-Occupied Homes*. Montclair, NJ: National Housing Institute.

Dean, Lois R. 1954. "Union Activity and Dual Loyalty." *Industrial and Labor Relations Review* 7(4):526–36.

De Lazowski. 1788. "Observations Made in a Tour in Swisserland [*sic*]." *Columbian Magazine* 2(12):688–93.

Della Vigna, Stefano, John A. List, and Ulrike Malmendier. 2011. "Testing for Altruism and Social Pressure." Unpublished paper, Department of Economics, University of California at Berkeley.

De Waal, Frans. 1990. *Peacemaking among Primates*. Cambridge, MA: Harvard University Press.

Diamond, Douglas, and Philip Dybvig. 1983. "Bank Runs, Deposit Insurance, and Liquidity." *Journal of Political Economy* 91(3):401–19.

Dixit, Avinash K., and Robert S. Pindyck. 1994. *Investment under Uncertainty*. Princeton, NJ: Princeton University Press.

Djilas, Milovan. 1982 [1957]. *The New Class: An Analysis of the Communist System*. New York: Harcourt Brace Jovanovich.

Douglas, William O. 1940. *Democracy and Finance*. New Haven, CT: Yale University Press.

Duflo, Esther. 2011. "Balancing Growth with Equity: The View from Development." Paper presented at the Jackson Hole Symposium, Federal Reserve Bank of Kansas City, August 1, http://www.kansascityfed.org/publicat/sympos/2011/2011.Duflo .Paper.pdf.

Dugan, Ianthe Jeanne. 2005. "Sharpe Point: Risk Gauge Misused." *Wall Street Journal*, August 31, C1.

Dugan, Ianthe Jeanne, Thomas M. Burton, and Carrick Mollenkamp. 2002. "Portrait of a Loss: Chicago Art Institute Learns Tough Lesson about Hedge Funds." *Wall Street Journal*, February 1, A1.

Edwards, George W. 1938. *The Evolution of Finance Capitalism*. New York: Longmans, Green.

Esterbrook, Frank H., and Daniel R. Fischel. 1985. "Limited Liability and the Corporation." *University of Chicago Law Review* 52(1):89–117.

Fabozzi, Frank J., and Franco Modigliani. 1992. *Mortgage and Mortgage-Backed Securities Markets*. Cambridge, MA: Harvard Business School Press.

Fabozzi, Frank J., Robert J. Shiller, and Radu Tunaru. 2010. "Hedging Real-Estate Risk." *Journal of Portfolio Management*, Special Real Estate Issue 35(5):92–103.

Fair, Ray C., and Robert J. Shiller. 1990. "Comparing Information in Forecasts from Econometric Models." *American Economic Review* 80(3):375–89.

Falke, Armin. 2004. "Charitable Giving as a Gift Exchange: Evidence from a Field Experiment." IZA Discussion Paper 1148. University of Bonn.

Fama, Eugene F. 1965. "Random Walks in Stock Market Prices." *Financial Analysts Journal* 21(5):55–59.

Fama, Eugene F., and Kenneth French. 2005. "Financing Decisions: Who Issues Stock?" *Journal of Financial Economics* 76(3):549–74.

Fehr, Ernst. 2009. "Social Preferences and the Brain." In Paul Glimcher, Colin Camerer, Ernst Fehr, and Russell Poldrack, eds., *Neuroeconomics: Decision Making and the Brain*, 215–30. Amsterdam: Elsevier.

Festinger, Leon. 1954. "A Theory of Social Comparison Processes." *Human Relations* 7:117–40.

———. 1957. *A Theory of Cognitive Dissonance*. Stanford, CA: Stanford University Press.

Fiorillo, Christopher D., Philippe N. Tobler, and Wolfram Schultz. 2003. "Discrete

Coding of Reward Probability and Uncertainty by Dopamine Neurons." *Science* 299(5614):1898–902.

Fisher, Irving. 1933. "The Debt Deflation Theory of Great Depressions." *Econometrica* 1(4):337–57.

Fliessbach, K., B. Weber, P. Trautner, T. Dohmen, U. Sunde, C. E. Elger, and A. Falk. 2007. "Social Comparison Affects Reward-Related Brain Activity in the Human Ventral Striatum." *Science* 318(5854):1305–8.

Frank, Robert H. 2011. *The Darwin Economy: Liberty, Competition, and the Common Good.* Princeton, NJ: Princeton University Press.

Franklin, Benjamin. 1787. "Information for Those Who Wish to Remove to America." *The American Museum or, Repository of Ancient and Modern Fugitive Pieces &c.* 2:211–16.

Fraser, Steve. 2009. *Wall Street: America's Dream Palace.* New Haven, CT: Yale University Press.

Freeman, Richard B. 2000. "Work-Sharing to Full Employment: Serious Option or Populist Fallacy?" In Richard B. Freeman and Peter Gottschalk, eds., *Generating Jobs: How to Increase Demand for Less-Skilled Workers*, 195–222. New York: Russell Sage Foundation.

Freeman, Richard, Douglas Kruse, and Joseph Blasi. 2008. "Worker Responses to Shirking under Shared Capitalism." National Bureau of Economic Research Working Paper 14227.

French, Kenneth R. 2008. "The Cost of Active Investing." *Journal of Finance* 3(4):1537–73.

French, Kenneth R., et al. 2009. *The Squam Lake Report: Fixing the Financial System.* Princeton, NJ: Princeton University Press.

Freud, Sigmund. 1952 [1930]. *Civilization and Its Discontents*, trans. Joan Reviere. The Major Works of Sigmund Freud. Chicago: William Benton / Encyclopaedia Britannica.

Friedman, Milton (with Rose D. Friedman). 1962. *Capitalism and Freedom.* Chicago: University of Chicago Press.

Friedman, Milton, and Simon Kuznets. 1945. *Income from Independent Professional Practice.* New York: National Bureau of Economic Research.

Gale, David., and Lloyd S. Shapley. 1962. "College Admissions and the Stability of Marriage." *American Mathematical Society Monthly* 69(1):9–15.

Gartner, John D. 2005. *The Hypomanic Edge: The Link between (a Little) Craziness and (a Lot of) Success in America.* New York: Simon and Schuster.

Gartzke, Erik, Quan Li, and Charles Boehmer. 2001. "Investing in Peace: Economic Interdependence and International Conflict." *International Organization* 55(2):391–438.

Geanakoplos, John. 2009. "The Leverage Cycle." In *NBER Macroeconomics Annual 2009*, 1–65. Cambridge, MA: National Bureau of Economic Research.

———. 2010. "Solving the Present Crisis and Managing the Leverage Cycle." Working Paper 1751. New Haven, CT: Cowles Foundation for Research in Economics, Yale University.

Gelman, Susan, and Paul Bloom. 2000. "Young Children Are Sensitive to How an Object Was Created When Deciding What to Name It." *Cognition* 76(2):91–103.

Gilpin, William J., and Henry E. Wallace. 1905. *Clearing House of New York City; New York Clearing House Association, 1854–1905*. New York: M. King.

Gintis, Herbert, Samuel Bowles, Robert Boyd, and Ernst Fehr. 2005. *Moral Sentiments and Material Interests: The Foundations of Cooperation in Economic Life*. Cambridge, MA: MIT Press.

Glezer, Laurie, Xiong Jiang, and Maximilian Riesenhuber. 2009. "Evidence for Highly Selective Neuronal Tuning to Whole Words in the 'Visual Word Form Area.'" *Neuron* 62(2):199–204.

Glick, Reuven, and Kevin J. Lansing. 2010. "Global Household Leverage, House Prices, and Consumption." *FRBSF Economic Letter* 2010-01, http://www.frbsf.org/publications/economics/letter/2010/el2010-01.html.

Glimcher, Paul. 2011. *Foundations of Neuroeconomic Analysis*. New York: Oxford University Press.

Goetzmann, William, Roger Ibbotson, Matthew Spiegel, and Ivo Welch. 2002. "Sharpening Sharpe Ratios." National Bureau of Economic Research Working Paper 9116.

Gollier, Christian. 2008. "Intergenerational Risk-Sharing and Risk-Taking of a Pension Fund." *Journal of Public Economics* 92:1463–85.

Gorton, Gary. 2010. *Slapped by the Invisible Hand: The Panic of 2007*. Oxford: Oxford University Press.

———. 2011. "Review [of books by Michael Lewis and Gregory Zuckerman]." *Journal of Economic Literature* 49:450–53.

Gorton, Gary, and Guillermo Ordoñez. 2012. "Collateral Crises." Unpublished paper, Department of Finance, Yale University.

Gorton, Gary, and Andrew Winton. 1995. "Bank Capital Regulation in General Equilibrium." National Bureau of Economic Research Working Paper w5244.

Graetz, Michael J. 1979. "Implementing a Progressive Consumption Tax." *Harvard Law Review* 92(8):1575–1661.

Granick, David. 1960. *The Red Executive: A Study of the Organization Man in Russian Industry*. Garden City, NY: Doubleday.

Griffiths, John C. 2003. *Hostage: The History, Facts & Reasoning behind Political Hostage Taking*. London: Andre Deutsch.

Grinblatt, Mark, Matti Keloharju, and Juhani Linnainmaa. 2011. "IQ and Stock Market Participation." *Journal of Finance* 66(6):2121–64.

Gross, L. 1982. *The Art of Selling Intangibles: How to Make Your Million($) by Investing Other People's Money*. New York: New York Institute of Finance.

Grossman, Sanford, and Joseph Stiglitz. 1980. "On the Impossibility of Informationally Efficient Markets." *American Economic Review* 70:393–408.

Gruber, Martin J. 1996. "Another Puzzle: The Growth in Actively Managed Funds." *Journal of Finance* 51(3):783–810.

Hacker, Jacob, and Paul Pierson. 2010. *Winner-Take-All Politics: How Washington Made the Rich Richer—and Turned Its Back on the Middle Class*. New York: Simon and Schuster.

Hansmann, Henry. 1990. "Why Do Universities Have Endowments?" *Journal of Legal Studies* 19:3–42.

Hansmann, Henry, Daniel Kessler, and Mark McClellan. 2003. "Ownership Form and Trapped Capital in the Hospital Industry." In Edward Glaeser, ed., *The Governance of Not-for-Profit Organizations*, 45–70. Chicago: University of Chicago Press.

Harbough, William T. 1998. "The Prestige Motive for Making Charitable Transfers." *American Economic Review* 88(2):277–88.

Harriss, C. Lowell. 1951. *History and Policies of the Home Owners' Loan Corporation*. New York: National Bureau of Economic Research.

Hayek, F. A. 1944. *The Road to Serfdom*. London: Routledge.

———. 1945. "The Use of Knowledge in Society." *American Economic Review* 35(4):519–30.

Heckman, James J., and Pedro Carneiro. 2003. "Human Capital Policy." In James J. Heckman and Alan B. Krueger, *Inequality in America: What Role for Human Capital Policies?*, 77–239. Cambridge, MA: MIT Press.

Hellman, Thomas, and Manju Puri. 2002. "Venture Capital and the Professionalization of Start-Up Firms: Empirical Evidence." *Journal of Finance* 57(1):169–97.

Hertzberg, Andrew. 2011. "Exponential Individuals, Hyperbolic Households." Unpublished paper, Graduate School of Business, Columbia University.

Higgins, Benjamin. 1943. "Problems of Planning Public Work." In Seymour E. Harris, ed., *Postwar Economic Problems*, 187–205. New York: McGraw-Hill.

Hill, Claire A. 1997. "Securitization: A Low-Cost Sweetener for Lemons." *Journal of Applied Corporate Finance* 10(1):64–71.

Hill, Rowland. 1837. *Post Office Reform*. London: William Clowes & Sons.

Hirschman, Albert O. 1977. *The Passions and the Interests*. Princeton, NJ: Princeton University Press.

Horesh, Ronnie. 2000. "Injecting Incentives into the Solution of Social Problems: Social Policy Bonds." *Economic Affairs* 20(3):39–42.

Iacocca, Lee (with William Novak). 1984. *Iacocca: An Autobiography*. New York: Bantam Dell.

Jaffee, Dwight, Howard Kunreuther, and Erwann Michel-Kerjan. 2008. "Long-Term Care Insurance (LTI) for Addressing Catastrophe Risk." National Bureau of Economic Research Working Paper 14210.

Jayachandran, Seema, and Michael Kremer. 2006. "Odious Debt." *American Economic Review* 96(1):82–92.

Jayadev, Arjun, and Samuel Bowles. 2006. "Guard Labor." *Journal of Development Economics* 79:328–48.

Jeon, Yoong-Deok, and Young-Yong Kim. 2000. "Land Reform, Income Redistribution, and Agricultural Production in Korea." *Economic Development and Cultural Change* 48(2):253–68.

Joseph, Jane E., Xun Liu, Yang Jiang, Donald Lynam, and Thomas H. Kelly. 2008. "Neural Correlates of Emotional Reactivity in Sensation Seeking." *Psychological Science* 20(2):215–23.

Jung, Jeeman, and Robert J. Shiller. 2005. "A Simple Test of Samuelson's Dictum for the Stock Market." *Economic Inquiry* 43(2):263–92.

Kahneman, Daniel, and Amos Tversky. 1979. "Prospect Theory: An Analysis of Decision under Risk." *Econometrica* 47(2):263–92.

Kamstra, Mark, and Robert J. Shiller. 2010. "Trills Instead of T-Bills: It's Time to Replace Part of Government Debt with Shares in GDP." *The Economists' Voice* 7(3), Article 5, http://www.bepress.com/ev/vol7/iss3/art5.

Kaplan, Steven N., and Antoinette Schoar. 2005. "Private Equity Performance: Returns, Persistence, and Capital Flows." *Journal of Finance* 60(4):1791–823.

Karlan, Dean, and Margaret A. McConnell. 2009. "Hey Look at Me: The Effect of Giving Circles on Giving." Unpublished paper, Yale University.

Karlan, Dean, and Jonathan Zinman. 2011. "Microcredit in Theory and Practice: Using Randomized Credit Scoring for Impact Evaluation." *Science* 332(6035):1278–84.

Kasper, Rob. 1980. "Jerry Rubin Goes Wall Street, but Still Can't Tie a Tie." *Baltimore Sun*, August 19, B1.

Kat, Harry, and Faye Menexe. 2003. "Persistence in Hedge Fund Performance: The True Value of a Track Record." *Journal of Alternative Investments* 5(4):66–72.

Kaufman, Henry. 2005. *On Money and Markets: A Wall Street Memoir.* New York: McGraw-Hill.

Kendall, Maurice. 1953. "The Analysis of Economic Time Series I." *Journal of the Royal Statistical Society, Series A* 116:11–25.

Keynes, John Maynard. 1936. *The General Theory of Employment, Interest and Money.* London: Macmillan.

———. 1937. "The General Theory of Employment." *Quarterly Journal of Economics* 51(2):209–23.

Khurana, Rakesh. 2004. *Searching for a Corporate Savior: The Irrational Quest for Charismatic CEOs.* Princeton, NJ: Princeton University Press.

Kleiner, Morris M., and Alan B. Krueger. 2009. "Analyzing the Extent and Influence of Occupational Licensing on the Labor Market." National Bureau of Economic Research Working Paper 14979.

Kremer, Michael, and Rachel Glennerster. 2004. *Strong Medicine: Creating Incentives for Pharmaceutical Research on Neglected Diseases.* Princeton, NJ: Princeton University Press.

Kroszner, Randall, and Robert J. Shiller. 2011. *Reforming the U.S. Financial Markets: Reflections before and beyond Dodd-Frank.* Alvin Hansen Symposium Series on Public Policy, Harvard University. Cambridge, MA: MIT Press.

Krueger, Alan B. 2003. "Inequality: Too Much of a Good Thing." In James J. Heckman and Alan B. Krueger, *Inequality in America: What Role for Human Capital Policies?*, 1–75. Cambridge, MA: MIT Press.

———. 2007. *What Makes a Terrorist: Economics and the Roots of Terrorism.* Princeton, NJ: Princeton University Press.

Kunreuther, Howard, and Michael Useem. 2010. *Learning from Catastrophes: Strategies for Reaction and Response.* Philadelphia: Wharton School.

Kupchan, Charles A. 2010. *How Enemies Become Friends: The Sources of Stable Peace.* Princeton, NJ: Princeton University Press.

Labuszewski, John W., John E. Nyttoff, Richard Co, and Paul E. Peterson. 2010. *The CME Group Risk Management Handbook.* Hoboken, NJ: Wiley.

Laird, John E. 2009. "Toward Cognitive Robotics." Unpublished paper, Department of Computer Science and Engineering, University of Michigan.

Lakoff, George, and Mark Johnson. 2003. *Metaphors We Live By*. Chicago: University of Chicago Press.

Lederer, Emil. 1915. "Zur Soziologie des Weltkriegs." *Archiv für Sozialwissenschaft und Sozialpolitik* 39:357–384. Translated as "On the Sociology of World War," *European Journal of Sociology* 47:241–68, 2006.

Lederman, Leon M. 2004. *Symmetry and the Beautiful Universe*. New York: Lederman and Hill.

Lee Kuan Yew. 2000. *From Third World to First: The Singapore Story 1965–2000*. New York: HarperCollins.

LeRoy, Stephen F., and Richard Porter. 1981. "The Present-Value Relation: Tests Based on Implied Variance Bounds." *Econometrica* 49(3):555–74.

Lessig, Lawrence. 2011. *Republic, Lost: How Money Corrupts Congress—and a Plan to Stop It*. New York: Twelve / Hachette Book Group.

Levine, Ross. 1997. "Financial Development and Economic Growth: Views and Agenda." *Journal of Economic Literature* 35(2):688–726.

Levitt, Arthur (with Paula Dwyer). 2003. *Take on the Street: How to Fight for Your Financial Future*. New York: Vintage.

Levy, Frank, and Richard J. Murnane. 2005. *The New Division of Labor: How Computers Are Creating the Next Job Market*. Princeton, NJ: Princeton University Press.

Lewis, Michael. 2010. *The Big Short: Inside the Doomsday Machine*. New York: W. W. Norton.

Li, Haitao, Rui Zhao, and Xiaoyan Zhang. 2008. "Investing in Talents: Manager Characteristics and Hedge Fund Performances." Unpublished paper, Department of Finance, University of Michigan.

Li, Zhisui. 1994. *The Private Life of Chairman Mao: The Memoirs of Mao's Personal Physician*. New York: Random House.

List, John A., and David Lucking-Reiley. 2002. "The Effects of Seed Money and Refunds on Charitable Giving: Experimental Evidence from a University Capital Campaign." *Journal of Political Economy* 110:215–33.

Locke, John. 1841 [1690]. *An Essay Concerning Human Understanding*. London: Thomas Tegg.

Long, Charles H. 1983. *Alpha: The Myths of Creation*. Oxford: Oxford University Press.

Lorenz, Konrad. 1966. *On Aggression*. New York: Bantam.

Luthar, Suniya S., and Shawn Latendresse. 2005. "Children of the Affluent: Challenges to Well-Being." *Current Directions in Psychological Science* 14(1):49–53.

Mac Cormack, Earl. 1985. *A Cognitive Theory of Metaphor*. Cambridge, MA: MIT Press.

Mailath, George, Larry Samuelson, and Avner Shaked. 2000. "Endogenous Inequality in Integrated Labor Markets with Two-Sided Search." *American Economic Review* 90(1):46–72.

Malmendier, Ulrike. 2005. "Roman Shares." In William Goetzmann and K. Geert Rouwenhorst, eds., *The Origins of Value: The Financial Innovations That Created Modern Capital Markets*, 31–42. New York: Oxford University Press.

Marcus, Alan J. 1984. "Deregulation and Bank Financial Policy." *Journal of Banking and Finance* 8(4):557–65.

Markopolos, Harry. 2011. *No One Would Listen: A True Financial Thriller.* New York: Wiley.

Martel, Gordon. 2008. *Origins of the First World War.* New York: Pearson Longman.

Martin, Sarah B., D. Jeff Covell, Jane E. Joseph, Himachandra Chebrolu, Charles D. Smith, Thomas H. Kelly, Yang Jiang, and Brian T. Gold. 2007. "Human Experience Seeking Correlates with Hippocampus Volume: Convergent Evidence from Manual Tracing and Voxel-Based Morphometry." *Neuropsychologia* 45:2874–81.

Marx, Karl. 1906. *Capital: A Critique of Political Economy.* New York: Modern Library.

Marx, Karl, and Friedrich Engels. 1906 [1848]. *Manifesto of the Communist Party.* Chicago: Charles H. Kerr & Co.

Mayer, Colin. 1990. "Financial Systems, Corporate Finance, and Economic Development." In R. Glenn Hubbard, ed., *Asymmetric Information, Corporate Finance, and Investment*, 307–32. Chicago: University of Chicago Press.

Melamed, Leo. 2009. *For Crying Out Loud: From Open Outcry to Electronic Screen.* Hoboken, NJ: Wiley.

Mian, Atif, and Amir Sufi. 2010. "Household Leverage and the Recession of 2007 to 2009." *IMF Economic Review* 58:74–117.

Mian, Atif, Amir Sufi, and Francesco Trebbi. 2011. "Foreclosures, House Prices, and the Real Economy." National Bureau of Economic Research Working Paper 16685.

Milgrom, Paul, and Nancy Stokey. 1982. "Information, Trade and Common Knowledge." *Journal of Economic Theory* 26:17–27.

Miller, John Perry. 1991. *Creating Academic Settings: High Craft and Low Cunning: Memoirs.* New Haven, CT: J. Simeon.

Miller, Joseph S. 2008. *The Wicked Wine of Democracy: A Memoir.* Seattle: University of Washington Press.

Miller, Merton H., and Franco Modigliani. 1961. "Dividend Policy, Growth, and the Valuation of Shares." *Journal of Business* 34:411–33.

Mishkin, Frederick. 1996. "Understanding Financial Crises: A Developing Country Perspective." National Bureau of Economic Research Working Paper 5600.

Modigliani, Franco, and Merton H. Miller. 1963. "Corporate Income Taxes and the Cost of Capital: A Correction." *American Economic Review* 53:433–43.

Mongelli, Lorena, and Dan Mangan. 2009. "The SEC Watchdog Who Missed Madoff; Don't Blame Me: Cheung." *New York Post*, January 7, http://www.nypost.com/p/news/business/item_IbjeXQwwTt0whXl6ojz3oJ.

Montague, Read. 2007. *Your Brain Is (Almost) Perfect: How We Make Decisions.* New York: Penguin Plume.

Montesquieu, Charles de Secondat. 1773 [1748]. *The Spirit of Laws*, Tenth Edition, trans. Thomas Nugent. London: S. Crowder, C. Ware, and T. Payne.

Moody, John L. 1933. *The Long Road Home.* New York: Macmillan.

Morrison, Alan D., and William J. Wilhelm, Jr. 2008. "The Demise of Investment-Banking Partnerships: Theory and Evidence." *Journal of Finance* 63(1):311–50.

Moss, David. 2004. *When All Else Fails: Government as the Ultimate Risk Manager.* Cambridge, MA: Harvard University Press.

Myers, Stewart. 1984. "The Capital Structure Puzzle." *Journal of Finance* 39:575–92.

National Commission on the Causes of the Financial and Economic Crisis in the United States (U.S. Financial Crisis Inquiry Commission). 2011. *Financial Crisis Inquiry Report*. Washington, DC: U.S. Government Printing Office, http://www.gpoaccess .gov/fcic/fcic.pdf.

Newcomb, Simon. 1879. "The Standard of Value." *North American Review* 129:223–38.

Nietzsche, Friedrich. 1968 [1901]. *The Will to Power*, trans. Walter Kaufmann and R. J. Hollingdale. New York: Vintage.

Nordenflycht, Andrew von. 2008. "The Demise of the Professional Partnership? The Emergence and Diffusion of Publicly-Traded Professional Service Firms." Unpublished paper, Beedie School of Business, Simon Fraser University.

O'Leary, Ann. 2012. "Risk Sharing When Work and Family Clash: The Need for Government and Employer Innovation." In Jacob Hacker and Ann O'Leary, eds., *Shared Responsibility, Shared Risk*, Chapter 9. New York: Oxford University Press.

O'Reilly, Randy, D. C. Noelle, Jon Cohen, and Todd Braver. 2002. "Prefrontal Cortex and Dynamic Categorization Tasks: Representational Organization and Neuromodulatory Control. *Cerebral Cortex* 12:246–57.

Owings, W. A. Dolph. 1984. *The Sarajevo Trial*. Chapel Hill, NC: Documentary.

Park, Sun Young. 2011. "The Safeness of AAA-Rated Subprime MBSs." Unpublished paper, Korea Advanced Institute of Science and Technology.

Patoine, Brenda. 2011. "Desperately Seeking Sensation: Fear, Reward, and the Human Need for Novelty: Neuroscience Begins to Shine Light on the Neural Basis of Sensation-Seeking," Dana Foundation, http://www.dana.org/media/detail.aspx?id=23620.

Pharoah, Cathy. 2009. *Family Foundation Philanthropy 2009: UK, Germany, Italy, US*. London: Alliance Publishing Trust.

Phelps, Edmund. 2007. *Rewarding Work: How to Restore Participation and Self-Support to Free Enterprise*. Cambridge, MA: Harvard University Press.

Phelps, Edmund, and Leo M. Tilman. 2010. "Wanted: A First National Bank of Innovation." *Harvard Business Review*, January–February, 1–2.

Philippon, Thomas, and Ariell Reshef. 2008. "Wages and Human Capital in the U.S. Financial Industry: 1909–2006." Unpublished paper, Department of Finance, New York University.

Pinker, Steven. 2011. *The Better Angels of Our Nature: Why Violence Has Declined*. New York: Viking Adult.

Pogrebin, Robin. 2011. "Resisting Renaming of Miami Museum." *New York Times*, December 6, C1.

Post, David. 2005. "Altruism, Happiness and Health: It's Good to Be Good." *International Journal of Behavioral Medicine* 12(2):66–77.

Prante, Gerald. 2007. "Most Americans Don't Itemize on Their Tax Returns." Tax Foundation, July 23, http://www.taxfoundation.org/news/show/22499.html.

Proust, Marcel. 2002 [1913]. *Swann's Way*, trans. Lydia Davis. New York: Penguin.

Pulvermüller, Friedemann. 2002. *The Neuroscience of Language*. Cambridge: Cambridge University Press.

Rajan, Raghuram. 2010. *Fault Lines: How Hidden Fractures Still Threaten the World Economy*. Princeton, NJ: Princeton University Press.

Rajan, Raghuram, and Luigi Zingales. 2004. *Saving Capitalism from the Capitalists: Unleashing the Power of Financial Markets to Create Wealth and Spread Opportunity.* Princeton, NJ: Princeton University Press.

Redleaf, Andrew, and Richard Vigilante. 2010. *Panic: The Betrayal of Capitalism by Wall Street and Washington.* Minneapolis: Vigilante.

Rhodes, Gillian. 2006. "The Evolutionary Psychology of Facial Beauty." *Annual Review of Psychology* 57:199–226.

Ross, Lee. 1977. "The Intuitive Psychologist and His Shortcomings: Distortions in the Attribution Process." *Advances in Experimental Social Psychology* 10:173–220.

Ross, Stephen A. 1976. "Options and Efficiency." *Quarterly Journal of Economics* 90(1):75–89.

Roth, Alvin E., Tayfun Sonmez, and M. Utku Unver. 2005. "Pairwise Kidney Exchange." *Journal of Economic Theory* 125(2):151–88.

Russett, Bruce, and John Oneal. 2001. *Triangulating Peace: Democracy, Interdependence and International Organizations.* New York: W. W. Norton.

Saint-Exupéry, Antoine de. 2000 [1943]. *The Little Prince*, trans. Richard Howard. Orlando, FL: Harcourt.

Salacuse, Jeswald W. 2003. "Corporate Governance, Culture and Convergence: Corporations American Style or with a European Touch?" *Law and Business Review of the Americas* 9:33–62, http://heinonline.org/HOL/Page?handle=hein.journals/lbramrca9&div=11&g_sent=1&collection=journals.

Sala-i-Martin, Xavier. 2006. "The World Distribution of Income: Falling Poverty and . . . Convergence, Period." *Quarterly Journal of Economics* 121(2):351–97.

Sargent, Frederic O. 1961. "Feudalism to Family Farms in France." *Agricultural History* 35(4):193–201.

Scharlach, Andrew E., and Amanda J. Lehning. 2012. "The Government's Role in Aging and Long-Term Care." In Jacob Hacker and Ann O'Leary, eds., *Shared Responsibility, Shared Risk*, Chapter 12. New York: Oxford University Press.

Schultz, Wolfram. 1998. "Predictive Reward Signal of Dopamine Neurons." *Journal of Neurophysiology* 80(1):1–27.

Schultz, Wolfram, Peter Dayan, and P. Read Montague. 1997. "A Neural Substrate for Prediction and Reward." *Science* 275(5306):593–99.

Schumpeter, Joseph A. 1962 [1950]. *Capitalism, Socialism and Democracy*, Third Edition. New York: Harper Torchbooks.

Schwed, Fred. 1940. *Where Are the Customers' Yachts? A Good Hard Look at Wall Street.* New York: Simon and Schuster.

Scoville, James G. 2006. "Labor Market Underpinnings of a Caste Economy." *American Journal of Economics and Sociology* 55(4):385–94.

Seavoy, Ronald E. 1972. "Laws to Encourage Manufacturing: New York Policy and the 1811 General Incorporation Statute." *Business History Review* 46(1):85–95.

Shapley, Lloyd, and Herbert Scarf. 1974. "On Cores and Indivisibility." *Journal of Mathematical Economics* 1(1):23–37.

Shefrin, Hersh. 2007. *Behavioral Corporate Finance: Decisions That Create Value.* Boston: McGraw-Hill.

Shefrin, Hersh, and Meir Statman. 1993. "Behavioral Aspects of the Design and Marketing of Financial Products." *Financial Management* 22(2):123–34.

Shiller, Robert J. 1981. "Do Stock Prices Move Too Much to Be Justified by Subsequent Changes in Dividends?" *American Economic Review* 71(3):421–36.

———. 1994. *Macro Markets: Creating Institutions to Manage Society's Largest Economic Risks.* Oxford: Oxford University Press.

———. 1997. "Public Resistance to Indexation: A Puzzle." *Brookings Papers on Economic Activity* 1:159–211.

———. 2003. *The New Financial Order: Risk in the 21st Century.* Princeton, NJ: Princeton University Press.

———. 2005a. "The Invention of Inflation-Indexed Bonds in Early America." In William N. Goetzmann and K. Geert Rouwenhorst, eds., *The Origins of Value: The Financial Innovations That Created Modern Capital Markets,* 239–48. New York: Oxford University Press.

———. 2005b. *Irrational Exuberance,* Second Edition. Princeton, NJ: Princeton University Press.

———. 2008. *The Subprime Solution: How Today's Global Financial Crisis Happened and What to Do about It.* Princeton, NJ: Princeton University Press.

———. 2009. *The Case for a Basket: A New Way of Showing the True Value of Money.* London: Policy Exchange.

———. 2012a. "Give People Shares of GDP." *Harvard Business Review* 90(1/2):50–51.

———. 2012b. "Irving Fisher, Debt Deflation and Crises." *Journal of the History of Economic Thought,* forthcoming.

Shiller, Robert J., Maxim Boycko, and Vladimir Korobov. 1991. "Popular Attitudes towards Free Markets: The Soviet Union and the United States Compared." *American Economic Review* 81(3):385–400.

Shiller, Robert J., Rafal M. Wojakowski, M. Shahid Ebrahim, and Mark B. Shackleton. 2011. "Continuous Workout Mortgages." Discussion Paper 1794. New Haven, CT: Cowles Foundation for Research in Economics, Yale University.

Shleifer, Andrei. 2000. *Inefficient Markets: An Introduction to Behavioral Finance.* Oxford: Oxford University Press.

Shubik, Martin. 2009. *A Proposal for a Federal Employment Reserve Authority.* Economics Policy Note 09-5. New York: Levy Economics Institute.

Simmons, Joseph P., and Nathan Novemsky. 2009. "From Loss Aversion to Loss Acceptance: Context Effects on Loss Aversion in Risky Choice." Working Paper. New Haven, CT: Yale School of Management.

Small, Deborah A., George Loewenstein, and Paul Slovic. 2007. "Sympathy and Callousness: The Impact of Deliberative Thought on Donations to Identifiable and Statistical Victims." *Organizational Behavior and Human Decision Processes* 102(2):143–53.

Smith, Adam. 1761. *The Theory of Moral Sentiments,* Second Edition. London: A. Millar in the Strand.

———. 1776. *An Inquiry into the Nature and Causes of the Wealth of Nations.* London: Ward, Lock & Bowden & Co.

Sprenkle, Case. 1964. "Warrant Prices as Indicators of Expectations and Preferences."

In Paul Cootner, ed., *The Random Character of Stock Market Prices*, 412–74. Cambridge, MA: MIT Press.

Stanley, Thomas J. 1991. *Selling to the Affluent*. New York: McGraw-Hill.

Stark, Oded, and Ita Falk. 1998. "Transfers, Empathy Formation, and Reverse Transfers." *American Economic Review* 88(2):271–76.

Stigler, George A. 1971. "The Theory of Economic Regulation." *Bell Journal of Economics and Management Science* 2(1):3–21.

Stratmann, Thomas. 1991. "What Do Campaign Contributions Buy? Deciphering Causal Effects of Money and Votes." *Southern Economic Journal* 57(3):606–20.

Summers, Lawrence H. 1986. "Does the Stock Market Rationally Reflect Fundamental Values?" *Journal of Finance* 41(3):28–30.

Swafford, Jan. 1996. *Charles Ives: A Life with Music*. New York: W. W. Norton.

Tarbell, Ida M. 1904. *The History of the Standard Oil Company*. New York: McClure, Phillips.

Tarlow, Steve. 2010. "Estate Tax Sends Elderly Racing to the Grave." newsytype.com, November 2, http://www.newsytype.com/3257-estate-tax/.

Tetlock, Philip E. 2006. *Expert Political Judgment: How Good Is It? How Can We Know?* Princeton, NJ: Princeton University Press.

Thaler, Richard H., and Cass R. Sunstein. 2008. *Nudge: Improving Decisions about Health, Wealth and Happiness*. New Haven, CT: Yale University Press.

Thomsen, Jens, and Verner Anderson. 2007. "Longevity Bonds: A Financial Market Instrument to Manage Longevity Risk." *Monetary Review* 46(4):29–44.

Thoreau, Henry David. 2008 [1863]. *Life without Principle*. Forgotten Books, http://www.forgottenbooks.org/.

Toppe, Christopher M., Arthur D. Kirsch, and Jocabel Michel. 2001. *Giving and Volunteering in the United States: Findings from a National Survey*. Washington, DC: Independent Sector, http://www.cpanda.org/pdfs/gv/GV01Report.pdf.

Townsend, Robert M. 1994. "Risk and Insurance in Village India." *Econometrica* 62(3):539–91.

Tufano, Peter, and Daniel Schneider. 2009. "Using Financial Innovation to Support Savers: From Coercion to Excitement." In Rebecca M. Blank and Michael S. Barr, eds., *Insufficient Funds: Savings, Assets, Credit and Banking among Low-Income Households*, 149–90. New York: Russell Sage Foundation.

Unger, Peter. 1996. *Living High and Letting Die: Our Illusion of Innocence*. New York: Oxford University Press.

United Nations. 1948. *The Universal Declaration of Human Rights*. http://www.un.org/en/documents/udhr/.

U.S. Commodities Futures Trading Commission and Securities and Exchange Commission. 2010. "Findings Regarding the Market Events of May 6, 2010: Report to the Joint Advisory Committee on Emerging Regulatory Issues." http://www.sec.gov/news/studies/2010/marketevents-report.pdf.

U.S. Congressional Budget Office. 2011. "Trends in the Distribution of Household Income between 1979 and 2007." http://www.cbo.gov/ftpdocs/124xx/doc12485/WebSummary.pdf.

U.S. Financial Stability Oversight Council. 2011. *Study & Recommendations Regarding*

Concentration Limits on Large Financial Companies. Washington, DC. http://www
.treasury.gov/initiatives/Documents/Study%20on%20Concentration%20Limits%20
on%20Large%20Firms%2001-17-11.pdf.

U.S. National Commission on Fiscal Responsibility and Reform. 2010. *The Moment of Truth.* Washington, DC.

Van Veen, Vincent, Marie K. Krug, Jonathan W. Schooler, and Cameron S. Carter. 2009. "Neural Activity Predicts Attitude Change in Cognitive Dissonance." *Nature Neuroscience* 12(11):1469–74.

Veblen, Thorstein. 1899. *The Theory of the Leisure Class: An Economic Study of the Evolution of Institutions.* London: Macmillan.

Vickery, Thomas J., Marvin M. Chun, and Daeyeol Lee. 2011. "Ubiquity and Specificity of Reinforcement Signals throughout the Human Brain." *Neuron* 72(1):166–77.

Visser, Jelle. 2003. "Unions and Unionism around the World." In John T. Addison and Claus Schnabel, eds., *International Handbook of Trade Unions,* 366–96. Cheltenham, UK: Edward Elgar.

Vuolteenaho, Tuomo. 2002. "What Drives Firm-Level Stock Returns?" *Journal of Finance* 57:233–64.

Weber, Max. 2010 [1905]. *The Protestant Ethic and the Spirit of Capitalism.* New York: CreateSpace.

Weller, Christian, and Amy Helburn. 2012. "Public Policy Options to Build Wealth for America's Middle Class." In Jacob Hacker and Ann O'Leary, eds., *Shared Responsibility, Shared Risk,* Chapter 7. New York: Oxford University Press.

Weyl, Hermann. 1952. *Symmetry.* Princeton, NJ: Princeton University Press.

Whitman, Walt. 1892. *Leaves of Grass.* Project Gutenberg Ebook, http://www.gutenberg
.org/files/1322/1322-h/1322-h.htm.

Wittgenstein, Ludwig. 1953. *Philosophical Investigations.* Oxford: Blackwell.

Wolfers, Justin, and Eric Zitzewitz. 2004. "Prediction Markets." *Journal of Economic Perspectives* 18(2):107–26.

Woodward, Bob. 2001. *Maestro: Greenspan's Fed and the American Boom.* New York: Simon and Schuster.

Working, Holbrook. 1934. "A Random-Difference Series for Use in the Analysis of Time Series." *Journal of the American Statistical Association* 29(185):11–24.

Yavlinsky, Grigory. 2011. *Realpolitik: The Hidden Cause of the Great Recession (And How to Avert the Next One),* trans. Antonina W. Bouis. New Haven, CT: Yale University Press.

Yunus, Muhammad. 2003. *Banker to the Poor: Micro-Lending and the Battle against World Poverty.* New York: Public Affairs.

Zuckerman, Gregory. 2009. *The Greatest Trade Ever: The Behind-the-Scenes Story of How John Paulson Defied Wall Street and Made Financial History.* New York: Crown Business.

Zuckerman, Marvin, Sybil B. Eysenck, and H. J. Eysenck. 1978. "Sensation Seeking in England and in America: Cross-Cultural, Age, and Sex Comparisons." *Journal of Consulting and Clinical Psychology* 46:139–49.

Index